P9-AOM-427

*A. Lincoln: His Last 24 Hours*

# A. Lincoln
# His Last 24 Hours

*by*

W. Emerson Reck

McFarland & Company, Inc., Publishers
*Jefferson, North Carolina, and London*

*Illustrations in this book,*
*unless otherwise credited,*
*were furnished by*
*the Louis A. Warren Lincoln Library and Museum*
*in Fort Wayne, Indiana, from*
*prints of photographs in its possession.*

**Library of Congress Cataloguing-in-Publication Data**

Reck, W. Emerson (Waldo Emerson), 1903–
*A. Lincoln, his last 24 hours.*

Bibliography: p. 199.
Includes index.
1. Lincoln, Abraham, 1809–1865 — Assassination.
2. Presidents — United States — Biography.
I. Title.
E457.5.R29 1987 973.7'092'4 85–43587

ISBN 0-89950-216-4 (acid-free natural paper) 

Printed in the United States of America.

McFarland Box 611 Jefferson NC 28640

*To Hazel*
*without whose encouragement and help*
*this book could not have been written*

# Contents

Preface 1

I "He Was Full of Hope and Happiness" 7
II Visitors Note His "Exuberant Mood" 19
III "There Must Be No Bloody Work" 31
IV Urgent Business, but Time for Good Deeds 41
V "I Never Saw Him So Supremely Cheerful" 47
VI Reluctantly He Starts for the Theatre 53
VII The Stage Is Set for Murder 63
VIII Lincoln's Guard Leaves His Post 81
IX Tragedy Strikes, Mary's Hand in His 89
X "It Is Impossible for Him to Recover" 113
XI "Now He Belongs to the Ages" 127

Appendix: Some Unsolved Mysteries 161
1. *Eli K. Price and His $500 Check* 161
2. *The Guard with a Shoddy Record* 162
3. *Light on the Missing Dispatch* 165
4. *Course of the Ball, Still Undetermined* 167

Notes 171
Bibliography 199
Index 223

# Preface

A college course in biography, an interview with a man who had known Lincoln, and the encouragement of a dedicated Lincoln scholar led me to write this book.

The course—under Dr. Paul F. Bloomhardt, a truly great teacher at Wittenberg College (now Wittenberg University)—first made my interest in Lincoln come alive. Later, while serving as a correspondent for the old *Omaha Bee-News*, during the 1930s, I had the privilege of interviewing an aging Fremont, Nebraska, banker, who had stood near the speaker's platform during a Lincoln-Douglas debate in 1858. It was to this old man, at that time a boy of nine, that Lincoln had referred when he said, in effect, "Not in my lifetime perhaps, but surely in the lifetime of this young lad, the slaves will be free." My interest in Lincoln quickened and led me to search for material to present before organizations interested in the sixteenth president of the United States.

The resolution to write this book finally came nearly thirty years ago when, after several visits to the Illinois State Historical Library, I made a trip especially to gather information on Lincoln's last day. It was on this visit that ever-helpful Marion Dolores Pratt of the library staff, and one of the editors for the Abraham Lincoln Association's massive nine-volume set, *The Collected Works of Abraham Lincoln*, spent much of two days making material available, answering questions, giving guidance, and finally emphasizing that a comprehensive, well-researched "last day" book ought to be written. Knowing of my long-time interest in Lincoln, Mrs. Pratt suggested that I might undertake the job.

The challenge motivated me, but duties at my university and other activities to which I was committed kept me from concentrating, except for short periods in summers, on the research demanded. Little by little, however, information was collected and carefully checked. This volume, based on material from several hundred sources, including over a hundred individuals who figured in activities and events of April 14–15, 1865, is the result.

The first problem faced was one met by all who have touched on Lincoln's last day: No schedule of appointments or meetings was kept,

*After Lincoln's death, a number of pictures appeared, each with the claim it was the President's last. For many years the one above, said to have been taken by Alexander Gardner on April 10, 1865, was regarded as his last. However, Matthew Wilson in his diary said that he had taken Lincoln to Gardner's studio on February 5 to get a model for the portrait he painted that month. The photo above is one of several Gardner took to provide a model. The picture opposite is a lithograph from the L. Prang Company of Boston, based on Wilson's painting for which Gardner had provided the model on February 5. The picture on page 4 was taken on the balcony at the White House on March 6 by H. F. Warren of Waltham, Massachusetts. Nicolay and Hay, in the Lincoln Memorial University edition of their* Complete Works of Abraham Lincoln *published in 1894 (Vol. II, opposite p. 94), said this was the last picture taken of Lincoln.*

and newspapers of the day provided little or no information about the President's activities. One of the resultant difficulties was determination of the hours when certain things happened, or indeed if they occurred at all.

For instance, Congressman Cornelius Cole always maintained that he and Speaker of the House Schuyler Colfax had their conference with the President in the afternoon. Colfax, who saw Lincoln in the morning and again in the evening, made no mention of Cole's presence either time, but he did use the plural pronoun as if Lincoln was speaking to more than one person during the morning conference. Since Colfax was about to leave for California, and Cole was a representative of that state, it is logical to assume that it was in the morning that the latter accompanied the Speaker. Certainly it was not in the evening.

How to spell the names of various individuals presented another problem. Names of several persons who figured in events of the day were spelled in different ways not only in newspaper stories, magazine articles, and letters of observers but in city directories and in records made during the trials that followed the assassination.

For instance, the alias of Lewis Thornton Powell, would-be assassin of Secretary William H. Seward, was spelled "Payne" by most newspapers and in official reports of the conspiracy trial, and is so spelled in many books today. It is spelled "Paine" in this book because that is the way the former Confederate soldier wrote it when he took the oath of allegiance in Baltimore on March 14, 1865.

A similar example is the tailor in whose house Lincoln died. In things written since 1865 his name has come out "Peterson" about as often as it has "Petersen," although the latter spelling is unquestionably correct. Some of the confusion may have resulted because his name was spelled both ways in city directories.

I have omitted things included in some accounts because evidence revealed that they were unrelated to April 14. One I wanted mightily to include was that which had Lincoln relating one of his prize stories to Congressman Samuel Shellabarger. The story is especially interesting to me because both Shellabarger and the man who often related the story as a "last day" happening—General J. Warren Keifer, Speaker of the House of Representatives in the forty-seventh Congress (1881–1883)—were residents of my hometown. Moreover, Keifer, who had risen from major of Ohio volunteers to brevet major general and brigade commander in the Civil War, was, at the age of ninety, awarded an honorary degree by Wittenberg College on the same day I received a bachelor's degree.

The story General Keifer liked to tell had Shellabarger calling at the White House to ask that one of his constituents be appointed to a staff position in the Army. "Your request, Shellabarger," Lincoln was quoted as saying, "reminds me of an Irishman out in Illinois who wanted a shirt for a special occasion and went to a woman who made shirts. When he got the shirt, he found that it had been starched all the way around instead of only in the bosom. A bit irked, he returned it remarking that he didn't want a shirt that was all collar. Now the trouble with you, Shellabarger, is that you want an army all staff and no army."

Shellabarger did make the request of Lincoln and the President's rejoinder was as reported. Unfortunately, the incident, as recounted by Shellabarger himself, had occurred at an earlier date.

For a long time the report that the Lincolns visited the *Montauk* during the afternoon was considered false because the ship's log for the day made no mention of the Lincolns. Testimony of the ship's surgeon and other reliable witnesses proved, however, that the President and his wife had indeed been there.

Piecing together testimony to produce the story of Lincoln's last day, told as fully and accurately as presently seems possible, has been a challenging task. I only hope the result will be as interesting to readers as it was to me over the years it was taking form.

No reader should assume, however, that all of the questions about Lincoln's last day have been answered. The appendix to this book proves that several mysteries remain to tantalize researchers and readers.

This book could not have been produced without the cooperation of scores of individuals who gave generously of their time to be of help. In addition to Marion Dolores Pratt, five others deserve special mention because of their outstanding contributions. They are Dr. Mark E. Neely, Jr., director of the Louis A. Warren Lincoln Library and Museum in Fort Wayne, Indiana, author of *The Abraham Lincoln Encyclopedia*, editor of *Lincoln Lore*, and coauthor of *The Lincoln Image: Abraham Lincoln and the Popular Print*; Frank Hebblethwaite, museum technician at Ford's Theatre National Historic Site; Lloyd Ostendorf, Dayton, Ohio, Lincoln collector, artist, and author; Dr. Robert G. Hartje, Wittenberg University professor of history and author, who read the manuscript and made many valuable suggestions; and my wife, Hazel W. Reck, who served as researcher, adviser, critic, and secretary before her death in August, 1983. Names of many others are listed with appreciation in the section on resources in the Bibliography. Still others gave help anonymously, and my great regret is that they cannot be recognized by name.

W.E.R.
Springfield, Ohio

# I
# "He Was Full of Hope and Happiness"

The North was delirious with joy. General Robert E. Lee had surrendered at Appomattox Court House on Sunday, April 9, 1865. The end of four years of bloody, fratricidal war now seemed certain.

Nowhere was jubilation more manifest than in the nation's capital. There, celebration reached its peak on the following Thursday night with an illumination that drew to the principal thoroughfares an exultant throng, garbed in holiday attire. Bells clanged. Cannons boomed. Bands played. Giant bonfires blazed in the street. Fireworks lit up the sky. Clusters of candles shone from the windows of public buildings and private homes. Never had Washington been so brilliantly lighted or its people so ecstatic as on this night.[1]

Then the dawn of April 14 – Good Friday – came to the capital with "all nature seeming to bask in the sunshine of assured peace."[2] The morning was balmy with a light breeze blowing from the south as the temperature climbed toward the 50-degree mark.[3] The gardeners at work early among the flowers in front of the White House, the sweet fragrance of lilacs, the dogwood and Judas trees in bloom, and the lacy green of the willows along the Potomac – all these gave evidence that spring was coming to Washington.[4]

Inside the White House, President Abraham Lincoln rose in his second-floor bedroom at seven, slipped into his faded dressing gown, pulled well-worn carpet slippers[5] over those exceptionally large feet,[6] and walked down the hall to the family sitting room and library above the Blue Room on the main floor. There, as was his custom, he sat down in his favorite chair in the middle of the room and read a chapter or two in the Bible,[7] the book an early biographer said Lincoln knew almost by heart.[8]

The President tarried in the library for a few minutes, possibly reflecting on the blessings of the day and prospects for the future. He had

## AREA OF MAJOR ACTIVITY IN WASHINGTON APRIL 14-15, 1865

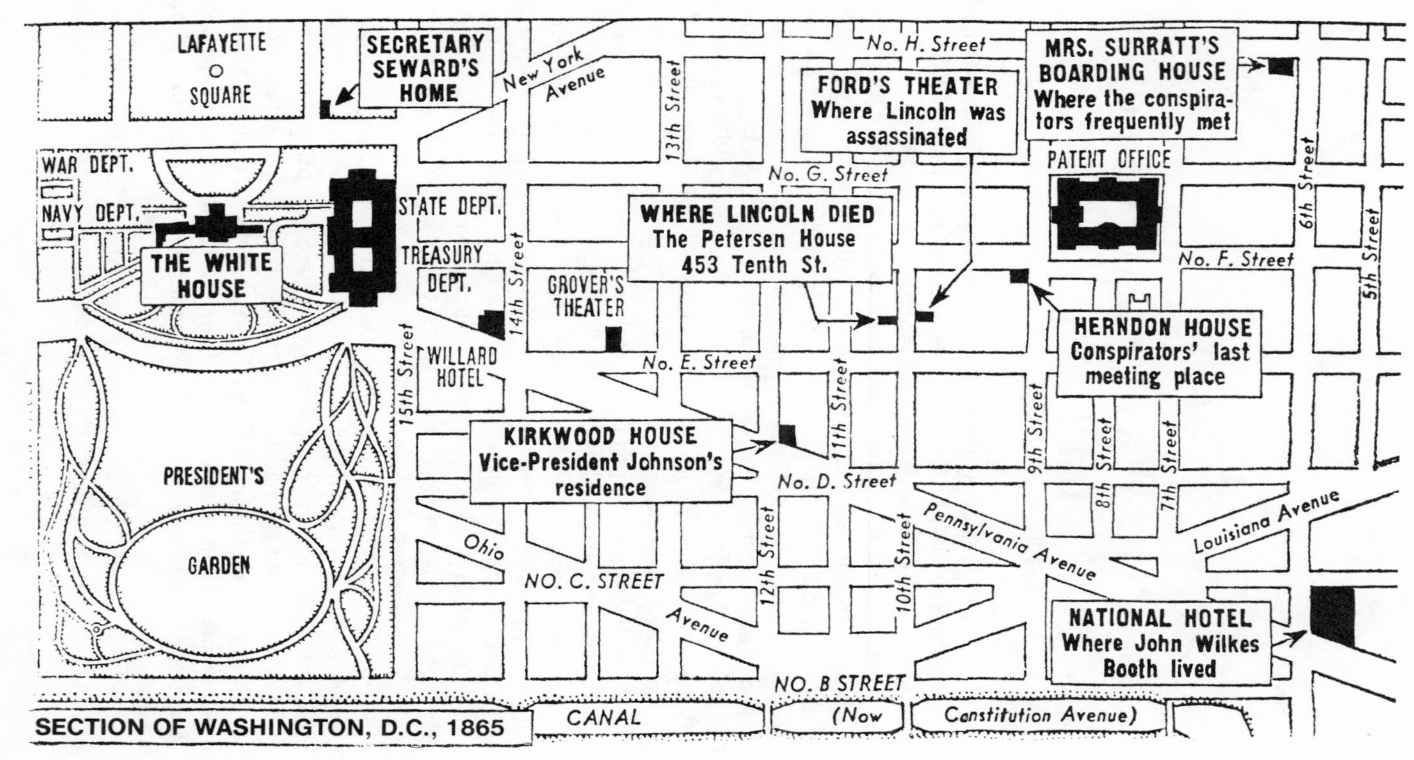


SECTION OF WASHINGTON, D.C., 1865

had some opportunity to relax since Lee's surrender but was still bone-tired. The burdens of the war—which he often called "this great trouble"[9]—had weighed heavily upon him, and during the winter of 1864–65 he had aged rapidly. He was "in mind, body and nerves a very different man . . . from the one who had taken the oath in 1861."[10] Several times he had been ill and confined to bed. The lines on his haggard, careworn face had grown deeper, the dusky gray eyes dark-ringed and sometimes dull.[11] The wiry frame of youth, now stooped, no longer reached the six feet four inches of which he had always been so proud.[12] Thirty pounds had dropped from his normal weight of 180.[13] One of his friends said that he looked like "a huge skeleton in clothes."[14]

Despite his fatigue, Lincoln was buoyed by hope and happiness he had not known since assuming the presidency.[15] The agonies of war had taken their toll but peace at last was near. Now he could anticipate success for the huge job ahead. Now he could devote himself to the task of healing war's wounds and reuniting the divided nation.

An editorial in the *New York Tribune* on this April 14 morning well expressed his mood and the reasons for it: "The path of Peace opens pleasantly before us. There may be thorns in the way as we advance, obstacles to overcome, pitfalls and snares to avoid, but we look back to the dread road we have travelled for four long and weary and painful years and the road before us smiles with summer sunshine. . . . Never before had a nation so much cause for devout Thanksgiving; never before had a people so much reason for unrestrained congratulation and the very extravagance of joy."

His meditation over, Lincoln walked down the hall to his office, and seated himself at the secondhand mahogany upright desk where he was wont to conduct official business, his back to a window opening upon a view of the Potomac.[16]

The morning's mail was already on his desk. Mail deliveries came to the White House twice a day, each bag usually containing about 125 items, exclusive of newspapers.[17] It was not unusual for the President to receive pretty photos or saucy notes from school girls and requests for autographs from college students. Much of his mail, however, consisted of letters, some of them twenty or thirty pages long, from men detailing the course they would take were they in his place.[18] Only a few of these letters—about one in fifty, according to John Hay, or one in a hundred, according to John Nicolay[19]—were read by Lincoln. The job of reading, sorting, and sometimes preparing replies for the President's signature devolved upon the secretaries.

Lincoln ignored most newspapers received, many of them with marked columns, editorials, or letters—complimentary, advisory, or

*Map (left) courtesy of the* Chicago Tribune.

abusive—which the senders hoped would be seen by the President. Early in his administration he had requested William O. Stoddard, a secretary assigned to the correspondence desk, to make a daily digest "of the course and comments of the leading journals, East and West." This was wasted work and soon discontinued for, said Stoddard, "Mr. Lincoln never found time to spend an hour upon laborious condensations."[20]

On the President's desk this morning was a check for $500 from Eli K. Price, a Philadelphia lawyer. Drawn on the Western Bank of Philadelphia on April 13, it was payable to "A. Lincoln on order." The President endorsed the check with the familiar "A. Lincoln," and it was deposited in the First National Bank of Washington.[21] Nothing to indicate why Price had sent the check has been discovered, a fact which leads to speculation that Price, a Quaker prominent in philosophical and historical circles, meant the money to be a gift for some charity in which the President or his wife was interested, possibly one related to the soldiers, for whom the Lincolns had great concern. (See Appendix for more on Price's check.)

The writing of four brief messages, three of them related to later activities of the day, was next on the President's agenda. The first of the notes was addressed to William H. Seward, Secretary of State, although that official was confined to his bed with serious injuries suffered when he was thrown from his carriage on April 5. This note, which Lincoln knew would be received by Frederick W. Seward, who was conducting business in his father's name, asked that the Cabinet be assembled at 11 A.M. that day. It also indicated that General Grant would meet with the Cabinet.[22] Lincoln on the previous evening had made an appointment with Grant for 9 A.M. Now he dispatched a note to the General: "Please call at 11 A.M. today instead of 9 as agreed last evening."[23]

A third note, addressed to William P. Dole, Commissioner of Indian Affairs, concerned the appointment of William T. Howell, whom Lincoln had nominated on March 10 to be agent for the Indians in Michigan, succeeding DeWitt C. Leach. The Senate had confirmed the nomination the following day, but James Harlan, who had been nominated and confirmed on March 9 to be Secretary of Interior, had not yet taken office. Apparently wishing to delay Howell's commission until Harlan had opportunity to approve it, the President wrote Dole: "Please do not send off the commission of W. T. Howell, as Indian agent in Michigan, until the return of Mr. Harlan, and hearing from me again."[24]

Lincoln's fourth note was addressed to General James H. Van Alen of New York. Van Alen had written Lincoln at least seven times about political and military matters since early January, 1861, and was sufficiently friendly with the President to invite him and Mary to be house guests.[25] He had recently urged Lincoln "for the sake of his friends and

The First National Bank of Washington

No. 8331 Philadelphia, April 13 1865

WESTERN BANK,

Pay to A. Lincoln or order

Five Hundred 00/100 Dollars

$500 Eli K. Price.

AN ORIGINAL CHECK OF ELI K. PRICE

A. Lincoln

*Top: Eli K. Price, Philadelphia lawyer, law reformer, and philanthropist, whose $500 check to President Lincoln created a mystery still unsolved. Bottom: front and back views of the check, which came into the hands of the Lincoln National Life Foundation in 1937 and is now a prized possession of the Louis A. Warren Lincoln Library and Museum in Fort Wayne, Indiana. (Price photo courtesy Historical Society of Pennsylvania.)*

the nation, to guard his life and not expose it to assassination as he had by going in to Richmond [on April 4 and 5]." To Van Alen the President now wrote: "My dear Sir: I intend to adopt the advice of my friends and use due precaution . . . I thank you for the assurance you give me that I shall be supported by conservative men like yourself, in the efforts I may make to restore the Union, so as to make it, to use your language, a Union of hearts and hands as well as of states."[26]

Van Alen was only one of many individuals who had been urging Lincoln to guard against the possibility of assassination. The President's mail, according to John Nicolay, "was infected with brutal and vulgar menace, and warnings of all sorts came to him from zealous and nervous friends."[27]

Rumors of assassination plots had increased as Lincoln's second term began. Secretary of State William H. Seward, who had held that "assassination is not an American practice or habit, and one so vicious and so desperate cannot be engrafted into our political system,"[28] was finally convinced that assassination was indeed a possibility. His change of mind had come when he received from F. M. Morse, American consul in London, two letters that had been forwarded by a private agent in France. The content of these letters was so portentous that Seward had consulted Secretary of War Edwin M. Stanton. They agreed that Seward should lay the matter before Lincoln. But before Seward could meet with Lincoln, he suffered the accident that left him confined to his bed, and the President was never apprised of the letters.[29]

It is commonly believed that Lincoln's secretaries—John Hay, John Nicolay, William O. Stoddard (1861–64), and Edward D. Neill (1864–65)—were instructed never to show threatening missives to the President but rather to destroy them at once and not mention their receipt to anyone. Nicolay, however, disputed this statement when he wrote: "Mr. Lincoln was shown every letter of this character containing any threat or intimation of such against his life . . . The whole question of possible danger to the President was discussed over and over by Mr. Lincoln with the officials surrounding him or with friends who called up the subject, as they frequently did."[30]

Despite the warnings and discussions, Lincoln paid little heed to the threats and "lived and moved about in utter disregard for them."[31] Because of Mrs. Lincoln's worry, he was provided with a thick oaken stick fashioned from a piece of timber from a sunken man-of-war, the ferrule an iron bolt from the *Merrimac*, and the head a bolt from the *Monitor*. However, he almost never carried it. "Mother [the title he always used for Mary] has got a notion in her head that I shall be assassinated," he told his good friend Noah Brooks, "and to please her I take a cane when I go over to the War Department at night—when I don't forget it."[32]

*John Nicolay, top, and John Hay, two of Lincoln's secretaries.*

"Soon after I was nominated in Chicago, I began to receive letters threatening my life," Lincoln once told F. B. Carpenter, who was in the White House to paint his famous Emancipation Proclamation picture. "The first one or two made me a little uncomfortable . . . but they have ceased to give me any apprehension." When Carpenter expressed some surprise, Lincoln declared, "Oh, there is nothing like getting used to things."[33] During Lincoln's presidency the number of threatening missives had mounted until by the summer of 1864 there were eighty in the envelope he had labeled "Assassination." As he dropped the eighty-first into the file, he declared to Carpenter, "I know I am in danger, but I am not going to worry over things like these."[34]

The threats to Lincoln brought constant worry to his aides. "What can we do to prevent assassination?" Hay wondered after the arrival of an especially threatening letter. "The President is so accessible that any villain can feign business, and, while talking with him, draw a razor and cut his throat, and some minutes might elapse after the murderer's escape before we could discover what had been done."[35]

Ward Hill Lamon, burly United States Marshal of the District of Columbia, long-time friend, and self-appointed bodyguard for Lincoln, worried so constantly about the President's safety that the chief executive declared he was a monomaniac on the subject of assassination. Hay declared that Lamon, driven almost wild with worry, one night in November, 1864, "went out, . . . lay down at the President's door, passing the night in that attitude of touching and dumb fidelity, with a small arsenal of pistols and Bowie knives around him. In the morning he went away . . . before I or the President were [sic] awake."[36]

Over and over Lincoln answered the entreaties of friends and aides with the declaration, "If they kill me the next man will be just as bad for them. In a country like this, where our habits are simple, and must be, assassination is always possible, and will come if they are determined about it."[37] His secretaries recorded that he would sum up the matter by saying that "both friends and strangers must have daily access to him in all manner of ways and places; his life was therefore in reach of anyone, sane or mad, who was ready to murder and be hanged for it; that he could not possibly guard against all danger unless he were to shut himself up in an iron box, in which condition he could scarcely perform the duties of a President; by the hand of a murderer he could die but once; to go continually in fear would be to die over and over."[38]

When it was decided in November, 1864, that there must be a guard at the White House and that a squad of cavalry must accompany him on his daily drive, Lincoln was greatly annoyed.[39] "It would never do," he argued, "for a President to have guards with drawn sabers at his door, as if he fancied he were, or were trying to be, or were assuming to be an emperor."[40]

Although Lincoln yielded to the judgment of those who prescribed the guard and cavalry escort, he was never comfortable with their presence. Riding to the Soldiers' Home one evening with a friend, he declared that the cavalry escort accompanying them had been forced upon him "by the military men," and that he could see no certain protection against an assassin if one had determined to take his life. "It [the escort] seems to me," he said, "like putting up the gaps in only one place when the fence is down all along."[41]

Having taken care of his four notes, Lincoln, before dressing and going to breakfast, addressed two endorsements to Attorney General James Speed, both of them on letters he had received from Congressman William H. Wallace of Idaho Territory on April 12. On a note in which Wallace had written, "I would respectfully recommend Milton Kelley of Idaho for the position of Associate Justice of the Supreme Court of the Territory of Idaho, made vacant by the resignation of Samuel C. Parks," Lincoln wrote, "If it is definitely concluded to accept Judge Parks' resignation, as I understand it is, let the appointment be made." On the other Wallace letter, recommending "James H. Alvord for the office of Marshall [sic] of the Territory of Idaho made vacant by the removal of Dolphus S. Payne," the President merely wrote the word "Appoint."[42]

The notes the President had written to Seward, Grant, Dole, and Van Alen carried the complimentary close, "Yours truly," with which he almost always ended letters. The notes, the commission endorsements, and items signed later in the day all bore his customary signature, "A. Lincoln," in a simple, unadorned hand. Seldom did he sign his full name except on state papers and political documents.[43]

Lincoln, it seems, did not particularly like his Christian name and liked the nickname "Abe" even less. John W. Bunn, a Springfield merchant-banker and longtime friend, said he had never heard anyone call Lincoln "Abe," and added, "He certainly was never spoken of as 'Abe' in his presence . . . His associates always called him "Mr. Lincoln."[44] Even Mary almost always addressed him as "Mr. Lincoln."[45] In their addresses and writing, most associates referred to him as "Mr. Lincoln." Exceptions were John Hay and John Nicolay, his secretaries for four years, who often, with affection and respect, referred to him as "the Tycoon."[46] Lincoln never referred to himself as "President," but rather used some circumlocution such as "Before I came here."[47] In fact, he seems to have disliked the term "Mister President." "Now call me Lincoln and . . . I shall have a resting spell from 'Mister President,'" he once told an intimate who had persisted in addressing him always by his proper title.[48]

It was now about eight o'clock and the President knew that Mary and Tad would be waiting for breakfast in the family's little dining room downstairs. Abraham Lincoln was not a man who lived to eat. His breakfast usually consisted of an egg and a cup of coffee.[49] This being a day of celebration, he may have had a bit of bacon, of which he was fond.[50] More important than food to him was the opportunity to chat and joke with his family, and today it was noted that he was more cheerful than he had been in a long while.[51]

Making this day's breakfast more enjoyable than those of most days was the fact that his eldest son, Captain Robert Lincoln, dropped in with interesting news from the front. Robert, in his twenty-second year, had been graduated from Harvard and wanted to join the Army. His mother not only objected violently but feared he would be drafted.

To allay her fears and satisfy Robert, Lincoln had finally, on January 19, written to General Grant asking, "Could he, without embarrassment to you, or detriment to the service, go into your Military family with some nominal rank, I, and not the public, furnishing his necessary means?"[52] Grant had replied two days later, using the blank half of Lincoln's letter, to say, "I will be most happy to have him in my Military family in the manner you propose."[53] Grant suggested that Robert be given the rank of captain, and it was as "Assistant Adjutant General of Volunteers with the rank of Captain" that Robert received on February 11 a commission signed by the President and Secretary Stanton.[54]

Lincoln was criticized by some for securing special treatment for his son, but Robert was soon popular with Grant's staff. Lt. Col. Horace Porter, Grant's aide-de-camp, wrote that he "entered heartily into all social pastimes at headquarters, was always ready to perform his share of hard work, and never expected to be treated differently from any other officer on account of his being the son of the Chief Executive of the Nation."[55] As a member of Grant's staff he had been among the officers at Appomattox when Lee surrendered on April 9.

Robert came into the dining room with a portrait of Lee in his hands. Lincoln took the picture, laid it on the table before him, and scanned the face thoughtfully. "It is a good face," he said. "It is the face of a noble, noble, brave man. I am glad the war is over at last." Then, looking up at Robert, he continued, "Well, my son, you have returned safely from the front. The war is now closed, and we soon will live in peace with the brave men that have been fighting against us. I trust that the era of good feeling has returned . . . and that henceforth we shall live in peace."[56]

Lincoln was hungry for details of the surrender at Appomattox. Robert, proud of his stint with Grant and of the fact that he had been on the porch of the McLean house while Lee surrendered inside, was happy to supply them and did so with boyish enthusiasm.[57] He had been impressed especially by the contrast between the commanding officers: "the stately, elegant Lee, with his white head and spotless uniform, his jeweled sword and gold spurs; and the small, stooping, shabby, shy man

*Portrait of the Lincoln family, apparently pictured sometime after February 11, 1865, because it was on that date that eldest son Robert received his captain's commission. This copy of the portrait was found in a Confederate home in Romney, West Virginia. (National Park Service.)*

in the muddy blue uniform, with no sword and no spurs—only the frayed and dingy shoulder straps of a Lieutenant General on the rumpled blouse of a private soldier. Oh, it was great," he concluded.[58]

Informed that Schuyler Colfax, Speaker of the House, was waiting to see him, the President rose. "Now, listen to me, Robert," he said in parting. "You must lay aside your uniform and return to college. I wish you to read law for three years, and at the end of that time I hope that we will be able to tell whether you will make a lawyer or not."[59]

# II
# Visitors Note His "Exuberant Mood"

Schuyler Colfax, the 42-year-old Speaker of the House of Representatives, had reached Washington from his South Bend, Indiana, home on April 13. He had been impelled, he wrote later, by "a strong and overruling desire to see him [Lincoln] once more before taking this long journey"[1] to the West on which he expected to leave soon. He also wanted to make certain the President was not planning to call a special session of Congress, an action which would require a revision of his plans.

The Speaker, accompanied by Cornelius Cole, one-time California prospector, later a Sacramento lawyer and editor, and now one of Lincoln's staunch friends in the House of Representatives,[2] found the President in "the most exuberant mood." The collapse of the rebellion was foremost in his mind and he spoke of it "with smiles." This, Colfax declared later, "was the happiest day of his [Lincoln's] life."[3]

Colfax and Cole expressed to Lincoln concern about recent announcements made by Major General Godfrey Weitzel, who was serving as military governor of Richmond. One of these related to prayers which would be permitted in the churches of Richmond.[4] Weitzel had given verbal permission for the churches to be opened, provided "no expression would be allowed in any part of the church service . . . which in any way implied a recognition of any other authority than that of the United States." No orders had been given "as to what would be preached or prayed for, but only as to what would not be permitted." The rebels had taken this statement to mean that ministers, while not permitted to pray for Jefferson Davis, would not be required to include the usual prayer for the President of the United States.[5]

Lincoln had wired Weitzel on April 12: "I have no doubt you acted in what appeared to you to be the spirit and temper manifested by me while there [in Richmond on April 5]."[6] He now assured his visitors that he had taken care of matters with Weitzel,[7] and Cole, about to start with his family for their California home, bade the President goodbye.

The President and Colfax talked about policies the government might follow in dealing with the defeated states and their citizens. Possibly because of the Cabinet meeting coming up, Lincoln seemed eager to get Colfax's opinion. The Speaker asserted with vigor that he "could forgive those who had been swept into the vortex of rebellion by the force of public sentiment in the South" but that there was another class he could not forgive: those men "who before rebellion, before secession, sitting in honor and trust in the Capitol, in the Cabinet and in the Halls of Congress, despite their oaths as officers of the Government . . . met in midnight conclave and deliberately plotted the secession . . . and sent messengers to organize and engineer the infernal rebellion, without ever asking the trouble to vacate their dishonored seats in the national Capitol."[8]

The President suddenly changed the subject by saying, "You are going to California, I hear." Colfax replied that he was, "if there was no extra session of Congress impending," and sketched his "proposed route and stoppages by the way."[9] Lincoln said there would be no extra session and expressed regret that he could not accompany the Speaker.

"How I would rejoice to make that trip!" he declared, "but public duties chain me down here, and I can only envy you its pleasures.[10] Now," he continued, "I have been thinking over a message I want you to take from me to the miners where you visit.

"I have," said he, "very large ideas of the mineral wealth of our Nation. I believe it practically inexhaustible. It abounds all over our Western country from the Rocky Mountains to the Pacific, and its development has scarcely commenced. During the war, when we were adding a couple of millions of dollars every day to our national debt, I did not care about encouraging the increase in the volume of our precious metals. We had the country to save first. But, now that the Rebellion is overthrown, and we know pretty nearly the amount of our debt, the more gold and silver we mine makes the payment of that debt so much easier. Now," he continued, speaking with much emphasis, "I am going to encourage that in every way possible. We shall have hundreds of thousands of disbanded soldiers, and many have feared that their return home in such great numbers might paralyze industry by furnishing suddenly a greater supply of labor than there will be a demand for. I am going to try to attract them to this hidden wealth of our mountain ranges, where there is room enough for all. Immigration, which even the war has not stopped, will land upon our shores hundreds of thousands more per year from overcrowded Europe. I intend to point them to the gold and silver that waits for them in the West. Tell the miners for me that I shall promote their interests to the utmost of my ability; because their prosperity is the prosperity of the nation. And we shall prove in a very few years that we are indeed the Treasury of the world."[11]

After Lincoln's death, Colfax spent four months in the West, and

*Schuyler Colfax, Speaker of the House, about to leave for California, conferred with Lincoln twice on April 14, mostly about political matters.*

during that time spoke "no less than fifty times,"[12] always eulogizing the man "whom I loved as I never loved man before."[13] Although his was not the most pleasant of voices, Colfax was a fluent speaker, "prone to eloquence whenever the subject admits of it,"[14] and often his immense audiences wept, even as he did while speaking.[15] In Salt Lake City he gave his eulogy on Lincoln at the Mormon Tabernacle before an audience said to have included six thousand persons, "one thousand more than Brigham himself had at his preaching in the afternoon."[16]

While in the mining districts of Colorado Territory, Utah Territory, Nevada, and California, Colfax presented Lincoln's message to miners as often as three times a day. Typical of reports published in mining area newspapers was that which occupied four columns of the *Black Hawk Mining Journal* of Black Hawk, Colorado Territory, after he had spoken in nearby Central City on May 29. "His vast audience," the paper reported, "packed all the streets within hearing of Clark and Co.'s bank and covered adjoining house tops."[17]

After giving Colfax his message for miners, Lincoln returned to the subject of policies relating to the defeated states. He apparently wanted Colfax to have complete background concerning his recent action that seemed to give the rebel legislature of Virginia authority to assemble.

On April 5 Judge John A. Campbell, the Confederacy's Assistant Secretary of War, had had an interview with Lincoln in Richmond in which he sought "an amnesty and a military convention" as a means of bringing Virginia back into the Union. The President had not promised amnesty but did say that, since he had the pardoning power, he "would save any repentant sinners from hanging."[18]

At the same time he had given Campbell a memo listing "three things indispensable" for peace: "(1) the restoration of the national authority throughout all the States. (2) No receding by the Executive of the United States on the slavery question, from the position assumed thereon, in the late Annual Message to Congress and in preceding documents. (3) No cessation of hostilities short of an end of the war, and the disbanding of all force hostile to the Government."[19]

On April 6 Lincoln had written General Weitzel from City Point that "the gentlemen who have acted as the Legislature of Virginia, in support of the rebellion, may now now [sic] desire to assemble at Richmond, and take measures to withdraw the Virginia troops, and other support from resistance to the General government. If they attempt it, give them permission and protection, until, if at all, they attempt some action hostile to the United States, in which case you will notify them and give them reasonable time to leave; & at the end of which time, arrest any who may remain. Allow Judge Campbell to see this, but do not make it public."[20]

After seeing this message, Campbell on April 7 had written Weitzel seemingly casting some doubt on the validity of Lincoln's proclamation on slavery. He also outlined numerous difficulties he said must be overcome before peace could be achieved and pressed for an armistice during which the Legislature of Virginia would be allowed to assemble and send commissioners "to adjust the questions that are supposed to require adjustment."[21] When Lincoln saw a copy of Campbell's letter on April 12, he had taken action to avoid further argument over the situation.

"Campbell assumes as appears to me that I have called the insurgent Legislature of Virginia together, as the rightful Legislature of the State, to settle all differences with the United States," he had wired Weitzel. "I have done no such thing. I spoke of them not as a Legislature, but as 'the gentlemen who have *acted* as the Legislature of Virginia in support of the rebellion.' I did this on purpose to exclude the assumption that I was recognizing them as a *rightful* body. I dealt with them as men having power *de facto* to do a specific thing, to wit 'to withdraw the Virginia troops, and other support from resistance to the General Government' . . . I meant this and no more. In as much however as Judge

Campbell misconstrues this, and is still pressing for an armistice, contrary to the explicit statement of the paper [memo] I gave him; and particularly as Gen. Grant has since captured the Virginia troops, so that giving a consideration for their withdrawal is no longer applicable, let my letter [of April 6] to you, and the paper to Judge Campbell both be withdrawn or, countermanded, and he be notified of it. Do not allow them to assemble; but if any have come, allow them safe-return to their homes."[22]

Lincoln told Colfax that his letter of April 6 to Weitzel may not have been wise, but he had hoped that it would result in the withdrawal of Virginia troops from service and thus save lives. Inasmuch as Lee's army had since then surrendered no further consideration of the matter was needed.[23]

Lincoln next read a memorandum summarizing the terms offered the Confederates at the Hampton Roads Conference on February 3. He emphasized that he had reiterated them in substance on April 5 in his memo given to Campbell, who was a Confederate representative at the conference. Campbell's letter of April 7 to Weitzel was, he felt, a breach of faith. For that reason he had ordered Weitzel in his wire of April 12 not to allow the men who had acted as Virginia's legislature to assemble.[24]

Lincoln said he had tried to be kind to those men Colfax could not forgive.[25] He believed, however, that restoration of peace would be difficult with the leading rebels in the country. He would therefore propose to have Union generals "skeer" them out by intimating that they would be punished if they remained.[26]

"Then," he said, "we can be magnanimous to the rest, and have peace and quiet in the whole land."[27]

Colfax told his brother-in-law, later his biographer, that Lincoln had spoken "with great impressiveness of his determination to secure liberty and justice to all, with full protection for the humblest, and to re-establish on a sure foundation the unity of the Republic after the sacrifices made for its preservation."[28]

As Colfax prepared to leave, William A. Howard of Michigan was admitted by the President's direction.[29] "Come again this evening" was Lincoln's parting request as Colfax bade the President good-bye.

No record has survived relative to Howard's brief visit with Lincoln, and it is presumed that the former Congressman, Detroit's postmaster by Lincoln's appointment since 1861,[30] had merely dropped in to congratulate the President and say good-bye before leaving for home.

Lincoln's next visitor was John A. J. Creswell of Maryland, who had become a senator in March after serving a term in the House of Representatives. "Hello, Creswell! The war is over!" was the President's greeting to the man who, as a loyalist in Maryland's House of Delegates, had done much toward keeping his state in the Union in 1861–62. Lincoln also remembered gratefully that Creswell, as assistant adjutant general a year later, had had the difficult job of raising Maryland's quota of troops for the Northern army.[31]

"He grasped my hand with the enthusiasm of a schoolboy, and repeated the exclamation, 'The war is over,'" Creswell later reported. "Indeed, with a spirit that was delightful to see, Mr. Lincoln several times exclaimed 'The war is over!' Then he stopped, grew serious, and added: 'But it has been an *awful* war, Creswell, it has been an awful war! But it's over.'"[32]

"But what are you here for?" Lincoln asked when he could leave the subject that was first on his mind. "You fellows don't come to see me unless you want something. It must be something big, or you wouldn't be so early."[33]

Creswell explained that a college classmate had received a letter from a cousin, a Confederate prisoner confined at Point Lookout, Maryland, asking him to persuade Creswell to secure his release. Creswell had endorsed the prisoner's appeal by writing on the letter, "I respectfully ask that the within named Benjn. F. Twilley be discharged on the usual terms."[34]

"That's not so hard," Lincoln said, and on the back of the letter merely wrote, "Let it be done. A. Lincoln. April 14, 1865."[35] Then he said to his visitor, "This makes me think of an old Illinois story, and I'm going to tell it to you.

"Years ago," he continued, "a lot of young folks, boys and girls . . . got up a Maying party. They took their dinners and went down to a place where they had to cross the Sangamon River on an old scow . . . When it was time to go back they were hilarious at finding that the scow had got untied and floated down stream. After a while the thing looked more serious for there was no boat and they could not throw out a pontoon. Pretty soon a young man, a little brighter than the rest, proposed that each fellow take off his shoes and stockings and pick up the girl he liked best and carry her over. It was a great scheme, and it worked all right until all had got over but a little, short, young man and a very tall, dignified old maid. Then there was trouble for one young man in dead earnest.

"Now, do you see," Lincoln concluded, "you fellows will get one man after another out of the business until Jefferson Davis and I will be the only ones left on the island. I'm afraid he'll refuse to let me carry him over, and I'm afraid there are some people who will make trouble about doing it if he consents."

When Creswell laughed heartily over the story and its application, Lincoln declared, "It's no laughing matter; it's more than likely to happen. There are worse men than Jefferson Davis, and I wish I could

*John A. J. Creswell, Maryland senator, who on April 14 obtained Lincoln's first pardon of the day for a Confederate soldier, and in the afternoon conferred with the President on patronage matters.*

see some way by which he and the people would let us get him over. However, we will keep going on and getting them out of it, one at a time."[36]

Still chuckling over Lincoln's story, Creswell took the President's endorsement and started for the War Department where, after a bit of fuss, the order for Twilley's release was honored.

The story told to Creswell was typical of the "little yarns" with which Lincoln garnished and illustrated his conversation. His anecdotes, according to an old friend, were seldom told for the sake of telling, "but because they fitted in just where they came, and shed a light on the argument [situation] that nothing else could." Lincoln disclaimed originality, however, declaring that five out of six of his stories were "the productions of other and better story tellers than himself" while the other sixth of those credited to him were "old acquaintances."[37]

Some of the men associated with the President did not appreciate his story telling, holding that it was undignified for a man of his position. The fact that he sometimes told broad stories was bruited about. Lincoln paid no attention. He couldn't understand people who didn't appreciate a good story, even said that he had "a dread of people who could not appreciate the fun of such things."[38]

Lincoln's story to Creswell also reflected his concern about the problem of Jefferson Davis, which was becoming increasingly touchy as callers and correspondents gave advice on what should be done with the Confederate president when captured. Commenting with some irritation to Slade, his mulatto doorkeeper, on a day when the suggestions had been numerous and varied, Lincoln had declared, "This talk about Davis tires one. I hope he will mount a fleet horse, reach the shores of the Gulf of Mexico, and drive so far into its waters we shall never see him again."[39]

After Creswell left, the President had an audience with John Parker Hale, whom he had recently appointed minister to Spain, following the New Hampshire politician's sixteen years (1847–53, 1855–65) in the Senate. Lincoln had known Hale since 1847 when the two began serving in Congress together, the former for his single term in the House, the latter for his first term in the Senate. He held his visitor in high regard for his strong anti-slavery stands and administrative ability. He had consulted with Hale, among others, on Cabinet appointments in 1861 and since then had frequently accepted his recommendations concerning patronage and affairs of the Army and Navy.[40] Their brief interview related largely to the return of peace and to problems Hale would face in Spain.

Lincoln's next caller was Charles M. Scott, Mississippi River steamboat pilot. Scott, caught in New Orleans at the outbreak of the war, had had a part interest in a boat load of cotton confiscated by Confederate General Gideon Pillow. Saying that he was completely out of money, Scott wanted the Federal government to make restitution. Lincoln merely took Scott's papers with a promise to look them over and take appropriate action if they were found to be correct.[41]

In the short time left before the Cabinet meeting at eleven o'clock, Lincoln wanted to visit the War Department. As he started to leave, he met two ladies who had just entered the corridor, shook hands, and asked their names. Recognizing that of Mrs. C. Dwight Hess, whose husband was one of the managers of Grover's Theatre, he expressed regret that he and Mrs. Lincoln would be unable to accept the theatre's invitation to be guests that night at Grover's performance of *Aladdin*.

Mrs. Hess and Helen Palmer Moss, her sister-in-law, said they had come to the White House to visit the conservatory, and Lincoln asked if they had seen his favorite lemon tree, at that time a mass of fruit and flowers. When they replied in the negative, he conducted them to it. Asked whether he was not feeling "very happy over the glorious news [about the war]," he replied, "Yes, madam, for the first time since this cruel war began, I can see my way clearly."[42] After picking a lemon for

*Secretary of War Edwin M. Stanton, worried about assassination rumors, urged Lincoln to have a competent guard, then after the President's murder took action that saved the capital from chaos in its time of crisis. (Lloyd Ostendorf Collection.)*

each of the visitors and asking the Scotch gardener to gather some flowers for them, the President departed.

Throughout the war Lincoln, when at home in the White House, had gone to the War Department at least twice a day to get news received by the Military Telegraph Bureau. He was eager this morning to learn whether word was in from General Sherman, whose forces were still chasing General Joseph E. Johnston's Army of Tennessee in North Carolina. None had arrived, but the President felt certain good news would come soon because of a dream he had had during the night. He would have been pleased to know that Johnston at that moment was preparing to initiate the steps that would lead to his surrender twelve days hence.

*Major Thomas J. Eckert was considered a likely guard by Lincoln, but excused himself, saying he would be busy with work referred to by Stanton.*

Lincoln engaged Edwin M. Stanton, Secretary of War, in conversation, after hanging over the screen door leading to Stanton's office the gray shawl Mary insisted that he wear.[43] He told Stanton that he had on Thursday invited General and Mrs. Grant to accompany him and Mary to the theatre on this Good Friday evening. Grant, in the city on matters relating to military business, including cessation of the draft and purchases of costly supplies,[44] had said they would go unless he could complete his work early enough on April 14 to catch a train for Burlington, New Jersey. Three of his children – Fred, Ellen (Nellie), and Ulysses, Jr. (Buck) – were in school there, and he was eager to see them again. If the General completed his work in time to catch the evening train, the Grants would not be going to the theatre. Stanton, unbeknownst to Lincoln, had been partially responsible for Grant's desire to get away if possible. He had learned of the proposed theatre party, told Grant that rumors of assassination were afloat, and urged him not to attend the theatre. Stanton now urged that Lincoln also give up his plans for the theatre. Failing in that, he told the President he should have a competent guard.[45]

"Stanton, do you know that Eckert [Thomas T. Eckert, General Superintendent of Military Telegraph] can break a poker over his arm?" was Lincoln's surprising rejoinder.

Not knowing what was coming, the Secretary answered, "No, why do you ask such a question?"

Lincoln had been present months before when Eckert had broken five soft iron pokers over his left forearm to demonstrate the poor quality of the tools purchased for use at the open fires heating the building. "Stanton," he said, "I have seen Eckert break five pokers, one after the other, over his arm, and I am thinking he would be the kind of man to go with me this evening. May I take him?"[46]

Stanton, still trying to discourage plans for the theatre party, declared that he had important work for Eckert to do that evening and could not spare him.

"Well," said Lincoln, "I will ask the Major [recently brevetted Brigadier General of Volunteers] himself, and he can do your work tomorrow." Going into the military telegraph headquarters Eckert had established for the War Department, Lincoln told Eckert of the theatre party and that he wanted the Major to be a member of the party but had been told by Stanton he could not be spared.

"Now, Major," Lincoln is said to have told Eckert, "come along. You can do Stanton's work tomorrow, and Mrs. Lincoln and I want you with us."[47]

Eckert, aware that Stanton objected to the theatre party, and that the Secretary had discouraged Grant's attendance, thanked the President but said he could not accept because the work referred to by Stanton must be done that evening.

Lincoln expressed his disappointment and indicated he would have to get someone else as a guard. "Stanton," he said, "insists upon having someone to protect me, but I would rather have you, Major, since I know you can break a poker over your arm."[48]

With that he returned to the office, gathered up his shawl, and departed for the White House, where it was now time for the Cabinet meeting he expected to be one of the most important of his administration.

# III
# "There Must Be No Bloody Work"

When the Cabinet met on April 14, Gideon Welles of Connecticut, Secretary of the Navy, was the only member of Lincoln's original Cabinet present. Secretary of State William H. Seward (of New York), who had also served since 1861, was confined to his bed. Now serving with Welles and Seward were Edwin M. Stanton of Ohio, Secretary of War; Hugh McCulloch of Indiana, Secretary of the Treasury; William Dennison of Ohio, Postmaster General; James Speed of Kentucky, Attorney General; and John P. Usher of Indiana, Secretary of the Interior. Usher, however, had submitted his resignation to become effective May 15.

Lincoln's Cabinet had never been a close-knit group and some members did not get along together.[1] "Considering the strong men who composed it [the Cabinet], the only wonder is that there was so little friction among them," John Nicolay wrote. "They disagreed constantly and heartily on minor questions, both with Mr. Lincoln and with each other, but their great devotion to the Union, coupled with his [Lincoln's] kindly forbearance, and the clear vision which assured him mastery over himself and others, kept peace . . . in his strangely assorted official family."[2]

Early in Lincoln's administration Tuesday and Friday had been set as the days for regular meetings of the Cabinet, but Lincoln was no stickler for following the schedule. Welles in September, 1862, described Cabinet meetings as "infrequent, irregular, and without system,"[3] while another member had said, "It would be well perhaps to postpone the Cabinet meetings altogether or indefinitely."[4]

Welles also reported that absenteeism at meetings was sometimes excessive. Often only three members, and occasionally only two, were attending meetings by 1864.[5]

Lincoln, whom Welles called a good listener and learner, endured the erratic behavior of some of his ministers with patience. "He [Lincoln] has good sense, intelligence, and an excellent heart, but is sadly perplexed, and distressed by events," the Navy Secretary wrote in September, 1862, when the war was going badly and some Cabinet members were questioning Lincoln's judgment.[6] Welles, always loyal, also wrote, "President Lincoln never shunned any responsibility and often declared that he, and not his Cabinet, was in fault for errors imputed to them, when I sometimes thought otherwise."[7]

However, when the chips were down, the President made the decisions, sometimes without consulting the Cabinet. "It was always plain that he was the master and they the subordinates," Charles A. Dana, Assistant Secretary of War, declared. "They constantly had to yield to his will in questions where responsibility fell upon him."[8]

At the hour of eleven scheduled for this Good Friday meeting, Welles and McCulloch were present along with Frederick Seward, serving as Acting Secretary of State in the absence of his father. Dennison and Speed soon arrived.[9] Still absent were Usher and Stanton. Both would be coming later, the latter especially delayed because of materials the President had asked him to bring.

The spirit of peace and joy prevailed. Relief and contentment showed in Lincoln's face as he sat in his study chair by the south window chatting about the "great news" with early arrivals.[10] At this very hour a prayer of thanksgiving was being spoken to open a great celebration at Fort Sumter attended by more than 4,500 persons, some of them as far away as New York. Precisely at noon Major General Robert Anderson, coming out of the retirement which had resulted from ill health generated by the happenings of April, 1861, would raise above the battered fort the same Stars and Stripes he had lowered before the opening guns of the rebellion exactly four years earlier.[11]

Some member of the Cabinet expressed curiosity about the heads of the Rebel government—whether they would flee the country or remain to be captured and tried. And if they were tried, what penalty would be imposed upon them? All present thought that, for the sake of general amity and good will, it would be desirable to have a minimum of judicial proceedings. But would it be wise to let the leaders in treason go entirely unpunished?

"It will be a difficult problem if it should occur," Speed commented.

"I suppose, Mr. President," Dennison asked, "you would not be sorry to have them escape out of the country?"

"Well," Lincoln replied slowly, "I should not be sorry to have them out of the country; but I should be for following them up pretty close to make sure of their going."[12]

Grant, arriving in accordance with Lincoln's earlier invitation, was welcomed cordially and showered with congratulations. Asked for details of the surrender at Appomattox, "he narrated them briefly and modestly."[13]

"What terms did you make for the common soldiers?" Lincoln inquired.

"I told them," Grant replied, "to go back to their homes and families, and they would not be molested, if they did nothing more."[14] Lincoln's face glowed with approval. And what about the present military situation?

Grant replied that he was hourly expecting word from Sherman. Lincoln expressed confidence it would come soon and be favorable "for he had last night the dream which he had had preceding nearly every great and important event of the war." The news coming after each time he had the dream had generally been favorable, and the dream itself had always been the same.

"It related to your element, the water," Lincoln replied when Welles asked for details. "I seemed to be in some indescribable vessel, moving with great rapidity toward an indefinite shore. I had this dream preceding Sumter, Bull Run, Antietam, Stone River, Gettysburg, Vicksburg, Wilmington, and others."

Grant declared that Stone River had certainly been no victory, that a few such victories would have ruined the country, and that he knew of no important results from it. Lincoln emphasized that victory did not always follow the dream but that the event or result was important. He had no doubt, however, that a battle had been fought or was about to take place.

"I had this strange dream again last night," Lincoln concluded, "and we shall, judging from the past, have great news very soon. It must relate to Sherman, my thoughts are in that direction, and I know no other very important event which is likely just now to occur."[15]

"At any rate," one of his auditors remarked, "it cannot presage a victory nor a defeat this time, for the war is over."

"Perhaps," Seward suggested, "at each of these periods there were possibilities of great change or disaster, and the vague feeling of uncertainty may have led to the dim vision in sleep."

"Perhaps," the President said thoughtfully, "perhaps that is the explanation."[16]

Cabinet members remembered the remarkable dream many times in the days thereafter and wondered whether it could possibly have presaged the tragedy which followed.

Usher arrived, and then Stanton came carrying a large roll of paper upon which he had been working. The discussions which followed were long and earnest, with evidence of "a hearty desire to restore peace and safety at the South, with as little harm as possible to the feelings or the property of the inhabitants."[17]

The matter of trade provided one problem needing solution. Stanton proposed that intercourse be opened by his issuing an order that the Treasury Department issue permits to all wishing to trade, and that he, Stanton, would order the vessels to be received in any port. Welles

*Frederick W. Seward was serving as Acting Secretary of State, taking over for his father, William H. Seward, who had been badly injured in a carriage accident.*

suggested that it would be better for the President to issue an executive order opening the ports of trade and prescribing therein the duties of the several departments represented by the Cabinet. He also proposed that the whole coast be opened to all wishing to trade, provided they had regular clearing and manifest and were entitled to a coast license. Stanton believed that the right to trade should not extend beyond the military line, but Grant thought it might embrace all east of the Mississippi. Lincoln said that the Secretaries of the Treasury, War, and Navy had given more thought to the subject than he had, and that he would be satisfied with any conclusion on which they united.[18]

Stanton then unrolled his sheets of paper on which he had drafted outlines for reconstruction. They had, he said, been prepared with much care, "embodying the President's views, and, as it was understood, those of the other members of the Cabinet." With a view to having something practical on which to base action, he had handed a copy to the President the preceding day.[19]

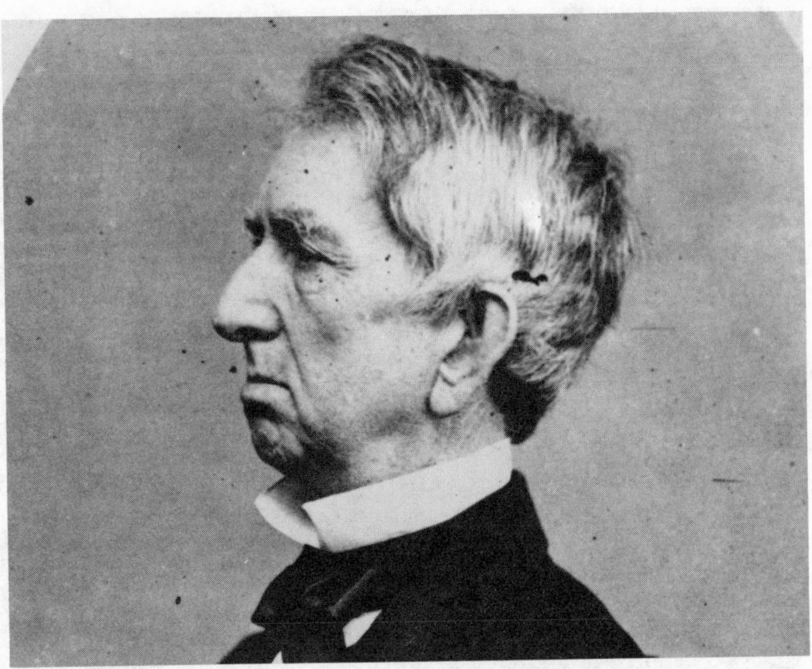

*William H. Seward of New York, Secretary of State 1861–1869. (National Park Service.)*

Frederick Seward later summarized the Stanton plans thus: "that the Treasury Department should take possession of the custom houses, and proceed to collect the revenues; that the War Department should garrison or destroy the forts; that the Navy Department should, in like manner, occupy the harbours, take possession of Navy yards, ships, and ordnance; that the Interior Department should send out its surveyors, land, pension, and Indian agents and set them to work; that the Postmaster General should reopen the postoffices and reestablish mail routes; that the Attorney General should look after the reestablishment of the Federal courts, with their judges, marshals, and attorneys; in short, that the machinery of the United States Government should be set in motion; that its laws should be faithfully observed and enforced; that anything like domestic violence or insurrection should be repressed; but that public authorities and private citizens should remain unmolested, if not found in actual hostility to the Government of the Union."[20]

Lincoln said that he had not had time to give attention to the details of the paper which Stanton had given him the day before but that it was substantially, in its general scope, the plan which the Cabinet had sometimes talked about in meetings.

*General Ulysses S. Grant. (National Park Service.)*

"He said that we would probably make some modifications, prescribe further details," Welles wrote in a magazine article later. "He said there were some suggestions he would wish to make, and he desired all to bring their minds to the question, for no greater or more important one could come before us or any future Cabinet. He thought it providential that this great rebellion was crushed just as Congress had adjourned, and there was none of the disturbing elements of that body to hinder and embarrass us. If we were wise and discreet, we would reanimate the states and get government in successful operation, with order prevailing and the Union reestablished before Congress came together in December. This he thought important. We could do better; accomplish more without than with them."[21]

"There are men in Congress, who, if their motives are good, are

*Gideon Welles, who served as Secretary of the Navy throughout Lincoln's administration, provided, through his comprehensive diary and magazine writing, a wealth of information about the administration, its Cabinet members and actions especially.*

nevertheless impracticable and who possess feelings of hate and vindictiveness in which I have no sympathy and could not participate," Welles quoted Lincoln as saying.

"I hope there will be no persecution, no bloody work, after the war is over. No one need expect me to take part in hanging or killing those men, even the worse of them. Frighten them out of the country, open the gates, let down the bars, scare them off," said the President, throwing up his hands as if scaring sheep. "Enough lives have been sacrificed. We must extinguish our resentment if we expect harmony and union. There has been too much of a desire on the part of some of our very good friends to be masters, to interfere with and dictate to those states, to treat the people not as fellow citizens; there is too little respect for their rights. I do not sympathize in these feelings."[22]

This led naturally to the question, who should be recognized as state authorities? Some of the Southern states now had military governors, but in several the legislatures were allegedly treasonable. Should these legislatures be allowed to continue until they committed some new overt act of hostility? Should the governors be requested to order new elections or should such elections be ordered by the Federal government?[23]

Stanton had proposed that a military or executive order be issued authorizing the War Department to reorganize those states whose individuality had supposedly been sacrificed. He also proposed establishment of a military department composed of Virginia and North Carolina with a military governor.[24]

Welles expressed concurrence with Stanton's belief that immediate action was needed, but he objected to military supervision or control and to the proposition of combining Virginia and North Carolina in the plan of a temporary government. Virginia, he argued, held a different position from that of any other state in rebellion. He pointed out that a Unionist minority, led by Francis H. Pierpont, had set up a rump government at Alexandria and had won from the Federal government recognition as the legitimate state of Virginia. Welles held that Virginia deserved different treatment because of the skeleton government maintained under Pierpont.[25]

Lincoln said that this was a point well taken. Dennison and Stanton felt that the general government would receive complete cooperation from Pierpont, and the former held with Welles that there should be separate propositions for the government of Virginia and North Carolina.[26]

It was now past 1:30 and little more was said about Stanton's proposals. Expressing belief that Virginia and North Carolina required different treatment, the President directed Stanton to draw separate plans for the two states and furnish copies to each member of the Cabinet for the next meeting on the following Tuesday.[27]

"We must not stultify ourselves regarding Virginia, but we must help her," he asserted. He then emphasized the importance of deliberating upon and carefully considering the matter discussed, and that in the interest of peace the Cabinet must begin to act.[28]

Lincoln was thinking of his "soldier boys" as the meeting broke up. "We must look to you, Mr. Secretary, for the money to pay off the soldiers," he said as he took McCulloch's hand.

"I shall look to the people," replied the Secretary of the Treasury, who had been in office only five weeks. "They have not failed us this far, and I don't think they will now."[29] McCulloch nevertheless knew that the funding job ahead would not be easy. The total debt of the nation now stood at more than $2,366,055,000.[30]

Grant lingered at the close of the meeting to tell the President that he was now certain he could leave for Burlington on the afternoon train as he had hoped earlier. When the memo from Lincoln had arrived requesting Grant to come to the White House at eleven o'clock instead of nine, the General had expressed to his wife the uneasy feeling that the change would make it impossible for him to leave the city that afternoon. When she insisted that she must leave, he had promised that he would go, too, if at all possible.[31]

*Mrs. Ulysses S. Grant, no friend of Mary Lincoln, had from the start resisted acceptance of the Lincolns' invitation to attend the theatre. Her note reaching the General as the Cabinet meeting ended may have kept him from changing his decision not to attend. (Lincoln Memorial University.)*

Lincoln was disappointed at Grant's decision. He said that the people would be delighted to see the General and that he ought to stay and go to the theatre with the Lincolns on that account. Although the prospect of facing another adulatory crowd did not appeal to Grant, he might have wavered but for the note from his wife that had arrived at just that moment, expressing much anxiety to start for Burlington on the afternoon train.[32] Grant later learned that a messenger had arrived from the White House at midday to tell Mrs. Grant, "Mrs. Lincoln sends me, Madam, with her compliments to say she will call for you at exactly eight o'clock to go to the theatre." Mrs. Grant did not like the messenger's looks and tone, and undoubtedly was wanting to avoid another contact with Mary, who had greatly embarrassed her in a fit of jealous rage in Richmond early in April. She consequently had commanded the messenger to "return with my compliments to Mrs. Lincoln and say I regret that as General Grant and I intend leaving the city this afternoon, we will not, therefore, be here to accompany the President and Mrs. Lincoln to the theatre."[33]

Seward, one of the last to leave, reminded the President that the country had a new British minister in Sir Frederick Bruce, who had arrived in Washington and was awaiting presentation. At what time would it be convenient for the President to receive him?

"Tomorrow at two o'clock," Lincoln replied after a moment's thought.

"In the Blue Room, I suppose?"

"Yes, in the Blue Room and," he added with a smile, "don't forget to send up the speeches beforehand. I would like to look them over."[34]

That exchange indicates that Lincoln did not, as some have claimed, write on this or any preceding day the remarks made when the British minister was received by President Andrew Johnson on April 20.[35]

As most of the Cabinet members went down the stairs together, several commented again on the cheerful mood so apparent in the President. "That's the most satisfactory Cabinet meeting I have attended in many a long day. . . . Didn't our chief look grand today?" commented Stanton.[36] Usher thought the President had never appeared to better advantage.[37]

# IV
# Urgent Business, but Time for Good Deeds

There is no evidence that Lincoln took time to eat lunch on April 14. Shortly after the Cabinet adjourned, he returned to his office eating an apple, his favorite fruit and often the only food he ate at noontime. Ahead of him was Edward D. Neill, an assistant secretary since the resignation of William O. Stoddard early in 1864. The colonel of a Vermont regiment, made a brigadier general while on furlough from the Army of the Potomac, was now at the White House to see if his commission had been signed by the President.

While Neill explained that he had been looking for the commission on the President's desk, Lincoln placed his hand on the bell pull. "He was," Neill said, "ringing for Andrew Johnson who was waiting below to see him in answer to a request sent the Vice President earlier." As Neill left, saying he would return later, Johnson was ushered in and Lincoln advanced and took him by the hand.[1]

What Lincoln and Johnson talked about can only be assumed. Since the Vice President had consistently preached a hard line attitude toward the South and its leaders—"that Davis and a few others of the arch-conspirators should be tried, convicted, and hanged for treason"[2]—Lincoln undoubtedly reviewed the discussions and decisions of the Cabinet meeting with the hope of softening his vice president's attitude and securing his support as Reconstruction started.

The hour following the interview with Johnson was a busy one for the President. Seldom, even on normal days, was he inaccessible to those asking to see him. On many days, when business was not too pressing, he would have his door thrown open between two and three o'clock for what he playfully called his "Beggar's Opera," an opportunity for all in the hall to enter and prefer their requests.[3]

There was no "Beggar's Opera" today. He was anticipating a drive with Mary at three o'clock, and before that hour there were visitors to see

*Vice President Andrew Johnson. (National Park Service.)*

on official matters, pardons to sign, and certainly some unscheduled business that would demand attention. Not all who wanted to see him would be able to do so.

"I went to the Executive Mansion to take leave of the President [before leaving Washington on a trip North]," L. E. Chittenden, Register of the Treasury, wrote later. "So many were waiting, the President seemed so busy with pressing business, that I came away without sending in my card."[4]

A memorandum signed by Lincoln on April 14 indicates that Governor Thomas Swann and Senator John A. J. Creswell of Maryland called concerning Maryland appointments. Swann, only recently elected governor of his state as the Union Party candidate, had called on Lincoln with others on March 9 to "personally complain of me about action in regard to the offices in Maryland."[5] On March 20, the President had wired Swann, saying, "I wish you would find Cresswell [sic] and bring him with you and see me tomorrow." Circumstances apparently kept Swann and

Creswell (who had been elected to the Senate on February 14 to succeed the late Senator Thomas H. Hicks) from seeing Lincoln for more than three weeks.[6]

Lincoln's memorandum of April 14, reading, "Gov. Swann and Senator Cresswell [sic] present the above today, which they do on a plan suggested by me," was accompanied by his endorsement of appointees for ten positions. Included was that of Edwin H. Webster of Bel-Air, Harford County, for the post of Collector of Customs.[7]

There are reasons to believe that Webster, also a former Congressman, accompanied Swann and Creswell but stayed only long enough to receive the President's endorsement on a petition seeking the release of George S. Herron, a member of Company C, 1st Maryland Cavalry, C.S.A., from Camp Chase, Ohio, where he had been confined since his capture in August, 1864. The prisoner's brother, the Reverend S. D. Herron of Baltimore, had written a memorial sometime earlier requesting clemency for his brother and put it in Webster's hands for presentation to the President. When no action had been reported, Herron on April 13 had addressed directly to the President an appeal on behalf "of a youthful brother confined as a rebel prisoner of war [who is] dangerously ill in the hospital at Camp Chase . . . with chronic diarrhea, is scarcely able to walk, and cannot possibly endure it beyond a short time in his confinement." Written by John Hay but signed by Lincoln, the endorsement on Herron's appeal read, "Let this prisoner be discharged on taking the oath of Dec. 8, 1863." War Department records show that young Herron was released on April 20, 1865, by order of the Commissary General of Prisoners, dated April 17.[8]

Tradition in the Webster family, supported by the colonel's obituary appearing in the *Baltimore Sun* of April 25, 1893, and a summary of his life supplied by the Maryland Historical Society, has it that Webster not only saw Lincoln on April 14 but that the latter's endorsement of his appointment as Collector of Customs at Baltimore was found on the President's person after his assassination.[9] The latter part of this story, however, was not verified when a box supposedly containing all items taken from Lincoln's pockets after his murder was opened at the Library of Congress on February 12, 1976.[10]

How many pardons Lincoln signed on April 14 will undoubtedly never be known. To him, however, "life was sacred, and he never would sign a paper that would take life away without deliberation."[11] Even in the midst of the war he had granted pardons to hundreds of Confederates who were facing death or long imprisonment. "They say," he commented to a member of his official family, "that I destroy discipline and am cruel to the Army when I will not let them shoot a soldier now and then. But I cannot see it. If God wanted me to see it, he would let me know it, and until he does, I shall go on pardoning and being cruel to the end."[12]

Since Lee's surrender Lincoln had been working harder than ever to consider all appeals for clemency. Explaining Lincoln's diligence, one of his biographers wrote: "Having some reason to fear that men who were in jail for disloyalty might, if they remained there, come up before military courts that would not be so sympathetic as he, the President worked diligently to clean up the docket that remained . . . Up to the twelfth of April he wrote the endorsements in his own hand; but on the thirteenth he found time to go hastily through a few more applications and, in order that he might work faster, he had John Hay write some slips, 'Let this man take the [loyalty] oath of Dec. 8, 1863, and be discharged.' These the President signed and attached them to as many applications as he had time to approve."[13]

Hay apparently varied the wording of endorsements as pressures mounted, the one for Herron being a shade different from that Lincoln had requested. Another known to have been written on April 14 reads, "Let the Prisoner be released on taking the oath of Dec. 8, 1863." In this case it is evident that Hay in his haste had started to write "President," then changed the word to Prisoner. The name of the individual pardoned is unknown.[14]

Among the pardons Lincoln signed on this afternoon was one for a soldier sentenced to be shot for desertion. As he signed, he is reported to have made a typical Lincolnesque observation: "Well, I think this boy can do more good above ground than under ground."[15]

Another order of April 14 written by Hay and signed by Lincoln appears on an appeal from a widow from Richmond, Maine, who had asked that her son be released from the Army because he was only seventeen years old. The cryptic order: "Let Thomas Geary be discharged from the service on refunding any bounty received."[16]

Despite the pressure of business, Lincoln took a few minutes to hear the plea of a servant who had lived with his family for several years in Springfield. She had married a man who was now in the Army. After managing to reach Washington, she was now asking for his release from the service. The President indicated pleasure at seeing her, gave her a basket of fruit, and directed her to come back the next day when he would provide a pass through the lines and money to buy clothes for herself and children.[17]

One of Lincoln's most important midafternoon business items, because it related to possibilities for readmitting Virginia into the Union, was an interview with James Washington Singleton of Mount Sterling, Illinois. Singleton, who carried the title of general because he had served as a brigadier of Illinois militia during the "war" of 1844 against the Mormons, was a native of Virginia and had ancestral connections in common with George Washington.[18] In Illinois after 1834 he had been numbered among Lincoln's friends, yet he was frequently a dissident in respect to party and governmental policies during the Civil War, which he declared could have been avoided but for the machinations of political "war hawks." He nevertheless labored persistently for peace, sometimes as a free-lance negotiator, apparently trusted by both Lincoln and Virginia authorities. Later in the war he made several trips to Richmond bent on peace efforts and was credited with playing a major role in bringing about the Hampton Roads Conference of February 3.[19]

Earlier in 1865 Singleton had also been involved with several prominent individuals—including Orville H. Browning, lawyer and ex-Senator from Illinois; Judge James Hughes of the Court of Appeals; and Robert E. Coxe of Canada—in a plan to get Southern produce such as cotton, turpentine, and rosin through Grant's lines under Treasure trade permits. Lincoln had at first approved the plan as a possible means of shortening the war, but withdrew support when it seemed that at least some of the men hoped to make a fortune while helping the North to get products in short supply.[20]

While withholding official sanction of Singleton's "negotiations" in behalf of peace and reconstruction, Lincoln was always ready to take action if encouraging proposals emerged from his friend's efforts.[21] On April 13 he had written a pass—"Allow Gen. Singleton to pass to Richmond and return"[22]—as Singleton prepared to leave for the Confederate capital on April 15. It can be assumed that the major objective of the interview on April 14 was to review with Singleton the proposals for reconstruction the Cabinet had heard earlier in the day.

The business of the afternoon seemingly complete, Lincoln stepped into a closet attached to his office to freshen up before the ride with Mary. There Charles A. Dana, Assistant Secretary of War, found him, his coat off and sleeves rolled up, washing his hands. Dana had received a telegram from the Provost Marshal in Portland, Maine, saying that he had positive information that Jacob Thompson of Mississippi, former Secretary of the Interior and now a semi-diplomatic agent in Canada for the Confederate government, would pass through Portland that night in order to take a steamer for England.

Dana had shown the telegram to Stanton, who had promptly ordered, "Arrest him," then added, "No wait, better go over and see the President."

"What is it? What's up?" Lincoln asked Dana. The Assistant Secretary read the telegram to Lincoln, who then wanted to know what Stanton had said.

"He says arrest him," Dana replied, "but that I should refer the question to you."

"Well," said Lincoln, slowly wiping his hands, "No, I rather think not. When you have got an elephant by the hind leg, and he's trying to run away, it's best to let him run."[23]

Congressman Edward H. Rollins of New Hampshire had now arrived to secure the President's endorsement on a petition from New Hampshire addressed to the Secretary of War. Lincoln took the petition and, resting it on his knee, wrote the endorsement: "Hon. Secretary of War, please see and hear Hon. Mr. Rollins, & oblige him if you consistently can."[24]

Lincoln also took time to speak briefly with Colonel William T. Coggeshall, who while reporting for the *Ohio State Journal* had won the friendship of the President-elect during the trip to Washington for the first inaugural. Early in the war Coggeshall had served as a military aide, going on secret missions for Lincoln. Now editor of the *Ohio State Journal*, he had been in the East and was seeing the President before leaving for home.[25]

It was now past three o'clock, but Lincoln paused for a kindly act before he and Mary departed. As he descended the stair, he chanced to hear a one-armed soldier say, "I would almost give my other hand if I could shake that of Abraham Lincoln."

"You shall do that and it shall cost you nothing, my boy!" the President declared as he walked forward and grasped the soldier's hand. Still holding it, he asked the man's name and regiment and where he had lost his arm and called him a brave soldier.[26]

He then hurried to keep his date with Mary, already waiting in the carriage.

# V
# "I Never Saw Him So Supremely Cheerful"

Fleecy white clouds feathered the sky, the temperature stood at a comfortable 68, and a gentle southwest wind played around their shoulders as the President and Mary started their drive.[1] Both were eager for this ride in their open carriage as the result of a little note, "playfully and tenderly worded," Lincoln had sent to Mary two days earlier, indicating the hour of the day he would be ready to go.[2]

In starting, Mary asked if anyone should accompany them. "No – I prefer to ride by ourselves today," Lincoln replied. Apparently, he wanted to converse with her alone.

Mary later wrote that she had never seen him so supremely cheerful. " . . . his manner was even playful," she wrote. "He was so gay, that I said to him, laughingly, 'Dear Husband, you startle me by your great cheerfulness. I have not seen you so happy since before Willie's death.'"[3]

"And well I may feel so, Mary," her husband replied. "I consider *this day*, the war, has come to a close." Then he added, "We must *both*, be more cheerful in the future – between the war and the loss of our darling Willie – we have both, been very miserable."[4]

Their conversation during the drive, as reported by Mary to friends and relatives later, covered a wide range of subjects with much emphasis on plans for the future.

"Mary," Lincoln said, "we have had a hard time of it since we came to Washington, but the war is over, and with God's blessing we may hope for four years of peace and happiness, and then we will go back to Illinois and pass the rest of our lives in quiet. We have laid by some money, and during this term we will try and save up more, but I shall not have enough to support us. We will go back to Illinois, and I will open a law office at Springfield or Chicago and practice law and at least do enough to help give us a livelihood."[5]

Perhaps Lincoln was recalling at this moment the request he had made of Herndon, his law partner of sixteen years, on the day before he left Springfield for Washington. "Let it continue to hang there," he had said of the sign board—*Lincoln & Herndon*—swinging from its rusty hinges. "Give our clients to understand that the election of a President makes no change in the firm of Lincoln & Herndon. If I live I'm coming back some time, and then we'll go right on practicing law as if nothing had happened."[6]

Earlier in the week, Lincoln had proposed to Mary that they go abroad for a time after the expiration of his second term. "He appeared to anticipate much pleasure from a visit to Palestine," she wrote her former minister.[7] He also wanted to cross the Rockies and visit California.[8] Indeed, he had talked at times about settling in California eventually because there might be more opportunity for his sons in that state.[9] Now, however, being released from the tensions under which he had lived for so long, his mind turned to things and events of days long past and "he was like a boy out of school." He recalled happenings of his boyhood and early manhood, spoke of his little brown cottage, his law office, the courtroom, the green bag for his briefs and law papers, adventures with old friends, and of experiences while riding the circuit.[10]

What route the Lincolns followed on this last ride together has never been established with finality. William H. Crook, one of Lincoln's bodyguards, said that Mrs. Lincoln had informed him that they drove to the Soldiers' Home.[11] Several individuals reported that they had seen and in some cases spoken with him at the Navy Yard. Inasmuch as the Lincolns could not have visited both the Soldiers' Home, about three miles northeast of the White House, and the Navy Yard in the time they were out, it is assumed that they drove *toward* the Soldiers' Home, then over to the Navy Yard in southeast Washington.

William H. Flood, who in April, 1865, was acting ensign and executive officer of the United States steamer *Primrose*, which was then anchored in the Navy Yard basin for repairs, recalled his conversation with Lincoln on this historic afternoon. Flood's grandfather, William G. Flood, had been in the Illinois legislature with Lincoln twenty-five years earlier, and the President had seen young Flood frequently when the latter was a boy. He had somehow learned that Flood was with the *Primrose*, and on arriving at the Navy Yard he sent for the young man.

"Which is the ship with a history?" he asked after introducing Mrs. Lincoln.

"Well, Mr. President," Flood replied, "they've all got histories, more or less. They've all been mussing around under fire quite a lot; but I guess you mean the *Montauk* over there. She's got the hardest hittin', and has been in the tightest spots."

"That's the one, Flood," Lincoln replied. "Take me over to her."

Flood said that by the time they got down to the *Montauk* officers were "popping up from all over to meet the President." "Lincoln," the young officer reported, "didn't seem to like the fuss at all." Neither, it seems, did Flood, who shortly excused himself – but not before the President had invited him to visit the White House.

"I was told later," Flood said, "that he went aboard the *Montauk* and looked all around her before driving home with Mrs. Lincoln."[12]

A letter which Dr. George B. Todd, surgeon on the *Montauk*, wrote to his brother, Harry P. Todd, on April 15 ties in with Flood's account.

"Yesterday about 3 P.M.," Todd wrote, "the President and wife drove down to the Navy Yard and paid our ship a visit, going all over her, accompanied by us all. Both seemed very happy, and so expressed themselves, glad that this war was over, or near its end, and then drove back to the White House."[13] As fate would have it, both Flood and Dr. Todd would be in attendance at Ford's Theatre that night when the President was assassinated.

Still another individual who verified statements that the President and Mary had visited the *Montauk*, a fact earlier in question, was Francis D. Blakeslee, in 1865 a 19-year-old clerk in the Quartermaster General's office. Blakeslee, later a Methodist minister and college president, had gone to the Navy Yard after government offices closed at noon in observance of Good Friday, and apparently saw the Lincolns before the President sought out Flood.

Writing in his diary, Blakeslee said, "Some fellow clerks and I went to the Navy Yard to see some monitors which had come in for repairs from the Fort Fisher engagement. Just before we left, President Lincoln and his wife drove into that part of the Yard where we were, and my fellow clerks and I saluted them as they sat in their carriage . . . My recollection is that the President acknowledged the salutes."[14]

When the Lincolns returned to the White House late in the afternoon, the President saw two friends, Richard J. Oglesby, Governor of Illinois, and General Isham N. Haynie, both of Springfield, going across the lawn toward the Treasury Building.

"Come back, boys, come back," Lincoln shouted.[15]

In his diary some time in the early evening, Haynie wrote, "At five o'clock this afternoon Governor Oglesby and I called at the White House. Mr. Lincoln was not in, but just as we were going away his carriage, with himself, wife and Tad, drove up. The President called us back. We went up into his reception room and had a pleasant, humorous hour with him. He read four chapters of Petroleum V. Nasby's book (recently published) to us, and continued reading until he was called for dinner, at about six o'clock, when we left him."[16] Apparently, Oglesby and Haynie were some distance away when the Lincolns drove up, and Haynie, knowing that Tad usually accompanied them on their drives, assumed the lad had been with them on this day.

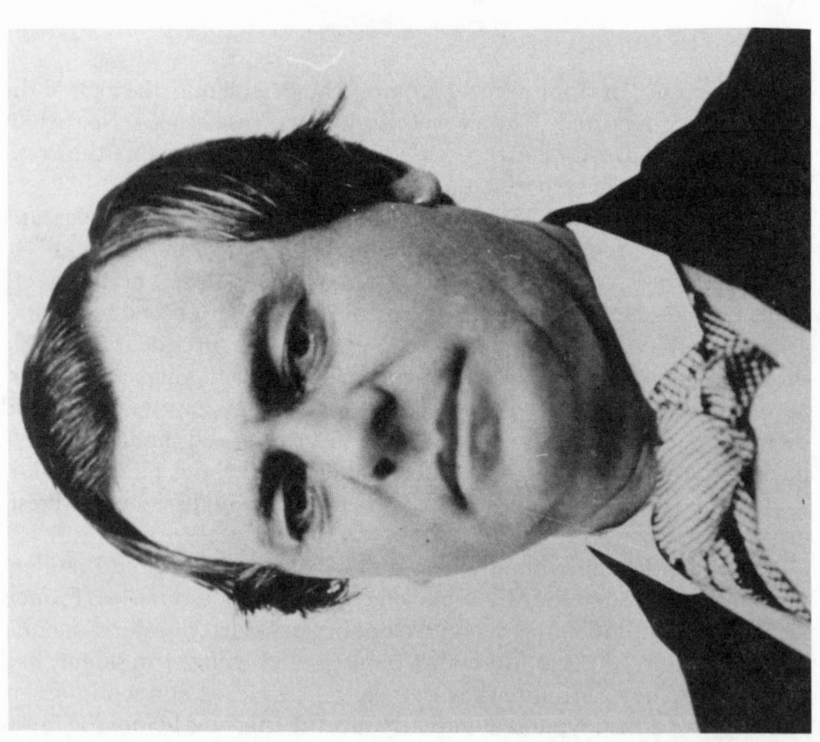

*The Nasby Papers*, produced with quaint satire, supposedly by an illiterate, hypocritical, dissolute country preacher, guilty of countless orthographical atrocities, were Lincoln's favorite form of light reading. He not only kept a pamphlet containing the first numbers of the series in his desk but also carried copies in his pocket.[17] These he was wont "to read on all occasions to visitors, no matter who they might be, or what their business was." It is recorded that he seriously offended many of the great men of the Republican Party in this way.[18]

"Grave and reverent Senators who came charged to the brim with important business," a book of reminiscences of Lincoln by prominent men reported, "took it ill that the President should postpone the consideration thereof while he read them a letter from 'Saint's Rest wich is in the state uv Noo Jersey.'"[19]

Lincoln, who felt that "grave statesmen, as a rule, do not understand humor, or comprehend its meaning or effect," showed little concern over the reaction of listeners. He is reported to have said that, next to a dispatch announcing a Union victory, he read a Nasby letter with most pleasure.[20]

Lincoln admired the author of *The Nasby Papers*, David Ross Locke, as much as he did his writings. Locke and Lincoln had become acquainted during the Lincoln-Douglas debates when Locke, at that time an itinerant printer and reporter, had conducted an interview.

Locke, who regarded Lincoln as a master satirist, was able to relate Lincoln anecdotes nowhere else recorded. In 1863, Lincoln wrote Locke a letter that concluded: "Why don't you come to Washington and see me? Is there no place you want? Come on and I will give you any place you ask for—*that you are capable of filling—and fit to fill.*"[21]

Locke could also furnish an interesting example of Lincoln's penchant for pardoning deserters.

"No man on earth hated blood as much as Lincoln did," Locke wrote for a book of reminiscences in 1888. He then told how, in 1864, he had gone to Washington to seek a pardon for a young Ohioan who had applied for a furlough to return home after hearing that the girl to whom he was engaged had taken up with a rival. Half mad and reckless of consequences, he had deserted after the furlough was refused. Although he had learned that the information received was partially true, he had married the girl, then been arrested as a deserter, tried, and sentenced to be shot. When Locke outlined the circumstances, Lincoln had at once signed a pardon.

*General Isham N. Haynie, left, and Governor Richard J. Oglesby of Illinois were entertained by Lincoln with four chapters from the latest book of quaint satire by political satirist Petroleum Vesuvius Nasby (David Ross Locke). Haynie and Oglesby were present at Lincoln's deathbed later. (Photos courtesy Illinois State Historical Library.)*

"Probably in less than a year the young man will wish I had withheld the pardon," Lincoln had commented. "We can't tell, though. I suppose when I was a young man I would have done the same fool thing."[22]

How much Lincoln enjoyed opportunity to visit with close friends and read passages from his favorite humorist to them is revealed by Governor Oglesby's comment about that late afternoon visit. "How long we remained there I do not know," he said later. "They kept sending for him to come to dinner. He promised each time to go, but would continue reading the book. Finally he got a sort of peremptory order that he must come to dinner at once. It was explained to me by the old man at the door that they were going to have dinner and then go to the theatre."[23]

After Tom Pendel, the doorkeeper, had explained about the theatre party and the need for the Lincolns to dine promptly, Governor Oglesby "called off" the visit. Lincoln was nevertheless reluctant to see them go, saying, "I'd much rather swap stories than eat."[24]

# VI
# Reluctantly He Starts for the Theatre

Lincoln was, in Mary's opinion, "more cheerful and joyous than he had been in years," yet during dinner with her, Robert, and Tad he complained that he was worn out. Nevertheless, he said, they would go to the theatre and have a good laugh at the play.[1]

Mary later told Dr. Anson G. Henry, one of the Lincolns' close friends, that she was suffering from a bad headache after their drive and had suggested that they stay home. Her husband, however, had insisted that he must go. If he stayed home, he had said, he would be obliged to see company all evening and would have no rest. Since he had seemed determined to go, Mary had decided she would go, too. She could not think of his going without her; never had she felt so unwilling to be away from him.[2]

The Lincolns usually had their evening meal at seven[3] but dined early this evening and did not tarry long at the table. The meal over, Lincoln was eager to make his usual after-dinner trip to the War Department, but Noah Brooks was waiting to keep an early evening appointment. Brooks had become acquainted with Lincoln while in business in Illinois in the middle 1850s and later had stumped the state with him during the Lincoln-Douglas debates. This association had ripened into intimate friendship, especially after Brooks became Washington correspondent for the *Sacramento Union* in 1862. He had become a frequent visitor to the White House, and Lincoln had invited him to become his private secretary to replace John Nicolay, who was soon to become consul in Paris.[4]

The President told Brooks that he "had had a notion to send for him to go to the theatre with them but Mrs. Lincoln had already made up a party with other guests to take the place of General and Mrs. Grant." He told Brooks that he had "felt inclined to give up the whole thing after the Grants decided to leave Washington early."[5]

According to Brooks, it was Mary who "had rather insisted they ought to go." The papers had announced that the Grants and Lincolns would be at the theatre and by the latters' going the public would not be wholly disappointed. Brooks, fighting a bad cold, left shortly and on his way home met and chatted for awhile with Schuyler Colfax, who was returning to the White House to keep the appointment made with the President that morning.[6]

William H. Crook, a twenty-six-year-old policeman and former soldier, was Lincoln's bodyguard during the trip to the War Department. Because of pressures exerted on Lincoln to pay more attention to his safety, he had finally yielded in November, 1864, to demands that he have bodyguards around the clock. After one of the four original guards, Thomas Pendel, became doorkeeper at the White House at the end of 1864, Crook had succeeded him on January 4, 1865.[7] On April 14 Crook had been on duty since 8:00 A.M. but was still at the White House because John Parker, the guard for the four-until-midnight shift, was late again. The President's mood by this time had evidently changed a great deal; as he and Crook started their walk for what Crook later described as "a hurried visit" to the War Department, the guard found that Lincoln "was more depressed than I had ever seen him and his step was unusually slow."

Seemingly impressed by the violent appearance of some drunken men they passed in crossing over to the War Department, the President said, "Crook, do you know I believe there are men who want to take my life?" Then, after a pause, he added in a calm tone, half to himself, "And I have no doubt they will do it."

"Why do you think so, Mr. President?" asked his startled companion.

"Other men have been assassinated," Lincoln replied, still in that manner of stating something to himself.

"I hope you are mistaken, Mr. President," Crook managed to say.

"I have perfect confidence in those who are around me—in every one of you men," Lincoln asserted after they had walked a short distance in silence. "I know no one could do it and escape alive. But if it is to be done, it is impossible to prevent it."[8]

At the War Department, Lincoln talked briefly with Stanton. There was still no word from Sherman, but both men were happy in the knowledge that the war was all but over. As they expressed their joy, Lincoln, from his greater height, dropped his long arm upon Stanton's shoulders, and a great surge of affection for his chief welled up in the Secretary.[9]

When Lincoln came out of the Secretary's office, Crook noted that every trace of his earlier depression had vanished. He chatted with his companion as usual, saying among other things that he and Mrs. Lincoln were going to see *Our American Cousin*. However, he showed no enthusiasm for going.

"It has been advertised that we will be there, and I cannot disappoint the people," he commented. "Otherwise I would not go. I do not want to go."[10]

Crook, who had become uneasy from thoughts of possible danger to his charge, urged the President not to go to the theatre. Lincoln again said he did not want to disappoint the people who would be present. Crook then urged that he be allowed to stay on duty and accompany the party to the theatre.

"No, Crook," Lincoln said kindly but firmly. "You have had a long hard day's work already and must go home to sleep and rest."[11]

By this time they had reached the portico of the White House. "Goodbye, Crook," the President said as they parted. It was the first time, Crook recalled later, that he had said other than "Good night." Lincoln, according to Crook, had several times talked about the possibility that an attempt might be made on his life but had never before expressed belief that he would be assassinated. Crook said he believed that Lincoln "had some vague sort of warning that the attempt would be made on the night of the 14th."[12]

After returning from the War Department, Lincoln snatched a few minutes to catch up on unfinished business in his office before Colfax arrived. It was undoubtedly during this period that he saw William Pitt Kellogg, Chief Justice of Nebraska Territory, who was being named Collector of the Port of New Orleans. Kellogg had been persuaded by Lincoln on April 12 to give up his judicial post to become the first collector at New Orleans since the war. Hugh McCulloch, Secretary of the Treasury, had informed him on April 14 that his commission had been sent to the White House. Kellogg called there but Lincoln had gone on his ride with Mary. Returning later, he was handed his commission by John Hay.

"Mr. Lincoln," Kellogg wrote, "was in his room, apparently signing papers. With a few words, to be careful and discreet in the discharge of my duties, he bade me goodbye."[13]

Among the other individuals Lincoln is supposed to have seen on the evening of April 14 was Robert L. Fraser, at that time an office boy at Grover's Theatre and later a prominent insurance man in Charleston, West Virginia.

According to Fraser, C. D. Hess, one of the theatre's two managers, had sent him to the White House with a note reminding the President that he and Mrs. Lincoln were expected to be guests at Grover's that night. At the White House, young Fraser looked about for Tad, whom he knew and liked. He was unable to find him. The President gave him a note for Hess indicating that the Lincolns had made plans to go to Ford's.

Robert Fraser claimed that after the assassination, he had gone through the theatre's wastebasket and retrieved a fragment of Lincoln's note, including the signature. He then sold it to a stranger for $20.[14]

Since the afternoon papers had announced the Lincolns' intention to go to Ford's, and also because Mrs. Lincoln had sent a note to Leonard Grover, Hess's partner, expressing regret that his invitation could not be accepted, some doubt is cast on the credibility of Fraser's story. Inasmuch as Grover was in New York on April 14, it is, of course, possible that Hess had not seen Mary's note.[15] But if Fraser did see Lincoln, it must have been just before or after the trip to the War Department.

It is probable, too, that Lincoln, just before Colfax was ushered in, signed the commission reappointing Alvin Saunders of Iowa Governor of Nebraska Territory. Saunders, governor of the territory since 1861, had seen the President on April 13 and been told to go back home and not be concerned about his reappointment; it would be made. After Lincoln's death the signed commission was found on his desk, unfolded.[16]

Colfax arrived at 7:30 and Pendel saw him up to the President's office.[17] For nearly half an hour the two men chatted until Mary came in and in a half-laughing, half-serious tone, said, "Well, Mr. Lincoln, are you going to the theatre with me or not?"

"I suppose I shall have to go, Colfax," Lincoln told the Speaker.[18]

At about that moment, Pendel arrived with the card of George Ashmun of Massachusetts, whom he had shown into the Red Room downstairs.[19]

After getting his hat and coat, Lincoln stopped at the door to Robert's room and said to his eldest son, "We are going to the theatre, Bob; don't you want to go?"

The weary young captain, who had not slept in a bed for two weeks, said he would prefer to stay home, finish the cigar he was smoking, and go to bed early.

"All right, my boy," the President replied. "Do just what you feel most like. Good night."

"Good night, Father," Robert answered.[20]

The Lincolns and Colfax then went downstairs to be with Mr. Ashmun. Lincoln mentioned his trip into Richmond and his guests told of the uneasiness felt in the North lest some traitor shoot him while in the Rebel capital.

"I would have been alarmed myself if any other man had been President and gone there," Lincoln asserted, "but I, myself, did not feel any danger whatever."[21]

"By the way, Colfax," Lincoln said to the Speaker, "Sumner has the gavel of the Confederate Congress, which he got at Richmond, and intended to give to the Secretary of War, but I insisted that he must give it to you."[22]

Lincoln was informed that two Southerners were waiting for a pass so they could go safely to Richmond and Petersburg. He hastily scrawled a note and had it delivered to them: "No pass is necessary now to authorize anyone to go & return from Petersburg & Richmond. People go & return just as they did before the war. A. Lincoln."[23]

The Lincolns, Ashmun, and Colfax presently came out of the Red Room and stood chatting in the inner corridor. Their conversation as they passed out of the corridor into the main vestibule was about Colfax's trip across the continent.[24] "Don't forget, Colfax," Lincoln reminded the Speaker, "to tell those miners that that's my speech to them, which I send by you. Let me hear from you on the road, and I will telegraph you at San Francisco."[25]

Colfax was going upstairs to see John Hay,[26] and Lincoln repeated an earlier invitation that he accompany him and Mary to the theatre. Colfax, expecting to leave for the West the next morning, and having other engagements for the evening, again begged off.[27]

Ashmun, who had been permanent chairman of the Republican National Convention which nominated Lincoln in 1860, and had "presided over the excited & enthusiastic assemblage with dignity, tact, and ability,"[28] referred to a matter of business connected with a cotton claim, preferred by one of his clients. Ashmun wanted to have a commission appointed to examine and decide upon the merits of the case.

With considerable warmth, Lincoln declared, "I have done with commissions. I believe they are contrivances to cheat the government out of every pound of cotton they can lay their hands on."

Ashmun, perturbed, expressed the hope that Lincoln meant no personal imputation. Seeing that he had hurt his friend, Lincoln quickly replied, "You did not understand me, Ashmun. I did not mean what you inferred, I take it all back. I apologize to you, Ashmun."[29]

Pendel at this time informed Lincoln that Senator William M. Stewart of Nevada and Judge Niles Searles were upstairs waiting to see him. Stewart had met Searles, a former law partner, in New York on April 13 and had invited him to come along to Washington after Searles expressed a desire to meet Lincoln. They had decided to call at the White House in the evening, anticipating that Lincoln would be seeing visitors then. Lincoln, about to help Mary into the carriage, wrote a note for Pendel to take upstairs: "I am engaged to go to the theatre with Mrs. Lincoln. It is the kind of engagement I never break. Come with your friend tomorrow at ten, and I shall be glad to see you. A. Lincoln."[30]

Ashmun was waiting to say that he had another matter in mind – an appointment to see the President with Judge Charles P. Daly of New York the following day. Before climbing into his carriage, Lincoln wrote his final note on a card: "Allow Mr. Ashmun and friend to come in at 9 A.M. to-morrow. A. Lincoln."[31]

Allow Mr. Ashmun
& friend to come in
at 9 - A.M. to-mor-
row

A. Lincoln

April 14. 1865.

Why Ashmun and Daly wished to see the President remains a mystery. Daly, Chief Justice of the Court of Common Pleas in New York, was a staunch Democrat but had supported Lincoln's administration wholeheartedly and on several occasions had been consulted by the President and his Cabinet. His advice in the case of James Murray Mason and John Slidell may in fact have averted war with Great Britain. Daly had maintained that seizure of the two Confederate representatives (bound for Europe to seek aid for the South) could not be justified in view of a decision made by Chief Justice John Marshall, and that they should therefore be surrendered. The liberation of Mason and Slidell soothed the angry British, who felt that the seizure had violated international law.[32]

Daly had come to Washington on April 12, had dined on Friday evening with Sir Frederick Bruce, the new minister from Great Britain, Mr. Geoffre, the French minister, and other officials, and planned to see Lincoln with Ashmun on Saturday.[33]

The only reference known to exist relative to the reason for the appointment is found in Mrs. Daly's diary: "Had Mr. Lincoln lived, the Judge would have succeeded in the business that took him to Washington. Lincoln told Mr. Evarts [William M. Evarts, powerful New York City attorney who had been sent to England twice on special missions] that he had the greatest respect for Judge Daly, first as a man of strictest integrity and reliability, and next as a lawyer, for the government had been much indebted to him in two cases, in the matter of the privateers, delivering them from a great embarrassment, and in the Trent business."[34]

As the President was about to get into his carriage, Senator Stewart and Searles came out of the White House. Lincoln spied them and shook hands with Stewart, who introduced Searles. Lincoln repeated that he would be glad to see them in the morning. (The note which Lincoln had written to Stewart is not known to be extant. Stewart had dropped it on the floor on the way out of the White House.)[35]

Lincoln had one more visitor before he left. As he was stepping into the carriage, Congressman Isaac N. Arnold, long a close friend, walked up. "Excuse me now," the President told him. "I am going to the theatre. Come and see me in the morning."[36]

Still another visitor had left at eight o'clock without seeing the President. He was ex-Senator Orville Browning, who had called in the afternoon, possibly on business related to Singleton, but had left after learning

*George Ashmun of Massachusetts, left, was the recipient of Lincoln's last writing, center, setting up an appointment for him and his friend, Judge Charles P. Daly, right, for Saturday morning. (Photo of Ashmun and of Lincoln's writing, Library of Congress; Daly picture by Lillian Butte as seen in* The American Portrait Gallery, *1877.)*

*Ward Hill Lamon, close friend and self-appointed guard for Lincoln, was in Richmond when Lincoln was assassinated.*

that Lincoln was through receiving for the day. In his diary under April 14, Browning wrote, "At 7:00 P.M. we went back to the President's. I went into his room and sat there till 8 o'clock waiting for him, but he did not come."[37] Only when one remembers that three second-floor areas were being used as reception rooms can one believe it possible that Browning could have missed the President.

With Ned Burke at the reins and Charles Forbes as footman, the Lincoln carriage rolled out of the White House grounds to pick up their guests of the evening, Major Henry R. Rathbone and Miss Clara Harris, his step-sister and fiancée, whom Mary had invited as guests to replace the Grants.[38] There was no escort from the Union Light Guard along to watch for possible danger. The President had flatly refused to allow the Guard to escort him to either church or theatre.[39]

John Parker, who had finally arrived to relieve Crook, had meanwhile started for the theatre. Tom Pendel, like Crook, apparently had a feeling of foreboding; he asked the departing bodyguard, "John, are you prepared?" meaning to determine if Parker had his revolver and was ready to protect the President in case of assault. Alfonso Dunn, another doorkeeper, had interposed, "Oh, Tommy, there is no danger," to which the uneasy Pendel had replied, "Dunn, you don't know what might happen."[40]

And the faithful Lamon, who had worried constantly over the possibility that Lincoln might be assassinated, was not in the city to keep his usual close watch over his friend. Before leaving for Richmond on a mission for the President on April 12, he had tried, but failed, to extract from Lincoln a promise that he would not, in Lamon's absence, go out at night, *particularly to the theatre*. To John Usher, who was present, Lincoln had declared that Lamon "is a monomaniac over the subject of my safety," then dismissed his friend's fears as nonsense.[41]

# VII
# The Stage Is Set for Murder

John Wilkes Booth, who played the villain's role in the final drama of Abraham Lincoln's life, was the ninth of ten children born to Junius Brutus Booth, the eccentric British-born Shakespearean actor, and Mary Ann Holmes, without benefit of marriage for the parents.[1] His Christian names were bestowed in memory of the celebrated English agitator who his grandfather claimed was a distant relative.[2]

Johnnie, as he was known in his early years, seemed to be a normal boy in almost every way, although less selfish, more affectionate and gentle of manner than many, more combative and compulsive than others.[3] As he entered his teens, however, contrasting actions and attitudes became more evident. Where formerly he had been cheerful and gay, he was now apt to lapse into sullen silence. In 1881 his brother Edwin, a famous actor in his own right, remembered the teen-age Johnnie as "wild brained," a "rattle-pated fellow filled with Quixotic notions."[4]

Johnnie's sister Asia, closer to him than any other member of the large Booth family, called him a "singular combination of gravity and joy." She recorded that he was "very tender of flowers, and of insects and butterflies," was "passionately fond of music . . . was full of merriment but hated jokes."[5] Kind to the extreme, he couldn't bring himself to kill animals he and Asia had caught in traps when the family was hungry during winter.[6] At the same time he hated cats and is said to have exterminated those around the family farm.[7]

Asia also said that there was a taint of melancholy about the teen-age Johnnie.[8] This melancholy may have been provoked in part by the jibes of schoolmates after it became known that his father had deserted a wife in England and come to America with Mary Ann Holmes. Not until May 10, 1851, the thirteenth anniversary of Johnnie's birth, were his mother and father married.[9]

In all probability a greater contributor to the boy's melancholy was the emphasis a gypsy gave to his "bad hand" while reading his palm when he was about fourteen. Declaring that she had never seen a worse hand,

*John Wilkes Booth in one of his favorite pictures.*

the gypsy saw only trouble in its lines. She declared that Johnnie had been born "under an unlucky star," had in his hand "a thundering crowd of enemies—not one friend," "would break hearts," "die young," and "make a bad end." These predictions, Asia asserted, troubled Booth on numerous occasions during his life.[10]

The predictions may also have had something to do with Booth's determination to perform some deed that would make his name live forever. Several schoolmates testified that his thoughts of such an act surfaced frequently in his conversations.

"It was," one said, "a name in history he sought; a glorious career he thought of by day and dreamed of by night. He always said he would make his name remembered by succeeding generations."[11]

Another testified that Wilkes had declared he would "do something that would hand his name down to posterity, never to be forgotten, even after he had been dead a thousand years."[12]

And years after Booth had killed Lincoln a former schoolmate wrote, "I am led to but one conclusion in regard to his taking the life of Abraham Lincoln, and that is . . . his great desire to do some deed or accomplish some act that had never been done by any other man, so that his name might live in history."[13]

Always athletic, Booth from his youth was an accomplished horseman and crack shot. Later he was a skilled fencer and excellent swordsman whose feats with broadswords thrilled theatre audiences.[14] Declared to be one of the handsomest men of his day—with a face that resembled Poe's but was far handsomer—Booth was particularly charming to women and consequently was reported to be the hero of numerous amours.[15] At the climax of one of these, Actress Henrietta Irving attacked him with a dirk, then stabbed herself almost fatally.[16]

By 1865 Booth was concentrating much of his attention on Bessie Hale, a daughter of Senator John Parker Hale. A letter from his brother Junius to Asia said that Wilkes had given "the great part of the day [Feb. 13, 1865] to the torturing composition of a Valentine acrostic to send to the lady of his love, . . . then kept me up until 3½ A.M. to wait while he wrote her a long letter . . . every now and then using me as a dictionary."[17]

Attracted to the stage, Booth made his acting debut at seventeen. At first he was inclined to be negligent in learning his parts and was sometimes hissed.[18] In 1860, however, his star as a Shakespearean actor began to rise and critics were soon proclaiming him a better tragedian than his famous brother Edwin. After bronchial trouble and efforts to become an oil speculator led him to abandon acting for a while, he returned to the stage in 1864 to win even greater plaudits.[19]

Booth had always believed that slavery was "one of the greatest blessings (both for themselves [the slaves] and us) that God had ever bestowed upon a favored nation," and from the start of the Civil War his sympathies were with the South.[20] He nevertheless made no serious attempt to join the Confederate Army. His only approach to armed service came when he persuaded the captain of the Richmond Grays to let him don a nondescript uniform and join the company entraining for Harper's Ferry, where John Brown was being held. When Brown was hanged, Booth was seen "to grow pale and almost faint as he turned his head away."[21] As the war continued, he came to see it more violently as a struggle between tyranny and freedom. Even Edwin Booth conceded that his brother was insane on that point.[22]

Asia, who wondered why Booth did not fight for the South, feeling as he did, came to realize that her brother was serving the Confederacy in other ways—as a dealer in drugs needed by Southern doctors, as a spy, a blockade runner, a rebel. "I knew [then]," she concluded, "that if he had twenty lives they would be sacrificed freely for that [Southern] cause."[23]

By September, 1864, Booth had conceived a daring plan which he hoped would end the war, or at least secure the exchange of Southern prisoners. It called for him, with the aid of carefully selected collaborators, to kidnap Lincoln and carry him off to Richmond. Success in such a daring effort, he believed, would startle the world and make heroes of the perpetrators.

Between September and March 1, 1865, Booth recruited six helpers for his project: Samuel Arnold and Michael O'Laughlin, two former schoolmates living in Baltimore after brief stints in the Confederate Army; John H. Surratt, a secret dispatch rider for the Confederacy and the son of Mary E. Surratt, who had recently moved to Washington from Surrattsville, Maryland; George A. Atzerodt, a middle-aged wagonmaker from Port Tobacco, Maryland; David E. Herold, a "light and trifling" Washington youth of nineteen and former drug clerk; and Lewis Thorton Powell, alias Lewis Paine, a twenty-year-old deserter from the Confederate cavalry.[24]

On the afternoon of March 17 Booth's band was waiting to capture the President on his way to the Soldiers' Home on the outskirts of the city.[25] Lincoln, however, did not appear, and the conspirators separated in the belief that their plot had been discovered. Arnold and O'Laughlin returned to Baltimore and took no further part in Booth's plans. What part, if any, Surratt took in those later plans was never clearly established. Booth himself took two trips out of town but was back in Washington for good by April 8.[26]

Booth's decision to murder Lincoln was probably made on April 11. On that night he, Paine, and Herold heard Lincoln, in what proved to be the President's last speech, advocate limited Negro suffrage in discussing the future of Louisiana. "That means Nigger citizenship; now, by God, I'll put him through!" Booth is alleged to have said. "That is the last speech he will ever make," he added. Before Lincoln had finished, Booth tried to get Paine to shoot the President but the latter, thinking such an act too dangerous in those surroundings, refused.[27] By this time Booth had become possessed "by an insane notion that Lincoln was an inhuman tyrant whose death was desirable."[28] He shortly confided to his diary, "Something decisive must be done."

That Booth was probably turning over possible procedures in his mind on April 13 is suggested by the fact that on the afternoon of that day he went into the office of C. D. Hess, a partner of Grover's Theatre [later known as the National], seated himself, and interrupted a business conversation between Hess and the theatre's prompter to ask about their plans for the next couple of days. This action, contrary to Booth's usual procedure unless invited, so surprised Hess that he put away the manuscript under discussion and entered into conversation with his uninvited visitor.

Booth was interested in Grover's plans for illumination. When Hess replied that Friday night would be the great night for illumination, because April 14 would mark the celebration of the fall of Fort Sumter, Booth wanted to know whether Hess planned to invite the President. "Yes," Hess replied, "and that reminds me I must send that invitation."[29] Hess shortly dispatched the invitation to Mrs. Lincoln in accordance with his usual procedure, but it arrived after she had already received and accepted an invitation from Ford's.

Leonard Grover, Hess's partner, later learned that Booth had requested his close friend, John Deery, who kept a billiard parlor directly over the front entrance of Grover's, to purchase a box at the theatre for the Friday night performance. He did not, he told Deery, want to put himself under obligation to the management by accepting the complimentary box which would be proffered if he sought to buy a ticket himself. Deery said that he took Booth's money and purchased a ticket that would have put the actor in the box adjoining the Lincolns had Hess's invitation been accepted by the Presidential family.[30]

No one seemed to know where Booth spent the night of April 13. When three men (presumably Herold, Paine, and Atzerodt) sought Booth at the National Hotel on the morning of April 14, it was discovered that the bed in his room, No. 228, had not been touched.[31] Somewhere, however, he had written at 2:00 A.M. a short letter to his mother, in which he excused his brevity with "am in haste."[32]

Booth's first known movement after breakfast at the National Hotel on April 14 took him to the barber shop of Booker and Stewart on E Street near Grover's Theatre. After Charles H. M. Wood shaved him and "trimmed his hair round and dressed it,"[33] he dropped in at Grover's Theatre, presumably eager to learn whether Lincoln had accepted Hess's invitation to attend Grover's presentation of *Aladdin* that night. There he was seen by Mrs. Hess and her sister-in-law as they started the walk that later took them to the White House. Booth greeted them with a handshake, a fact which made the ladies remember for the rest of their lives that they had shaken the hands of both the assassin and his victim on April 14.[34]

From Grover's Booth went to the Kirkwood House at Twelfth Street and Pennsylvania Avenue, hoping to see Vice President Johnson. Booth had spoken to Atzerodt about getting from Johnson a military pass which would enable the conspirators to get into southern Maryland that night. He apparently had not heard that passes were no longer needed by travelers going south. Learning that neither Johnson nor his secretary, William Browning, was in, Booth wrote on a card: "Don't wish to disturb you; are you at home? J. Wilkes Booth." The clerk placed the card in Browning's box, and it was not picked up until the secretary returned at five o'clock.[35]

From the Kirkwood House, Booth started back toward the National Hotel. Thomas R. Florence, editor of the *Daily Constitutional Union*, wrote on April 15 that he had talked with Booth on the preceding day, and it is believed that their conversation took place at this time. Booth told Florence that he might soon be going to Canada, where several theatre managers were offering him engagements. He also claimed that he had lost about $6,000 in oil as a result of the recent floods at Oil City, Pennsylvania.[36]

At the National Hotel Booth saw Michael O'Laughlin who had called "to collect a debt."[37] At eleven Henry E. Merrick, a clerk at the National, saw Booth in the hotel office and noted that he looked unusually pale.[38]

Booth feared that he would be unable to get, through Vice President Johnson, the passes he believed necessary for travel south. His next movement therefore took him to Mrs. Surratt's boarding house on H Street near Sixth. He knew Mrs. Surratt was planning to go to Surrattsville with a boarder, Louis Weichmann, that afternoon. She could determine whether pickets were out three miles south of Washington along the route he was expecting to travel that night.[39] That request made, Booth stopped briefly at the stable he had rented back of Ford's Theatre several weeks earlier in which to keep a horse or horse and carriage. Mary Jane Anderson, a Negro woman who lived back of the theatre, testified at the conspiracy trial that she had seen Booth near the stable on this morning.[40]

Booth's next objective was the theatre itself, and he arrived there about noon. "There comes the handsomest man in Washington," Harry Clay Ford, the theatre's treasurer, commented as Booth approached.[41] Although he had played at Ford's only once since early November, 1863 (as Pescara in *The Apostate* on March 18, 1865), Booth had free access to the theatre as a longtime friend of the owner, John T. Ford, and had his mail sent there. Several letters from other cities were awaiting him, and he sat down on the theatre steps to read them. One letter apparently contained something amusing because he laughed every now and then as he read it.[42]

While at Ford's, Booth learned that a messenger from Mrs. Lincoln had come to the theatre about 10:30 and received tickets for the "state box" for that evening from James R. Ford, the business manager.[43] Clay Ford told Booth that the Grants were coming with the Lincolns. Then, just to tease Booth, he added that Jefferson Davis and General Lee would also be there, captives in another box.[44] Booth denounced Lee in vigorous terms for surrendering at Appomattox, but expressed hope that

*Ford's Theatre (with arched doorways, center) at the time of the assassination. The Star Saloon, where Booth did much of his drinking on that day, is to the right.*

the Confederate commander would not be paraded "as the Romans did their captives."[45]

From Ford's, Booth went to the stable of James W. Pumphrey at 224 C Street, near the National Hotel, to arrange for a saddle horse to be ready by four o'clock. When in the city in recent weeks, he had been riding a sorrel horse furnished by Pumphrey, but on this day the sorrel was engaged. Booth suggested that Pumphrey put off the person who had engaged the sorrel, but the stableman refused, saying that he would furnish a very good saddle horse in its place. "Well, don't give me any but a good one," Booth demanded, then settled on a bay mare, to be picked up about four.[46]

Booth seems next to have gone down Pennsylvania Avenue to the Willard Hotel at Fourteenth Street where the Grants were staying. When

Mrs. Grant and her young son, Jesse, went to luncheon, she was disturbed by the fact that "a man with a wild look" sat down at a table nearby and stared at her continually, at the same time seeming to be listening to what she said. Later she claimed positively that the man was Booth.[47]

On his way back to the National to change to riding clothes and get field glasses (which he wanted Mrs. Surratt to leave at Surrattsville), Booth stopped at the Kirkwood House. He wanted to try again to get a pass from Vice President Johnson. It would come in handy if Mrs. Surratt learned that sentries still guarded the road south. Johnson was not in. By that time he was at the White House for his appointment with the President.[48]

About 2:30 Booth called on Mrs. Surratt. Louis Weichmann, on his way to get the horse and buggy for the drive to Surrattsville, saw Booth and Mrs. Surratt talking. When he returned, Booth was gone. As they were about to leave, Mrs. Surratt said, "Wait, Mr. Weichmann. I must get those things of Booth's." The package she got contained the field glasses Booth later picked up at Surrattsville for use during his flight.[49]

From Mrs. Surratt's, Booth went to the stable behind Ford's to make certain everything was ready for sheltering the mare he had hired at Pumphrey's, apparently so she would be nearby for use that evening. He then stood at the back door of the theatre, chatting with a lady for "a considerable time." Mary Jane Anderson testified at the conspiracy trial that she saw Booth talking to a lady sometime around three o'clock and had stood at her gate "and looked right wishful at him." Her neighbor, Mary Ann Turner, testified that she had also seen Booth with the lady.[50]

The rehearsal for *Our American Cousin*, begun shortly after eleven, had just ended, but members of the company and a quartet hired by William Withers, director of the orchestra, were still practicing a song titled "Honor to Our Soldiers." It had been composed by H. B. Phillips, an actor associated with Ford's, with music by Withers, to be sung between acts in honor of General Grant and President Lincoln.[51]

When the rehearsal ended, Booth entered the theatre, where William J. Ferguson, the call boy, was sitting at the prompter's desk writing detailed mechanical arrangements for stage employees to follow during the play.[52] After observing preparations being made in the state box for the Presidential party, Booth went to Taltavull's Star Saloon next door for a drink with Ferguson and James Maddox, the theatre's property man, before walking toward Pumphrey's.[53] Before leaving Ferguson, Booth remarked that he had pleurisy and was not feeling well.[54]

Preparations for the visit of the Presidential party, and for making the most of the publicity it afforded, had begun almost immediately after the White House messenger came for the tickets at 10:30. After checking with Clay Ford, his younger brother, on the propriety of such action, James Ford wrote notices for the afternoon papers.[55] Thomas J.

Raybold, purchasing agent and sometimes ticket seller, was dispatched to the *Evening Star*[56] with the notice: "Ford's Theatre. 'Honor to Our Soldiers.' A new and Patriotic Song and Chorus has been written by Mr. H. B. Phillips and will be sung this evening by the entire Company to do honor to Lieutenant General Grant and President Lincoln and lady, who visit the Theatre in compliment to Miss Laura Keene, whose benefit and last appearance is announced in the bills of the day. The music of the above song is composed by Prof. W. Withers, Jr." Ford took the notice for the *National Republican* himself, and the announcements were published in the papers' editions appearing about two o'clock. New handbills, giving notice that the Presidential party would be present that evening, were also ordered.[57]

After writing announcements for the papers, James Ford went to the Treasury Building on Fifteenth Street about noon, seeking a thirty-six-foot flag. He found none this size but returned to the theatre with the blue Treasury Department flag. On the return trip he exchanged a few words with Booth at Tenth and E Streets.[58]

The Presidential box at Ford's was actually two boxes, numbers 7 and 8, on the south side of the building on the same level as the dress circle and over the forestage. It was reached by a vestibule, four feet wide and about ten feet long, that opened off the south side of the dress circle. Each box had its own door, approximately two and a half feet wide and seven feet high, with the door for Box 7 facing south and that for Box 8 facing west. Each box normally accommodated four persons, but as many as twelve could be seated in the enlarged space once a partition, about seven feet high and three inches thick, had been removed. When the President attended the theatre, the door to Box 7 was shut (and supposedly locked) and entry made through that to Box 8.[59]

Ford's boxes, four over the stage at each side of the house, were the ultimate in elegance in a theatre admired for its general grandeur. Dark red, figured paper covered the walls, Turkish carpet the floors, while yellow satin draperies overhanging Nottingham lace curtains provided greater privacy for occupants. Hanging directly in front of the center of the two arches enframing the box and extending out at about four feet from a point on top of the cornices, a chaste chandelier allowed soft lighting to reach the interior of the box.[60]

The theatre building originally housed the First Baptist Church of Washington but in December, 1861, was leased by John T. Ford, Baltimore theatre entrepreneur, for five years with an option to buy (despite predictions that a dire fate awaited anyone who turned a former house of worship into a theatre). Following renovations, the theatre opened as Ford's Atheneum on March 19, 1862, and achieved good success until a fire caused by a defective gas meter left only blackened walls remaining on December 31.[61]

After buying or leasing additional adjoining ground, Ford on February 28, 1863, had laid the cornerstone for an enlarged theatre, with James J. Gifford as builder. The new theatre, with three floors plus basement, would be 72 feet wide, 110 feet long. Five arched doors would provide entrance or exit on Tenth Street. After overcoming numerous difficulties, including foundation cave-ins because of quicksand, war-supply problems, a scarcity of workmen, and bad weather, the theatre was ready for opening night on August 27, 1863.[62]

First floor seating in orchestra and parquet would accommodate 602, and the cane-bottomed wooden chairs might be removed so the area could be boarded level with the stage for dancing and festive events.[63] The horseshoe-shaped dress circle, composing the second floor and seating 422 persons, had chairs similar to those on the first floor. The family circle, also horseshoe-shaped, composed the third floor and offered seating on wooden benches for about 600.[64] Ornamental plaster work, an elaborately decorated, inverted, saucer-shaped dome, and white and gold paint throughout the auditorium added to the beauty of the theatre, which received generous praise from the city's newspapers.

"In magnitude, completeness, and elegance it has few superiors, even in our largest cities," declared the *Washington Sunday Chronicle* on August 23, 1863. "In fact, every improvement that genius could devise, and skill and wealth achieve, has Mr. Ford brought to his aid in the erection of this magnificent theatre."

Preparing for the Lincolns and the Grants on this Good Friday, Clay Ford and seven of his employees set about making the Presidential box even more comfortable and elegant for the expected guests. Directed by Gifford, the theatre's builder and carpenter, Edmund Spangler,[65] the carpenter's helper and scene shifter, assisted by Joseph ("Peanuts John") Burroughs, began converting Boxes 7 and 8 into a single box by removing the partition between them.[66] While working, Spangler made a remark which was used against him at the conspiracy trial two months later.

"Damn the President and General Grant," he exclaimed.

"What are you damning the man for—a man that has never done any harm to you?" Peanuts asked.

"He ought to be cursed when he got so many men killed," was Spangler's reply.[67]

With the partition out, Clay Ford and his men began to move in furniture—a chair from the stage, a velvet-covered sofa and three velvet-covered armchairs from the reception room just off the dress circle, and a rocking chair from Clay and James Ford's room adjoining the family circle above. The rocker, of black walnut and also velvet-covered, belonged to the set with the sofa but Clay had had it taken to his room from the reception area because ushers lounging there had greased it with their hair.[68]

Joe Simms, a Negro helper who was eating a belated luncheon up in the flies, was called to go upstairs for the chair and came carrying it on his head.[69] When the partition was taken down, a triangular corner was formed in Box 7 and the rockers of the chair, as on previous occasions when the President had occupied the box, went into the corner with the rockers pointing toward the audience.[70] In any other position the rockers would have been in the way. (This explanation by Thomas J. Raybold, general overseer of conditions in the house, was made later to indicate that the rocker had not been positioned purposely to help Booth in his assassination scheme.)[71]

The job of decorating would usually have been done under Thomas Raybold's direction, but he had been bothered by neuralgia for three days.[72] Clay Ford therefore did most of the decorating with some help from James Maddox, property man of the house,[73] and John E. Buckingham, the night doorkeeper, who was not on his daytime job at the Navy Yard because it was Good Friday.[74] Maddox brought two flags to the box,[75] and with Raybold's help, Ford positioned these on staffs at each end of the expanded box.[76] Two more flags were festooned over the velvet-covered balustrade, and the Treasury Guard's blue regimental flag was placed at the center post above the American flags. To add a bit of patriotic color for this historic occasion, Ford brought a gilt-framed engraving of George Washington from the reception room and placed it on the center pillar.[77] To arrange the flags and engraving, Ford needed hammer and nails. Spangler, on stage fixing flats, threw the nails up to Ford, then handed up the hammer.[78]

To cut strings to tie up the flags and the engraving, Ford used his own penknife, then forgot to retrieve it when the job was finished.[79] At the conspiracy trial in June, effort was made to indicate that Booth had used a penknife to round out the hole that had been found in the door leading to Box 7, the thought apparently being that Booth had used Ford's knife to do this part of his work.[80] This supposition seemed logical at the time inasmuch as George Bunker, a clerk at the National Hotel, had found in Booth's trunk after the assassination a left-handed gimlet of the type with which the hole had supposedly been started.[81]

However, new light on the origin of the quarter-inch hole, which had been bored at the rising of the panel so close to the moulding that only a sharp eye would normally have seen it,[82] was provided in the 1960s by Frank Ford, elderly son of Clay Ford. In a letter written on April 13, 1962, to Dr. George J. Olszewski, Ford's Theatre historian, Ford said:

> I say . . . unequivocally that John Wilkes Booth did not bore the hole in the door leading to the box President Lincoln occupied the night of his assassination . . . The hole was bored by my father, Harry Clay Ford, or rather on his orders, and was

> bored for the simple reason that it would allow the guard . . . easy opportunity whenever he so desired to look into the box rather than open the inner door to check on the Presidential party . . . My father always "blew his top," to use today's slang, whenever he read or heard of this historical absurdity . . . and would often finish his vehemence by saying, "John Booth had too much to do that day other than go around boring holes in theatre doors." And while it is true Mr. Booth might use "professional courtesies" to attend performances, it is laughable to imagine he had such free access to Ford's Theatre that he could perform feats of carpentry whenever he wished, to say nothing of doing it the very day the decision was made by President Lincoln to attend the performance at the Theatre.[83]

The author, curious about a niche that had been cut in the wall to provide a firm resting place for a bar which would hold shut the door leading from the dress circle into the passageway to the President's box, queried Frank Ford about this niche in a letter written on November 26, 1965. In a reply dated December 2, Ford insisted that his letter to Dr. Olszewski also covered the matter of the bar.

> If you will refer to it [the letter to Olszewski] once more you will see that I speak of feats of carpentry. These words, I submit, cover the point [the matter of the bar] you say I make no mention of . . .
>
> May I comment that as the years go by it becomes more incredible to believe that a man bent on assassination would provide a barrier that in itself might be the very means of keeping him away from his intended victim. All Major Rathbone had to do was insert the bar, somewhat like a two by four, into the cavity in the wall, and the crime would not have been committed—that night at least . . . The hole in the door and the bar and the niche were to secure privacy and security. Such were the makeshift methods used to safeguard a president.[84]

Who actually cut the mortice into the wall, with the expectation that it would be used to seat a bar to hold shut the door to the passageway, will probably never be known. The cut, from all appearances, had been made with a knife,[85] was about four or five inches long, two inches deep and one and a half or two inches wide,[86] and could have been made in four or five minutes.[87] The bar used was about three feet six inches long,[88] with one end beveled, the other containing two two-inch nails, supposedly to keep the bar from slipping once it had been wedged in place.[89]

*Four American flags, a Treasury Guard flag, and a gilt-framed engraving of George Washington were used to make unusually colorful the front of Ford's Presidential box for the night of April 14. (Lincoln Memorial University.)*

According to John T. Ford, owner of the theatre, the bar was part of a music stand made hastily on February 22 after it was discovered that the band scheduled to play for a ball being held that night was short of stands. The bevel had been made and the nails placed in fashioning the stand.[90] Because the door leading into the passageway from the dress circle had neither lock nor latch,[91] it is possible that the bar had been used to keep the door securely shut even before April 14.

No sign of plaster was found on the floor of the passageway after the assassination.[92] If the niche in the wall was cut on April 14 and Booth, as Frank Ford claimed, could not in the theatre "perform feats of carpentry whenever he wished," the action must have been taken by an accomplice.

Belief that Booth or an accomplice had fixed the doors to Boxes 7 and 8 so they could be opened easily was erased by testimony at both the conspiracy trial and the trial of John Surratt in 1867. Thomas Raybold, in charge of the front of the theatre, testified at the latter that the locks on Boxes 4, 6, 7, and 8 were all out of order on April 14. That for Box 7, he said, "has been broken for some time." He had personally burst off the keepers on the lock to Box 8 on March 7 when he found the door locked but needed to let a party into the box in the absence of the usher who had the key and was out of the theatre.[93] (Frank Ford's letter to the author echoes this statement: "The keys to the boxes were mislaid, few of the door locks functioned, and the presidential box itself had some time previously suffered being broken into.")

After chatting with some of the actors in mid-afternoon, observing decorations in the state box, and having a drink with Ferguson and Maddox, Booth started for Pumphrey's stable for his horse. In front of the theatre he met Joseph Hazelton, Ford's twelve-year-old program boy.

"Well, Joseph, have you made up your mind yet to become an actor?" he asked, patting the boy on the shoulder.

"I don't know, Mr. Booth," Joseph answered. "Perhaps I wouldn't do for the stage."

"Try it, Joseph, when the time comes," Booth said, holding the lad at arm's length and studying his face for a moment. "Try it. You have the face of an actor . . . The world will think better of the actor some day and treat him more liberally."

Booth started away, then turned back and said, "We have been good friends, Joseph, eh? Well, try to think well of me and this will buy you a stick of candy." He then handed the boy a ten-cent "shinplaster" and walked quickly down Tenth Street leaving young Hazelton, later an actor for more than fifty years, looking after him a bit puzzled.[94]

Before getting his horse, Booth stepped into the National where he stopped at the counter and asked Henry Merrick, the day clerk, for a sheet of paper and an envelope. Merrick jocularly asked Booth if he had made a thousand dollars that day. Looking startled, Booth replied, sotto voce, "No, but I have worked hard enough to have made ten times that amount."

When about to write, Booth seemed to fear that someone might see his letter and asked if he might do his writing in the office. He had written only a few lines when he said, "Merrick, is this the year 1864 or 1865?" When Merrick said he must be joking, Booth replied, "Sincerely, I am not," then, assured it was 1865, he resumed writing. Only then did Merrick notice something troubled and agitated in the actor's appearance, "entirely at variance," Merrick said later, "with his usual quiet deportment."[95]

His writing complete, Booth sealed the letter, placed it in his pocket and left for Pumphrey's. At the entrance to the stable, he met an old schoolmate, Col. C. F. Cobb, and asked if his friend had heard "that dirty tailor [Vice President Johnson] from Tennessee speak in front of Willard's Hotel. Cobb said he had not but that he had read Johnson's speech in a newspaper. When Booth began a harangue against Johnson, Cobb concluded he was drunk. "If I had been there I would have shot the son of a bitch," Booth declared.[96]

Leaving Pumphrey's, Booth trotted his horse down Sixth Street to Pennsylvania Avenue, then let her run toward the White House for four blocks until he spied Charles Warwick, an actor friend who was out for a stroll while trying to regain strength from a recent illness. Booth reined the mare to the sidewalk and shook hands with Warwick.

"Glad to see you so much better," Booth declared. Warwick later said that Booth appeared to be in unusually good spirits.[97]

Booth then turned right on Tenth Street and in front of Ford's chatted briefly with James Maddox. When James P. Ferguson, owner of the restaurant that adjoined the theatre on the north, stepped out on his porch, Booth saw him and said, "See what a nice horse I've got. Now watch; he [sic] can run like a cat!" He then wheeled, struck his spurs into the mare and went back down Tenth Street toward Pennsylvania Avenue.[98]

On Pennsylvania, at the triangular enclosure between Thirteenth and Fourteenth, Booth saw John Matthews, an old friend who played the part of the unscrupulous agent, Richard Coyle, in *Our American Cousin*. Booth appeared so pale and nervous as he greeted Matthews that the latter asked what was the matter. Booth assured him it was nothing. Matthews just then drew Booth's attention to a group of ragged Confederate soldiers being escorted by, and Booth, with a gesture of seeming despair, exclaimed, "Great God! I have no longer a country."[99]

Booth next asked Matthews to do him "a little favor." "Perhaps I may leave town tonight," he said, "and I have a letter here which I desire to be published in the *National Intelligencer*. Please attend to it for me, unless I see you before ten o'clock tomorrow; in that case I will see to it myself."[100]

As Matthews pocketed the letter, apparently the one written at the National Hotel a short time earlier, he saw a coach passing rapidly toward the Capitol. Recognizing Grant as one of the passengers, he exclaimed, "Why, there goes Grant. I thought he was coming to the theatre with the President this evening."

"Where?" demanded Booth. When Matthews pointed, Booth set off at a gallop after the coach.[101]

When a horseman rode by the coach and peered at its occupants, Mrs. Grant turned to her husband and said, "That is the same man that sat at the luncheon table near me. I don't like his looks." As the carriage turned off on First Street, heading for the Baltimore and Ohio station at C Street and New Jersey Avenue, Booth rode back by and looked intently at the Grants.[102] He then galloped to Willard's and learned from individuals standing there that Grant was departing for New Jersey.[103]

After the assassination Matthews opened the letter. Frightened by its concluding paragraphs and fearing that he might become implicated, he burned it. Later he remembered the approximate wording of the final paragraphs:

> For a long time I have devoted my energies, my time, and money to the accomplishment of a certain end. I have been disappointed. The moment has now arrived when I must change my plans. Many will blame me for what I am about to do; but posterity, I am sure, will justify me.
>
> Men who love their country better than gold or life, John W. Booth, Payne, Herold, Atzerodt.[104]

After observing the Grants and learning their destination, Booth stopped at the Kirkwood House for a few minutes, supposedly to see Atzerodt and possibly to try once more to see Johnson. On the steps he talked briefly with John Devenay, a former Maryland infantry officer and longtime acquaintance. Devenay asked if he would be playing in Washington again, and Booth replied, "No, I am not going to play again. I am in the oil business."

A few minutes later Devenay saw Booth riding down the street, apparently on his way to the stable back of Ford's,[105] where he left the mare with Peanuts John and went into the theatre to get a halter from Spangler. Because he was busy preparing the stage for the evening performance, Spangler sent Jacob Ritterspaugh to get one, then went to the stable to put the halter on the horse. He started to take off the saddle but Booth said, "Never mind, I do not want it off but let it and the bridle remain."[106] Booth, Peanuts John, Maddox, and Spangler then went to the restaurant next door and had a drink at Booth's expense.[107]

Booth's movements for the hour after leaving the three theatre employees sometime after five o'clock are unrecorded. Those who still hold to the belief that he bored the peephole in the door to Box 7 and prepared the means for barring the passage door think that it was sometime around six that he performed these "feats of carpentry."

According to Henry Merrick, Booth was at the National Hotel for tea at 6:30. He then went to his room, presumably to get the weapons needed for the action planned.[108]

At about seven Booth passed out of the hotel for the last time. "Are you going to the theatre tonight?" he asked George Bunker, the room clerk, as he tossed his key on the desk. When Bunker answered in the negative, Booth said, "You should. There will be some fine acting there tonight."[109]

William Withers, director of the orchestra at Ford's, claimed that he had a drink with Booth about 7:30 and heard the actor make a startling prediction.

"During the conversation . . . about different members of the theatrical profession," Withers said, "I laughingly remarked that Booth would never be as great as his father. An inscrutable smile flitted across his face as he replied, 'When I leave the stage, I will be the most talked about man in America.' At the time the statement had no significance for me. Afterward I remembered it with a shock."[110]

By prior arrangement, Booth and his fellow conspirators met at the Herndon House for a final conference about eight o'clock. Booth indicated that he would murder Lincoln. Paine would take care of Secretary Seward, then be guided out of the city by Herold. Atzerodt would assassinate Johnson. Atzerodt replied that he would not do it—that he had entered into the plot to abduct but not to kill. Booth said Atzerodt was a fool, that he would be hanged anyhow, and that it was death for any man who backed out now. Atzerodt held to his determination not to kill the Vice President, wandered about the streets most of the night, then went to the home of a cousin in Montgomery County, Maryland, where he was arrested on April 19.[111]

# VIII
# Lincoln's Guard Leaves His Post

While the conspirators were holding their conference, the Lincolns were en route to pick up their guests, Major Henry Reed Rathbone and Clara Harris, at the Harris home at H and Fifteenth Streets, two short blocks northeast of the White House. Miss Harris was the daughter of New York's Senator Ira Harris, a Lincoln friend, who had married Rathbone's mother after the latter's husband died. Clara was regarded as a "dear friend" by Mary and had been a guest at her side at the White House as Lincoln delivered his last address on April 11.[1]

When the Grants announced that they could not accompany the Lincolns to the theatre, Mary had at once thought of Clara and her fiancé and made arrangements for them to be guests. Lincoln was probably glad for her action. The Major had served with distinction during the war and could be regarded as the protector Stanton had urged that the President have.

The Lincolns and their guests were in the best of spirits as they traveled the seven blocks between the Harris residence and the theatre.[2] Fog was beginning to settle over the city, but its happy people were still celebrating, a victory parade being in progress down Pennsylvania Avenue.[3] As the carriage drew up in front of Ford's, its occupants could see toward Pennsylvania Avenue the yellowish flame of smoking tar torches stuck in barrels. They were part of the theatre's effort to attract patrons, with a barker standing by each barrel yelling, "This way to Ford's."[4]

Inside the theatre the audience was becoming restive. Many had come because they wanted to see the President or General Grant or both. When neither was in evidence as the curtain rose, a considerable number of complaints were heard. Some patrons were apparently "irritated at themselves for being such fools as to part with their money just to see a play that ordinarily would not cost them more than from 25 to 50 cents to see at any other time."[5] At Ford's only family circle seats sold for 25

*Major Henry Reed Rathbone, as seldom pictured in civilian dress, and Clara Harris, his step-sister and fiancée, who were guests of the Lincolns on assassination night. The Major never recovered from the shock of that night in the Presidential box, and in Hanover, Germany, on Christmas morning, 1883, he killed the former Miss Harris, his wife since 1867. (Harris photo from Lloyd Ostendorf Collection.)*

cents. Other admission prices were as follows: orchestra, $1; dress circle and parquet, 75 cents; boxes, $6 and $10.

As indicated earlier, the theatre accommodated approximately 1,675 persons when seating in each of the eight boxes was held to six. How large the audience was on April 14 is one of the unknowns of the day because those in the best position to know disagreed, just as many in the theatre disagreed about various things seen and heard between 8:00 and 10:30 P.M. One thing is certain: The only box in use that night was the one occupied by the Lincoln party.[6] Miss Harris and four members of the cast—Harry Hawk, E. A. Emerson, Helen Truman, and Mrs. J. H. Evans, who were seen as Asa Trenchard, Lord Dundreary, Augusta, and Sharpe, respectively—claimed that the theatre was crowded. Miss Truman, in fact, said it "was packed to the walls, there being no fire restrictions."[7] On the other hand, William Ferguson, the call boy, who was also playing the part of Lieutenant Vernon, R. N., said "only a fair-sized crowd had turned out . . . and it was an audience that seemed singularly unresponsive."[8] Daniel DeMotte, in Washington as Indiana's Military and Sanitary Agent, and A. C. Richards, Washington's Superintendent of Police, also held that the theatre was not overcrowded.[9] The fact that several patrons moved about to get better seats would seem to verify the latter view.

When the Lincoln party entered the theatre's southwest door and turned left toward the stairs leading to the dress circle, Joseph Hazelton, the young program boy, seemed in doubt whether to give Lincoln a program. He did so, however, after the President smiled, said something in an aside to Mrs. Lincoln, and held out his hand. Hazelton also gave one of the printed sheets to each of the other members of the party and received a smile from Mary.[10] Led by Usher James O'Brien, and escorted by John Parker and Charles Forbes, the party climbed the stairs, then crossed behind the seats in the dress circle to the south side of the building, thence down the aisle to the passageway leading to the state box.

As with so many things concerning the night, there has been disagreement as to the scene being enacted when the party crossed behind the dress circle. Hawk declared that the Lincolns arrived during the first act just as Lord Dundreary (E.A. Emerson) had asked one of his foolish conundrums, then added in a lisping way, "They don't thee it." Hawk claimed that he personally had put in a "gag line" at this point, "No, but they see him," whereupon the house laughed and cheered.[11]

The author of a book on Lincoln's death wrote that George C. Maynard of the War Telegraph Office had indicated on his playbill the point at which the Lincolns were first seen. He had written down the lines being spoken, these indicating that Florence Trenchard (Laura Keene) was trying to tell a joke to Dundreary who—of course—did not see it.[12] Maynard himself later wrote that the arrival came in the dairy scene, during which, he said, Georgiana (Miss M. Hart) was telling Lord Dundreary an American joke whose point eluded him.[13]

There are apparent inaccuracies in all these versions. Hawk was not on stage when Dundreary was telling his conundrums. Florence Trenchard at no time told a joke to Dundreary. The dairy scene did not take place until the second scene of the second act and even then Georgiana told no jokes. Although not more than twenty-five minutes could have elapsed after the curtain finally arose, the Lincolns, as Dr. George J. Olszewski wrote, probably passed through the dress circle lobby as the following exchange took place:

Dundreary: Why does a dog waggle his tail?

Florence: Upon my word. I never inquired.

Dundreary: Because the tail can't waggle the dog! Ha! Ha![14]

Lincoln on this night, as on all his nights at the theatre, seemed to hope that he could reach his box unnoticed. His intimate friend, Noah

Brooks, claimed that the President had "an almost morbid dread of what he called a 'scene'—that is, a demonstration of applause such as always greeted his appearance in public."[15]

When, however, the audience became aware of his presence and many of its members began rising in their seats, he stopped and acknowledged their recognition with a solemn bow. "His face was perfectly stoical; his deepset eyes gave him a pathetically sad appearance," Dr. Charles A. Leale, the young Army physician who would shortly be seeking to save the President's life, wrote later. "The audience seemed to be enthusiastically cheerful, yet he looked peculiarly sorrowful as he slowly walked with bowed head and drooping shoulders toward the box."[16]

All who later wrote about the President's reception agreed that the orchestra under William Withers' direction immediately struck up "Hail to the Chief." Although the President had attended several performances in the course of the season, this was, according to William Ferguson, the first time the orchestra had "heralded his arrival in this way."[17]

There was, however, considerable disagreement as to the warmth and extent of the applause that greeted the Presidential party. Major Rathbone, Dr. Leale, Joseph Hazelton, Charles A. Sanford, a young paymaster clerk, Mrs. Helen DuBarry, wife of the assistant to the Commissary General of Subsistence, and James Suydam Knox, a young Princeton graduate who soon would become a physician and have a distinguished career as Professor of Obstetrics at Rush Medical College in Chicago, were among the many who wrote or testified that the audience rose and cheered.[18]

Withers even declared that "the uproar was deafening as Lincoln walked down the narrow aisle leading to his box." The orchestra director added that when Lincoln reached the end of the aisle, he stopped, placed his right hand over his heart and bowed twice to the audience.[19]

Withers' brother, Reuben, drummer in the orchestra, was another witness who maintained that there was "a lot of cheering." Even after the President stood up in his box, again to bow his acknowledgment, the demonstration seemed to go on for some time. "For," said Reuben, "we played away vigorously two or three of the national airs."[20] Mrs. Annie Wright, wife of Ford's stage manager, John B. Wright, agreed that the audience rose and applauded, many waving handkerchiefs, but she had no recollection of cheers.[21] William Ferguson maintained that there was nothing more than a ripple of applause even when Lincoln, before sitting down, drew aside the draperies and bowed to the audience.[22] Thomas H. Sherman, a War Department telegrapher, later secretary to James G. Blaine and American consul in Liverpool, claimed that "only a polite burst of applause greeted Lincoln. The crowd," he added, "had come principally to see General U. S. Grant, the war hero."[23]

*Mrs. Lincoln is often pictured as wearing a wreath of flowers on that night at Ford's, but women who observed her headdress said she wore a black bonnet. (Lloyd Ostendorf Collection.)*

Among those known to have shown great enthusiasm at the Lincolns' arrival was Edmund Spangler, who had damned the President only a few hours earlier. Standing at the passage to the back stage close to the President's box, Spangler applauded loudly both by clapping his hands and stamping his feet.[24]

When members of the President's party seated themselves, Lincoln, as expected, took the rocking chair in the left hand corner of the box, and Mary sat in a chair between the President and the pillar in the center. Miss Harris sat in one of the two chairs at the opposite side of the box. The small sofa stood at her left hand along the wall running from the end of the box to the rear, and Major Rathbone sat at the end of the sofa next to his fiancée. The arrangement placed the Major seven or eight feet from the President and about the same distance from the open door to Box 8. Lincoln was only four or five feet from the door.[25] Later Clay Ford and Thomas Raybold testified that Booth, when he decided to see a play at the theatre, had always asked to have Box 7, the area in which Lincoln sat that night.[26]

Pictures of Mary as she was supposedly dressed on the night of April 14 have usually shown her in evening gown and wearing a wreath of flowers. However, Miss Truman and Mrs. Evans, who paid close attention to her appearance, both noted that she wore neither evening dress nor a headdress of flowers. Miss Truman said that Mary wore a spring silk dress, light gray in color with black pinhead check and bonnet to match. Mrs. Evans described Mary's headdress as "an old fashioned black coal scuttle bonnet." Miss Truman added that they had all remarked about the fact that Mary was not in evening dress.[27] Mrs. Wright, who sat in the fourth row of orchestra seats on the opposite side of the auditorium from the President's box, said that Mary and Miss Harris wore their bonnets and wraps the entire evening, "probably because it was rather cold. Mrs. Lincoln," she added, "had on a black velvet bonnet trimmed with white satin and a black velvet cloak edged with ermine."[28]

Shielded by the draperies, the President could be seen from the theatre floor only when he leaned forward. "I think that during the entire intermission [following the second act]," Mrs. Wright told a reporter, "he leaned forward in his low rocking chair, both elbows resting on the box railing, his chin and both cheeks buried in his hands. He was studying the audience as if to ascertain how many persons there he recognized."[29]

Long before this John Parker had left his post in the passageway to the President's box to take a seat in the gallery and watch the play. It is altogether possible that he had done so, not willfully, but at the suggestion of the President, who believed there was no need for a guard and that Parker should be privileged to watch the comedy. But during the intermission Parker and Charles Forbes went next door for a drink. And when the play's final act began that fateful evening, the guard was again absent from his post, either still at Taltavull's or back in the gallery seat to follow the action.[30] (For more on the strange case of John Parker, see Appendix.)

# IX
# Tragedy Strikes, Mary's Hand in His

Although he had, by his own admission, "seen very little of the drama,"[1] Abraham Lincoln was a great lover of the theatre. He was especially fond of Shakespeare and once remarked, "It matters not to me whether Shakespeare be well or ill acted; with him the thought suffices."[2] His favorites were *Macbeth, Hamlet,* and *Richard III*, and to friends he often quoted long passages from them from memory.

"I think nothing equals *Macbeth*," he once wrote the actor James H. Hackett. Commenting further, he wrote, "Unlike you gentlemen of the profession, I think the soliloquy in *Hamlet* commencing 'O, my offense is rank' surpasses that commencing 'To be or not to be.'"[3] Another of the President's favorite passages was Richard's soliloquy:

> Now is the winter of our discontent
> Made glorious summer by this sun of York;
> And all the clouds that lower'd upon our house
> In the deep bosom of the ocean buried.

Somewhat awed by the force and power with which Lincoln rendered this soliloquy from memory, Francis B. Carpenter, the artist, once told the President, "I am not sure but that you made a mistake in your choice of a profession."[4]

When Lincoln went to the theatre during the trying days of the war, he preferred comedy. "A farce, or a comedy, is best played; a tragedy is best read at home," he told Noah Brooks.[5] Lincoln's liking for comedy undoubtedly accounted for the fact that, unlike most theatregoers of the day, he nearly always remained to see the farce or comedy which customarily followed the evening's drama. Helen Truman, who played the role of the fortune-seeking Augusta Mountchessington in *Our American Cousin*, not only noted this fact but also observed that the President "never applauded with his hands, but laughed heartily on occasion and by his face spoke plainly of his approval."[6]

Perhaps Mary Lincoln, in deciding to make reservations at Ford's rather than at Glover's for April 14, was influenced by the knowledge that *Our American Cousin* was a farcical comedy whose humorous situations and eccentric rhetoric would serve as a relaxant to the President. Or perhaps knowledge that the performance was to be a benefit for Laura Keene, making her last appearance in the play after some 999 presentations, was the deciding factor.

*Our American Cousin*, described by John T. Ford, owner of the theatre, as "a very plain play,"[7] had been written by Tom Taylor, a young English barrister, in 1851 and sold for eighty pounds while Yankee mania gripped England. It had, however, never been produced, and in 1858 Taylor tried to peddle it to Lester Wallack, a well-known American manager, through John Chandler Bancroft Davis, secretary of the U. S. legation in London. Wallack, not interested, suggested that Davis take the play to Laura Keene at the Metropolis Theatre. Initially, she was not much interested. Later, needing a substitute vehicle for *A Midsummer Night's Dream*, whose opening was being delayed by troubles with costumers and scene painters, she bought the play for one thousand dollars. It was a hit and paved the way to fame for Joseph Jefferson, E. A. Sothern, and Miss Keene.[8]

By coincidence, *Our American Cousin* was presented at McVicker's Theatre in Chicago on May 20, 1860, when the Republican Convention came to a close after Lincoln's nomination for the Presidency. It had been presented eight times at Ford's before April 14, 1865, but never with Laura Keene in the cast. She had played at Ford's only ten times previously, all since early April. In seven of these, the vehicle was *The Workingmen of Washington*, a play she had written and adapted for widespread presentation by substituting for Washington the name of the city in which she chanced to be appearing.[9]

In brief, *Our American Cousin* revolved around Asa Trenchard, an American country bumpkin who comes to England to claim a fortune he has inherited from old Mark Trenchard, a British emigrant of noble blood. Soon he falls in love with Mary Meredith, old Mark's granddaughter, who is now a dairy maid and poor because her mother was disinherited by Asa's good fortune. Asa forfeits his inheritance by burning his benefactor's will, but meantime is being pursued by a scheming English matron, Mrs. Mountchessington, intent on snaring him and his inheritance for her daughter, Augusta.

Laura Keene, who played the part of Florence Trenchard, a nobleman's daughter and a principal in *Our American Cousin*'s other romance, was a versatile individual who at her death in 1873 could be remembered as an actress, theatre manager, editor, and lecturer. Born in London in 1826, the daughter of a builder, she got her stage experience in that city, then made her first American appearance as Albina Mandeville in *The Will* at Wallack's New York Theatre on September 20,

*At 39, Laura Keene was making her last appearance in* Our American Cousin *on April 14, and the performance had been booked as a benefit for her. After Lincoln was shot, she sought to calm the audience, reportedly carried water to the state box, and is said to have held the President's head in her lap.*

1852. After making a name for herself in the United States and Australia, she added managing to her duties by opening the Metropolitan Theatre in New York with *Laura Keene's Varieties* in 1855.

Lauded as "an unexcelled actress" by the *New York Sun* (January 12, 1862) and as "the greatest stage manager I have ever known" by J. H. Stoddart, she was also an innovator. She spent large amounts of money for advertising and in 1867 became the first American manager to encourage native writers by offering one thousand dollars for the best play written by an American. In 1872 she founded at great expense a short-lived magazine, *The Fine Arts*, which published at length on the best of paper and with the finest of engravings articles on such subjects as English painters, art treasures, sculpture, outstanding buildings, drama, and actors. At the same time she became as popular a lecturer as she was as an actress.

Miss Keene was described as "a very charming woman," a person "slender and graceful with an aquiline face, delicate features, dark eyes, and a musical voice." Although she lived eight years after Lincoln's assassination, the horror of that tragedy was held to have done much to ruin her physically.[10]

For two hours on this Good Friday night there was an exhilarating air of good cheer in Ford's Theatre. The large audience, including hundreds of ladies in rich gowns and many officers in splendid uniforms, the lively music of the orchestra, the knowledge that President and Mrs. Lincoln were present, and the feeling of relief and joy over the end of the war conjoined to lift the spirits of all present.

Only a few individuals in the audience – those seated at the extreme north side of the dress circle and orchestra directly opposite the state box – could see all members of the Lincoln party, and even to them only the left profile of the President was visible. To observers from these seats it seemed that the sweethearts were in a festive mood and that the President and Mrs. Lincoln were enjoying the play highly. John Deering, a clerk in the Treasury Department, and Dr. Charles Sabin Taft, who later would be the second surgeon to reach the stricken President's box, were among those who noted that occupants of the box laughed heartily at times. Taft also said that Mary seemed to take great pleasure in witnessing her husband's enjoyment. But Deering added that Lincoln, appearing distracted, at times "rested his face in both his hands, bending forward, and seemingly buried in deep thought."[11]

Only once did the President rise from his chair. The theatre had no central heating system, and when it became chilly in the box he got up to put on his overcoat. He was using on this night the black wool coat tailored for him by Brooks Brothers of New York and bearing on its dark silk quilted lining the figure of an eagle holding in its mouth two festoons bearing the words, "One Country, One Destiny."[12]

Occasionally, the President's messenger (presumably Forbes, who was often identified with this designation) came in to see if anything was wanted.[13] Shortly after the third act began, Forbes also took in to the President an official-looking envelope delivered to him by S. P. Hanscom, editor of the *National Republican*. Hanscom had been to the White House and there was entrusted with a "dispatch" for the President. When he reached the theatre and found the play in progress, he delivered the envelope to Forbes, who was seated in the chair nearest the vestibule door.[14] (For information about the recovery of this dispatch and its later disappearance, see Appendix.)

Scarcely five minutes later a handsome young man, immaculately dressed in black, moved slowly back of the dress circle until he was near the door to the passage leading to the President's box. Several persons in the audience who chanced to glance his way recognized him as John Wilkes Booth.[15]

After leaving his henchmen following the meeting at the Herndon House, Booth had gone back to the theatre. As he passed the box office, he looked into the window and, putting his arm through, placed a partially smoked cigar on a shelf inside. To Clay Ford in the box office he said "in a mock heroic bombastic furioso style," "Who e'er this cigar dares displace must meet Wilkes Booth face to face." Ford recognized the doggerel as a parody of the first two lines of General Bombastes' tristich, ending "Thus do I challenge the human race," in the popular burlesque of the day, *Bombastes Furioso*. He realized only later that it was meant by Booth to be a challenge to authority in the light of action to come.[16]

This was the first of half a dozen times Booth was inside Ford's during the evening. And much of the time he was not going in and out of the theatre seems to have been spent in Taltavull's Star Saloon next door. Robert Gourlay, brother of Jeannie Gourlay,[17] the Mary Meredith of the play, was among those who saw Booth drinking in the saloon during the intermission after Act I, which ended about nine o'clock.[18]

From Taltavull's, Booth apparently went to the stable in the alley back of the theatre to get the bay mare left there earlier. Leading her by the bridle rein, he walked to the rear door of the theatre.

"Tell Spangler to come to the door and hold my horse," he told John Debonay, often a scene-shifter on stage right, who was standing near the door after completing a brief appearance as a servant in the play's dairy scene. Debonay went to the basement and up the other side to deliver Booth's message to Spangler at his post as scene-shifter on stage left.

While Spangler was outside, Booth came in and asked if he could cross the back stage. Debonay informed him that it was in use during the dairy scene in Act II and he would therefore have to go under the stage and up on the other side. As Booth descended the stair, Spangler called to Debonay, "Tell Peanuts [who often attended Booth's horses, seeing they were fed and groomed] to come here and hold this horse. I have not time. Mr. Gifford is out in the front of the theatre and all the responsibility of the scene lies on me."[19]

Debonay obediently went after Joseph Burroughs, who was sitting at the stage door entrance at the east end of the passage leading to Tenth Street to keep out strangers and those who had no business behind the scenes. Told by Spangler to hold the horse, Peanuts protested that he could not—that he had to sit at his door.

"Hold the horse," commanded Spangler, "and if there is any difficulty lay the blame on me." So the simple-minded youth held the horse, most of the time sitting or lying on a carpenter's bench nearby.[20]

After another pause at Taltavull's, Booth was in and out of the theatre frequently and aroused some curiosity in John Sessford, the ticket taker. Joseph Hazelton, the program boy, returned to the lobby from the dress circle about 9:40 and saw Booth come in, speak to Buckingham and then move on.

"Wonder what he's up to?" muttered Sessford, standing close beside the door, as he looked after Booth. "He was in here this afternoon, too."[21]

"In looking back over the occurrences," John Buckingham said later, "I can see that Booth must have been under great stress of excitement, although his actions did not seem to me at that time to be at all strange. He was naturally a nervous man and restless in his movements."

"What time of night is it?" Booth had asked Buckingham, taking hold of two of the doorkeeper's fingers, during an early trip into the theatre.

"I told him to step into the lobby and there he could see the clock [on the east wall]. Next, he came and asked me to give him a chew of tobacco which I readily did. Afterward I went into the saloon just below the theatre to get a drink, and Booth was there drinking brandy. I went back to the door and he soon came in again. He passed into the house and stood a moment looking at the audience, and then went out again."[22]

To some extent Buckingham's testimony ties in with that given by Sergeants Joseph M. Dye and Robert Cooper, members of Battery C, Independent Pennsylvania Artillery, who were in front of the theatre or nearby from about 9:30 until 10:10. On the way back to Camp Barry, located at the junction of H Street and the Baltimore Turnpike, they stopped to rest in front of the theatre. Dye said that he sat down on the platform onto which patrons arriving by carriage alighted. Cooper spent much of his time walking up and down both sides of Tenth Street between E and F. The Lincolns' carriage was standing at the platform, Coachman Burke in the driver's seat.

Dye testified that some fifteen minutes after he and Cooper arrived at the theatre, and a few minutes before the second act ended at about 9:50, he saw a man he identified as Booth come out of the passage between the theatre and Taltavull's Star Saloon and engage in conversation with an individual whose description tallied roughly with that of George Atzerodt. Shortly, another man he later identified as John Surratt appeared, and the three conversed. Dye heard one of the men, presumably Booth, say "I think he will come out now," and later thought the speaker must have been referring to the President.

After the theatre patrons had gone back for Act III (many after visiting the Star Saloon), the two better-dressed individuals, claimed by Dye to be Booth and Surratt, were in and out of the theatre several times, the latter calling out the time as observed on the theatre clock, and Booth once going into the saloon. Dye said that the individual identified as Surratt called out the time, "ten minutes past ten," then hurried north toward G Street. Booth, the sergeant testified, whispered briefly to the rough-looking individual at the passageway before reentering the theatre.

Dye and Cooper then walked up Tenth Street to H, where they entered an oyster saloon. They were still there when a man rushed in some fifteen minutes later to announce that the President had been shot.[23]

In a letter to his father a few hours later, Dye declared that Lincoln's death had deeply affected him. "And why shouldn't it," he wrote, "when I might have saved his precious life?" He then told of his observations the evening before and how, as he later testified at the conspiracy and Surratt trials, he had become suspicious of Booth and his companions.

"I stood awhile between them and the carriage with my revolver ready," he told his father. "The act ended, but the President did not appear, so Booth went into the restaurant and took a drink . . . He came back and whispered to the other rascal, then stepped into the Theatre!"[24]

Although the testimony Dye gave during the conspiracy trial was accepted generally at the time, that given by others at the trial of John Surratt in 1867 strongly suggested that the sergeant was mistaken—or stretched the truth—about much of what he had allegedly heard and seen.

This was true despite the fact that Dye, while on the stand for much of two days during the Surratt trial, repeated his earlier testimony, and Cooper, who had not been heard at the conspiracy trial, supported the testimony of his friend.[25]

Later in the 1867 trial, James Gifford, Ford's builder-carpenter, Louis J. Carland, the theatre's former costumer, and Courtland Hess, an actor whose only assignment on April 14 was to appear with the group scheduled to sing "Honor to Our Soldiers," presented testimony strongly indicating that they were the individuals Dye and Cooper had supposed to be Booth, Surratt, and Atzerodt.[26] According to their testimony, the various positions they had taken between the end of the play's second act and 10:10 were much the same as those of the men Dye and Cooper had seen.

Hess said he had been in and out of the theatre frequently before it was time for him to get dressed for his appearance with the chorus. After walking up to F Street to buy a cigar, he had asked what time it was as he joined Carland and Gifford. The latter had said, "I fixed the clock in the vestibule . . . today, and it is right by that," whereupon Carland had stepped into the vestibule, noted the time and announced, "It's ten minutes past ten."[27]

"Ten minutes past ten," Hess had replied. "I am wanted in a few minutes," meaning that he would have about fifteen minutes to get into his black suit and ready to appear before the President. After a brief pause he had then walked south a few feet and turned left to enter the theatre by the stage door near the end of the corridor between Ford's and the Star Saloon.[28]

Carland, Gifford, and Hess all maintained that they had at no time seen Booth while they were in front of the theatre.[29] According to Hess's testimony, he had heard the report of Booth's shot almost immediately after reaching the stage, a fact which would place the moment of the President's assassination at approximately 10:13.[30]

Other individuals claimed that they had seen Booth outside during the intermission, among them Charles L. Willis and John A. Downs, two Washington teenagers who had stepped out for a breath of fresh air. While standing in front of the theatre, they saw Booth come out and enter the Star Saloon. By the time they reentered the theatre, Booth was back and talking to Buckingham.[31]

When the testimony of Gifford, Carland, and Hess is compared with that of Buckingham, Dye, and others, one puzzling question arises: How did the three Ford's Theatre associates while in front of the house fail to observe the frequent in-and-out trips made by Booth as reported by others? Gifford and Carland testified that they knew the actor well, and Hess, a recent arrival in the city, knew him by sight.

As the third act opened about ten o'clock, Jeannie Gourlay (Mary Meredith), on stage with Harry Hawk (Asa Trenchard), saw Booth standing in the lobby, hat in hand. "He was so pale," she declared, "that I thought he was ill."

When her scene with Hawk (the one in which he burned the will making him the heir to Mark Trenchard's fortune) ended, Miss Gourlay looked out over the footlights and saw that Booth had disappeared.[32]

It was at this time, probably while Hanscom was delivering to the President the message with which he had been entrusted, that Booth was in Taltavull's for the last time.

"He just walked into the bar, and asked for some whiskey," Taltavull reported at the trials of 1865 and 1867. I gave him the whiskey; put the bottle on the counter . . . It is customary to give water, but I did not give him water right off; and he called for some water, and I gave him some. He put the money on the counter and went right out. I saw him go out of the bar alone, as near as I can judge, from eight to ten minutes before I heard the cry that the President was assassinated."[33]

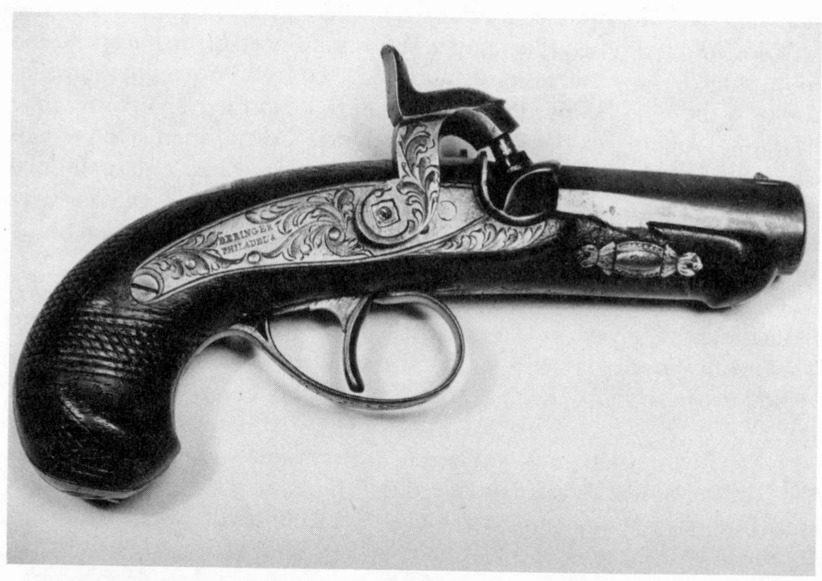

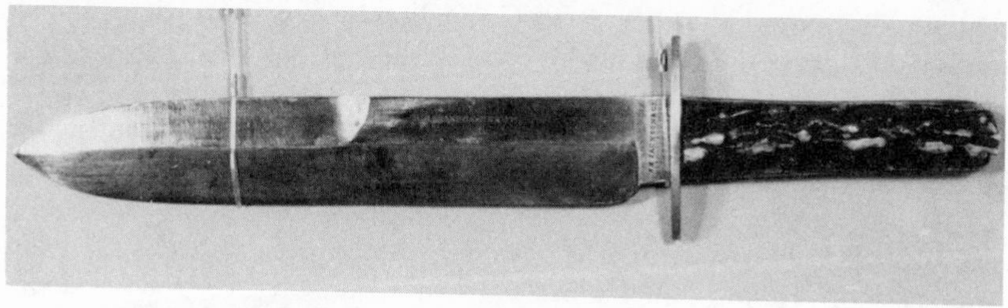

*The derringer with which Booth assassinated Lincoln and the long knife with which he wounded Major Rathbone. Both weapons are now on display at Ford's Theatre National Historic Site. (National Park Service.)*

Evidently it was after this trip to Taltavull's that Booth returned to the theatre, passed by Buckingham and went up the stairs to the dress circle, humming a tune.[34]

Walking through the dress circle lobby, Booth ultimately entered an aisle, or rather a passage of near-trapezoidal shape, only a few feet from the door of the corridor leading into the state box. The theatre management had put chairs in this space apparently in anticipation of an overflow crowd, and seated there were Captain Theodore McGowan and Lieutenant Alexander McL. Crawford, who had moved from their original positions on the north side of the dress circle. Captain McGowan later testified that shortly after they had seen the man (apparently Hanscom) deliver an official-looking envelope to the President's messenger, a dark-haired man of medium height, dressed in a black coat and dark pants and wearing a stiff-rimmed, flat-topped, round-crowned black hat, persisted in passing through the aisle behind them. To let him pass by and step down to the level below, the officers had to bend their chairs forward. The man, looking at the stage and orchestra below, then stood a step above the President's messenger (Forbes), seated in a chair next to the lobby leading into the state box. McGowan said that the man took several cards from his pocket, descended to the messenger and showed him a card.

"I do not know whether the card was carried in by the messenger, or his consent given to the entrance of the man who presented it," McGowan stated. "I saw a few moments after, the same man entering the door of the lobby leading to the box and the door closing behind him."

McGowan thought it was two or three minutes later that he heard the fatal shot, and he was convinced that the man who leaped from the state box was the same one who had passed behind him and Lieutenant Crawford.

"I had," stated McGowan, who had been irked by the man's pushy manner, "supposed him to be an ill-bred fellow who was pressing a selfish matter on the President in his hours of leisure."[35]

Writing to his brother, Henry, on April 15, Dr. George B. Todd, surgeon on the *Montauk* visited by the Lincolns in the afternoon, described Booth's approach to the Presidential box much as Captain McGowan did.

"I heard a man say 'there's Booth,'" he wrote, "and I turned my head to look at him. He was still walking very slow, and was near the box door, when he stopped, took a card from his pocket, wrote something on it, and gave it to the usher, who took it to the box. In a minute the door was opened and he walked in."[36]

In a book some years later William O. Stoddard, a former Lincoln secretary, said that Booth, in presenting his card to the President's messenger, stated that the Chief Executive had sent for him and on the basis of that statement was permitted to enter the state box. John Nicolay made a similar statement in his *Short Life of Lincoln*, published more than three decades after the assassination.[37] If the statements of Stoddard and Nicolay were true, they could have been based solely on information from Charles Forbes. They would, moreover, indicate that Forbes himself did not take the card into the President as Todd had believed.

Dr. Charles A. Leale, the twenty-three-year-old army surgeon who soon would be called upon to administer to the President, also saw the action near the passageway to the state box, although his estimate of the time may have been several minutes off.

"*Our American Cousin*," he wrote on July 21, 1867, to General Benjamin Butler, chairman of the Special Assassination Committee appointed by the House of Representatives, "was progressing very pleasantly until about five minutes past 10 when on looking towards the box I saw a man speaking with another near the door and endeavoring to enter, which he at last succeeded in doing after which the door was closed."[38]

Seated with friends in the dress circle diagonally opposite the Lincolns, Captain Roeliff Brinkerhoff, Washington Post Quartermaster who later became famous as an Ohio editor, lawyer, reformer, politician, banker, and philanthropist, also saw Booth approach the corridor leading to the state box, but saw no one delay his entry.

"When," wrote Brinkerhoff, "one of my friends called my attention to the President's box, with the remark, 'There's a reporter going to see Father Abraham,' I looked and saw a man standing at the door of the President's box, with his hat on, and looking down upon the stage. Presently he took out a card case, or something of this kind, from his side pocket and took out a card. It is said that he showed it to the President's messenger outside, but I saw nothing of the kind, in fact I saw no other man there aside from those seated in the audience. He took off his hat, and put his hand upon the door knob, and went into the little hall or corridor, back of the box." Brinkerhoff said it was "two, three or five minutes" later that the pistol shot was heard.[39]

William Withers, director of the orchestra, had received word from Stage Manager John B. Wright at the end of the second act that Miss Keene was not ready for the singing of "Honor to Our Soldiers." The rendition of the song dedicated to the President would therefore have to be delayed to the end of the play. Somewhat exercised, Withers decided after Act III began to find Wright and express his concern.

"I started to go upon the stage," he wrote later, "when I saw Booth in the balcony walking down the aisle in the direction of the President's box. I did not think strange of this, as Booth was a frequent visitor in the building, and his appearance at this time created no suspicion whatever. He was seemingly attentive toward the acting, for the curtain had again gone up [presumably for Scene II]."[40]

Captain Oliver C. Gatch of Company G, 89th Ohio Volunteer Infantry, saw Booth near the passage to the state box and was impressed by the actor's appearance and actions.

"It was during a lull in the action of a scene," Gatch recalled, "that my brother and I, cramped from long sitting in one position, rose from our seats to stretch ourselves. While we were standing in the aisle close to the wall, my brother called my attention to a young man who seemed to be watching the play from a position against the wall near the entrance to the President's box. My brother remarked [about] this young man's striking appearance, and I agreed with him, thinking him the handsomest man I had ever seen. He had a haughty demeanor, but his face was so calm that one would never have thought of suspecting him of any dreadful purpose. I noticed, though, how his eyes flashed and how sharp was their contrast to his pallid countenance. Presently, I saw him edge toward the box without changing his attitude, and then enter the passage-way and close the door behind him."[41]

James P. Ferguson, operator of the restaurant adjoining Ford's Theatre on the north, had learned from Clay Ford shortly after noon that General Grant was expected to be with the Lincolns that night. Because of his desire to see Grant, he had acted quickly to get seats at the front of the dress circle directly opposite the President's box. Still hoping that Grant would put in an appearance, Ferguson looked toward the state box frequently during the evening.

"I saw Booth pass along near the President's box, and then stop and lean against the wall," he testified at the conspiracy trial. "He stood there a moment. Something directed my attention to the stage, and I looked back and saw him step down one step, put his hands on the door and his knee against it, and push the door open—the first door that goes into the box."[42] In his testimony at the Surratt trial two years later Ferguson omitted the reference to Booth's knee and merely stated that the actor "pushed open the door to the passage leading to the private boxes."[43] Inasmuch as the passage door had no latch, there should have been no need to use the force Ferguson's original statement implied.

Still another member of the audience who saw Booth near the door of the President's box was Mrs. John B. Wright, wife of the stage manager, who was sitting in the orchestra section with friends. "I wondered why he should be there," she recalled, "and I shall never cease to regret, idle as the wish is, that no sort of intimation of his real purpose entered my mind. Had it done so, I might have prevented the awful tragedy."[44]

Once inside the passage to the state box, Booth quickly barred the door with the piece of music stand which had been left in the corner. He then drew a six-inch, single-shot derringer and a long knife from his coat and began the ten-foot walk to the entrance of Box 8. Through the open door he could see that Major Rathbone, who could be the most dangerous obstacle in his path, was intent on the play.[45] Whether he had stopped to peek through the hole in the door to Box 7 or even knew it existed will never be known.

In the state box the Lincolns and their young guests had been having a happy evening. All four found much in the "eccentric drama" to laugh about and between acts and scenes they chatted genially.[46] Mary seemed to take great pleasure in seeing her husband's enjoyment, and she sat close to him, her hand in his, in the moments before Booth's intrusion.[47]

*Harry Hawk, as Asa Trenchard, the American country bumpkin whose lack of good society manners afforded Lincoln his last laugh. (National Park Service.)*

Aware that their guests might note their affectionate posture, she said, "What will Miss Harris think of my hanging on to you so." "She won't think anything about it," he had replied, accompanying the statement with "a kind and affectionate smile."[48]

On stage, Asa Trenchard, Mrs. Mountchessington, and her daughter, Augusta, were responding to the audience's enthusiasm by playing their roles with zest. Asa, realizing that he was being sought only because of the fortune he was believed to have inherited, had just announced with sly satisfaction that he had no fortune but was "biling over with affection." Mrs. Mountchessington, shocked by the fact that Asa appeared to be offering her daughter his heart and hand "with nothing in 'em," had ordered Augusta to her room.

"Yes, ma, the nasty beast," the disillusioned Augusta had responded as she exited. "I am aware, Mr. Trenchard," Mrs. Mountchessington had then said before sweeping haughtily from the stage, "you are not used to the manners of good society, and that alone will excuse the impertinence of which you have been guilty."

"Don't know the manners of good society, eh?" Asa was saying as he looked after her, apparently greatly amused. "Well, I guess I know enough to turn you inside out, old gal—you sockdologizing old mantrap."[49]

Booth knew *Our American Cousin* well, and this was apparently the moment at which he had planned to act. He stepped into the state box unobserved, and now, from close behind the President, he pulled the trigger of his .44 caliber weapon. If the President's eyes had been on the stage, the bullet would have crashed into the right side of his head. At the moment he was shot, however, Lincoln was not looking toward the stage. He was looking down at a person in the orchestra seats. To do so he had pulled aside the flag that decorated the left side of the box and was looking between the post and the flag.[50] Consequently the derringer's heavy ball, homemade of Britannia metal, entered the head about three inches behind the left ear and ploughed seven and a half inches through the brain before coming to rest above one orbit.[51] (For information on the discordant reports on the Lincoln autopsy—concerning the path of the ball—see Appendix.)

Major Rathbone, who had his back to the door, looked around at the sound of the shot and saw Booth through the smoke. The actor shouted something Rathbone thought to be "Freedom," dropped his pistol, and shifted his knife to his right hand as the Major sprang forward and seized him. Booth wrested free and struck at Rathbone's breast with his knife. The Major parried the blow by striking it up but received a wound several inches deep and an inch and a half long in his left arm, between the elbow and shoulder. Booth then turned to the front of the box, placed his left hand on the rail on Mary's right, and dropped downward as Rathbone

*Jeannie Gourlay, the "Mary Meredith" benefitted by action of lovesick "Asa Trenchard," saw Booth in the lobby about 10 o'clock and thought he must be ill. (Georgetown University Library.)*

tried to seize him again. Failing in this effort, Rathbone could only shout, "Stop that man!"[52]

Most members of the audience thought that the shot was part of the play.[53] At least one individual thought the sound came from the barroom next door.[54] Some, remembering that the war was just over, and shooting in the city was still common, gave the sound no particular thought.[55]

Members of the play cast reacted to the shot in a variety of ways. John Matthews, playing the part of Richard Coyle, heard the shot as he waited behind the withdrawn flats and thought it was something interpolated to frighten the butt of the comedy, Lord Dundreary.[56] E. A. Emerson, who on this night was playing the part of Dundreary for the first time, was standing just under the Lincoln box reading some of his lines. Thinking the shot had come from the audience, he stepped out on the stage just in time to see Booth descending from the box.[57] To Harry Hawk, still on stage, the shot sounded muffled and he thought it had come from the theatre's property room.[58] Mrs. J. H. Evans and Maggie Gourlay, playing the parts of the serving maids, Sharpe and Skillet, were in the green room and wondered if the property man had accidentally

dropped a revolver.[59] William Ferguson, the call boy who was taking the part of Lieutenant Vernon, R. N., in the absence of the regular for that role, was standing near the prompter box with Miss Keene, and he also thought the property man was responsible. "The property man," he explained, "was in the habit of discharging old firearms in the alley back of the theatre in order to reload them."[60] Clay Ford was in the treasurer's office with Joe Sessford, the ticket seller. When they opened the little window opening into the theatre, they saw Booth on the stage, knife in hand, and thought he was pursuing someone who had insulted him.[61]

The claims of patrons concerning what they heard and saw during the minute after their eyes were drawn to the state box were as varied as the number of persons making them.

When Booth's memorandum book (diary) was found after his death, there was noted in it this entry for April 14:

> I struck boldly and not as the papers say. I walked with a firm step through a thousand of his friends, was stopped, but pushed on. A colonel was at his side. I shouted *Sic Semper* before I fired. In jumping broke my leg. I *passed* all his pickets, rode sixty miles that night, with the bone of my leg tearing the flesh at every jump. I shall never repent it, though we hated to kill. Our country owed all her trouble to him, and God simply made me the instrument of his punishment.[62]

It could be conjectured that Booth did not complete the phrase, *Sic semper tyrannis* ("Thus always to tyrants," the motto of the state of Virginia), in his diary because he could not remember how to spell "tyrannis." Only the day before the assassination he had asked a young student of Latin, visiting in Washington from a New York convent, how to spell the word. "Is it with two n's or two r's?" he had asked.[63]

The *New York Times* in its first Saturday edition carried nine dispatches about the assassination filed between 11:30 P.M. and 2:12 A.M. The second of these said the assassin shouted, "*Sic semper tyrannis,*" while still in the President's box. Lawrence Gobright's Associated Press dispatch, filed about eleven o'clock, said the same.[64] None of these dispatches carried the assassin's name.

Harry Hawk, Samuel R. Ward, a student at Georgetown University, and John Devenay, the former Maryland infantry officer who claimed that he knew Booth well, also declared that the assassin uttered the words while still in the box.[65] James P. Ferguson and General T. M. Harris, later a member of the military commission that tried the

*Assassination of President Lincoln as visualized by Albert Berghaus, artist for* Frank Leslie's Illustrated Newspaper, *April 29, 1865.*

conspirators, claimed to have heard a shout from Booth in the box but both of them asserted his words were, "Revenge for the South!"[66]

Many more individuals, including James R. Morris, who had just completed his second term as an Ohio Congressman[67]; Joseph B. Stewart, Washington attorney, who would soon be one of two patrons to pursue Booth[68]; Thomas Bradford Sanders, a descendant of General William Bradford of Plymouth Colony[69]; Henry J. Raymond, whose biography of Lincoln would appear later in 1865[70]; William H. Flood, the Navy officer who had directed the Lincolns to the *Montauk* in the afternoon[71]; A. L. Mace, a Massachusetts soldier on furlough from duty in a Federal hospital near Alexander, Virginia[72]; and Captain McGowan[73] declared that Booth uttered, "*Sic semper tyrannis*," while leaping from the box. Captain Silas Owens, Flood's companion of the evening, agreed that Booth called out something as he was about to leave the box but he could not make out the words.[74]

While most of those who wrote or told about what they saw in Ford's that night used "leaped" or "jumped" to describe Booth's descent from the box, a number of other interesting verbs, such as "vaulted," "plunged," "tumbled," "clambered," "sprang," and "fell," were used. Lieutenant John T. Bolton, a member of the 7th Regiment, U. S. Veteran Reserve Corps, Daniel DeMotte, George C. Maynard, later curator of technology at the National Museum, and Captain Brinkerhoff presented a different concept of Booth's descent. Bolton said the assassin "lowered himself by his left hand from the plush cushion on the railing in front of the box and dropped to the stage."[75] DeMotte wrote that Booth, "holding to the front [of the box] with his hands, lowered himself to the stage floor."[76] Maynard declared that the actor "slid down from the front of the box onto the stage."[77]

Captain Brinkerhoff wrote that Booth went over the railing "not with a clean sweep, but with a kind of scramble, first one leg and then the other. It evidently was his intention," he added, "to swing over as we swing over a fence, but his spur, as appeared afterward, caught in the flag, and hence the scramble."[78]

How high the state box was from the stage in Ford's Theatre has not been determined with assurance. More than a score of individuals made judgments for publication after the assassination and their estimates ranged from six or seven feet[79] to fifteen,[80] with nine, ten, and twelve feet the figures mentioned most often and ten the median. The distance from the floor line of the stage to that of the Presidential box in the restored theatre is given as ten feet ten inches,[81] but considering the fact that Edmund Spangler, an individual of medium height, had handed a hammer up to Clay Ford during decoration of the box,[82] it is improbable that the distance from the box to stage floor in the original theatre was as much as that in the restored theatre. Osborn H. Oldroyd, founder of the Lincoln Museum, located for many years in the house in which Lincoln died, always claimed that the distance from the stage floor was nine feet.[83]

Even if the box had been as much above the stage as the higher estimates, Booth under normal circumstances could have made the leap without difficulty. Testifying at the conspiracy trial, John T. Ford, manager of the theatre, said that Booth was "a bold, fearless man" who "introduced in some Shakespearean plays, some of the most extraordinary and outrageous leaps, deemed so by the critics, and condemned by the press at the time." Booth never rehearsed his leaps, Ford testified, and recalled one the actor had made in *Macbeth* "as high or higher than the box."[84]

The fact that Booth placed his left hand on the plush top of the balustrade of Box 7 and swung his feet over almost against the column in the center of the state box seems to indicate that he meant to vault to the stage, probably dropping or sliding down much as Bolton and Maynard described his movement.[85]

Rathbone, however, had grabbed the assassin's coat as he started over the balustrade.[86] As a consequence, Booth's left toe hit Washington's picture and his right spur caught in the Treasury Guard flag on the center post and also tipped the moulding that ran around the edge of the box.[87] Thus, off balance, the actor struck the floor on his left foot and knee, tearing a semicircular hole in the green baize carpet and fracturing the fibula of his left leg just above the ankle.[88]

Despite his injury, Booth was on his feet almost instantly and moving toward the entrance to the offstage passage on the north side of the theatre nearly forty feet away, a piece of the flag trailing from a spur. Many patrons declared that he "ran," "dashed," "rushed," or "strode." Others described his motion more graphically. Dr. Leale said that he "hopped . . . dragging his leg."[89] James N. Mills, formerly a drummer boy with Company I, 67th New York Infantry, and more recently a clerk in the Adjutant General's Office, testified that Booth disappeared, "limping slightly."[90] To the eyes of Charles H. Johnson, regimental quartermaster sergeant of the 3rd Massachusetts Heavy Artillery, he "stalked off with a noticeable limp."[91] Mrs. Wright, the stage manager's wife, was most graphic of all. "He crossed the stage," she said, "with a motion . . . like the hopping of a bull frog."[92]

Although a few in the audience said that they heard Booth shout, "*Sic semper tyrannis*," as he leaped from the President's box, most of the scores who later reported on things seen and heard claimed that the assassin uttered these or other words after reaching the stage. A large majority said that he shouted only, "*Sic semper tyrannis*." Others thought that he added another phrase or said something entirely different. And most of the reporters asserted that Booth, at the time he spoke,

brandished, flourished, or waved around his head the weapon carried from the box – to some only a dirk or dagger, to others a knife ten, twelve, or even fifteen inches long.[93] The phrase most often said to have been added to *Sic semper tyrannis*, or uttered alone was "The South is avenged,"[94] or in one case "Virginia is avenged."[95]

A handful of patrons said that Booth uttered something while crossing the stage but that they could not understand what he said.[96] Others said they had not heard Booth speak but did see him brandish his knife.[97]

Daniel Ballauf, a Washington manufacturer, and William Ferguson, the call boy-actor, were certain Booth had said nothing.[98] Dr. Andrew Jackson Huntoon, longtime member of the U. S. Civil Service Commission, was equally emphatic in claiming that Booth had said, "*Sic semper tyrannis*." "They [those who denied Booth had spoken] don't know what they are talking about," declaimed Dr. Huntoon, who was sitting with his wife in the dress circle directly opposite the Presidential box. "Booth positively did make that remark. I'll swear to it."[99] William Flood, who had said he heard Booth utter the phrase in the box, and Police Superintendent A. C. Richards were equally emphatic. Both of them declared that Booth uttered, "*Sic semper tyrannis*," not once, but twice while crossing the stage.[100] James P. Ferguson put in still another claim – that Booth said, "I have done it," as he disappeared into the passage leading to the alley.[101]

Booth's face as he crossed the stage is said to have borne "a hideous and fiendish expression,"[102] but to no one did he look more frightening than to Harry Hawk, who was standing toward the front of the stage opposite the President's box when his soliloquy on Mrs. Mountchessington was interrupted.

"Booth dragged himself up on one knee and was slashing the long knife around him like one who was crazy," Hawk recalled. "It was then, I am sure, I heard him say: 'The South shall be free!' I recognized Booth as he regained his feet and came toward me, waving his knife. I did not know what he had done or what his purpose might be. I did simply what any other man would have done – I ran. My dressing room was up a short flight of stairs and I retreated to it."[103]

Laura Keene, who was to have come on stage just as Hawk completed his soliloquy, was standing with William Ferguson near the prompter's desk at the front entrance on the north side of the theatre

*This Albert Berghaus drawing in* Frank Leslie's Illustrated Newspaper *for May 20, 1865, shows Booth pausing to brandish his knife as he crossed the stage. The figure at right rear might be considered that of the character Lord Dundreary (E. A. Emerson), who was near that spot as Booth descended from Lincoln's box. (National Park Service.)*

*William Withers, orchestra leader who had tippled and joked with Booth earlier in the evening, was knifed and sent sprawling as the actor made his rush for the theatre's back door. (National Park Service.)*

when the shot was fired. After Booth crossed the stage he ran between them, striking Miss Keene's hand with his own holding the dagger, then passing so close to Ferguson that the boy felt the assassin's breath on his face.[104]

William Withers, returning to the orchestra after his conference with the stage manager, was standing at the third entrance on the north side talking to Jeannie Gourlay, his back to the first entrance, when the shot was heard. "I stood with astonishment, thinking why they should fire off a pistol in *Our American Cousin*," Withers testified later. "As I

*The alley in the rear of Ford's Theatre through which Booth escaped after striking and kicking the boy who had been holding his horse.*

turned around, I saw a man running toward me with his head down . . . I saw it was John Wilkes Booth."[105]

Withers, who said he stood "completely paralyzed," declared that Booth cursed him fiercely and shouted, "Let me pass! Let me pass!"

"Should I live a thousand years," the orchestra leader said, "I shall never forget the ten seconds of my life that I spent between Booth and his liberty . . . he looked terrible. His eyes seemed starting from their sockets, and his hair stood on end. In his left hand there was a long dagger . . . He glared at me like a wild beast for a few seconds, then lowered his head, and, with arms flying, made a rush . . . With the dagger, he made a desperate lunge at me. I was so bewildered that I made no move to defend myself and his second stab sent the sharp blade ripping through the collar of my coat, penetrating my vest and under garments and inflicting a flesh wound in my neck." Withers was sent sprawling by Booth's rush, and as he lay on the floor he saw the actor pull the alley door open, then caught a glimpse of a horse's head and Peanuts John holding the animal by the bridle.[106]

Jake Ritterspaugh, a theatre carpenter, was standing on stage behind the scenes when he heard the shot and Major Rathbone's plea, "Stop that man!" When shortly he glimpsed Booth running down the passageway, he ran after him, reaching him just as the assassin was opening the door. Booth struck at the carpenter with his knife, and Ritterspaugh jumped back. Running out, Booth slammed the door, which then stuck until given a yank.[107] In the few seconds it took Ritterspaugh to open the door, Booth had time to demand his horse from Peanuts John, standing near the carpenter's bench, strike the boy with the butt of his knife, and kick the youngster as he mounted the bay mare.[108] By the time the door was opened, Booth was already riding away.

In a few more moments Booth was turning from the alley back of the theatre into that leading to F Street. His objective was the Navy Yard bridge, which he hoped would lead to liberty in the countryside beyond. In his flight he missed by only a few yards a grand torchlight procession which was marching up Tenth Street in the spirit of celebration that still gripped many of the city's inhabitants.[109]

# X
# "It Is Impossible for Him to Recover"

"My God—the President's shot!"

This cry, coming from restaurateur James P. Ferguson and echoed an instant later by sixteen-year-old Harley Butt, gave members of the audience their first inkling of the tragedy being enacted. Ferguson and Butt, sitting in dress circle chairs on the far north side of the theatre, had chanced to be looking toward the state box at the moment Booth shot the President.[1]

At almost the same moment came the cry from Major Rathbone, "Stop that man," a phrase Miss Harris immediately repeated, adding "Won't somebody stop that man?"[2] Mary Lincoln at the same time was on her feet, screaming incoherently in her horror and fright. Then she sank to her knees at the feet of her husband, still uttering in her panic and grief words no one could understand.[3] Having failed in his effort to stop the assassin, Rathbone turned his attention to the President, who had scarcely moved, his head drooped slightly forward, his eyes closed. The Major saw that he was unconscious and, supposing him mortally wounded, rushed to the outer door of the passage to call for medical aid.[4]

Despite the cries of Ferguson and Butt and the noise coming from the President's box, the audience sat—or in a few cases stood—transfixed as Booth crossed the stage and disappeared.

"There was deathly silence; you could have heard a pin drop," young William Ferguson declared.[5] "For a few moments," asserted Captain Henry W. Mason, "the audience was struck dumb; no one seemed to realize what had happened."[6] Then someone in the audience called, "What is the matter?" And Miss Harris replied, "The President is shot!"[7]

"In an instant the theatre was in an uproar," said Mrs. J. H. Evans, seen as Sharpe in the play. "Everyone had risen in his seat. Men were shouting and climbing out into the aisles."[8]

"In the pandemonium which followed, no one seemed to know just what to do," declared E. A. Emerson, the play's Lord Dundreary.[9]

"The crowd went mad," according to Captain Oliver Gatch, "A wilder night I never saw, not in battle, even."[10]

"I had never witnessed such a scene," asserted Attorney Seaton Munroe, who had rushed to the theatre after a man went running down Tenth Street, wilding exclaiming, "My God, the President is killed at Ford's Theatre." "The seats, aisles, galleries, and stage," Munroe continued, "were filled with shouting, frenzied men and women, many running aimlessly over one another; a chaos of disorder beyond control, had any visible authority attempted its exercise."[11]

Helen Truman, Augusta Mountchessington in the play, declared that the house was turned into an inferno of noises. "There will never be anything like it on earth," she said. "Through all the ages it will stand out in my memory as the hell of hells."[12]

"All was in an uproar," Andrew Huntoon declared, echoing the words of many in the audience. "Many men and women were crying like broken-heartened children," he added. "Several women fainted, and determined men hurled strong words at the brute who had shot our beloved President."[13]

Among those so shouting was former Congressman James R. Morris of Ohio, who climbed on his chair and cried, "Hang the — — scoundrel!" using expletives he later admitted "were not very creditable to myself."[14]

Many in the audience had recognized the assassin as he dropped from the state box and crossed the stage. When someone shouted, "That was Wilkes Booth,"[15] the cry was taken up louder and still louder, "Booth! Booth! *Booth*!"[16] Soon Morris was not the only one crying for violent vengeance. Shouts of, "Kill him!" "Shoot him!" Lynch him!" came from many.[17]

Suddenly there was conjoined movement. The actors behind the scenes crowded on the stage, while individuals in the front of the house pressed forward and tried to reach the stage.[18]

"The crowd behind us surged forward, and before long our party found itself wedged against the orchestra," recalled Miss Porterfield (later Mrs. William A. Brown), a teen-aged school girl from near West Point, New York, who had been sitting in the parquet with her mother and the Washington friends they were visiting. "As I was somewhat shorter than those about me, my mother, fearing for my safety, undertook to lift me up on the stage; but the pressure from behind became so great she was unable to extricate me. I might have been injured . . . but . . . a somewhat muscular man . . . picked me up and literally threw me over the footlights upon the stage." When the girl became "deathly sick" because of the excitement, actor E. A. Emerson took off his wig and fanned her vigorously. Because people were clambering upon and filling the stage, some well-intentioned person lifted her into the empty box immediately below that of the stricken President.[19]

Miss Porterfield was not the only child endangered and frightened at Ford's that night. Henry Polkinhorn, twelve-year-old son of the theatre's program printer, was home for the Easter vacation from a Georgetown school, and he had sneaked out expecting to see the President and General Grant after his mother had denied him permission to attend. As the son of the theatre's printer, he had entrée to Ford's with permission to slide into the best seat he might find available. He was able this night to find one in the orchestra. Shocked and terrified by what he had seen and by the tumult around him after the shouting for Booth's life began, the youngster howled unremittingly until someone helped him to leave saying, "Let the kid go home—he is not guilty." Wild-eyed, breathless, his face streaked with tears, Henry ran all the way home six blocks away to break the news to unbelieving parents.[20]

Only two men who saw Booth drop to the stage claimed to have sensed that the actor had committed a crime and took immediate action. One was Joseph B. Stewart, a Washington attorney, the other James Suydam Knox, temporarily a clerk in the War Department before entering medical school at Columbia. The latter, from his place in the second row of orchestra seats just below the President's box, followed close behind Stewart but became lost in the scenery and gave up the chase.[21]

Stewart, sitting in the first chair in the first row of orchestra seats on the left-hand side of the aisle nearest the President's box, was talking with his sister when the assassin's shot sounded. Looking up, he saw Booth coming over the balustrade, a curl of smoke directly above him. According to testimony Stewart gave during the conspiracy trial in May, 1865, and at the trial of John H. Surratt two years later, he stepped to the balustrade of the orchestra as Booth rose and faced the audience. After his foot slipped on the covering of the railing, Stewart stepped on his chair and jumped over to the stage. Looking up at the box, he could see everyone there except the President.

By the time Stewart turned back toward the fleeing actor, Booth was disappearing in the passage to the alley. Three times while crossing to the passage, Stewart claimed, he shouted "Stop that man!" to persons he said were on the stage. After a second or third step into the passage, when he was still about twenty-five feet from the narrow back door, he heard it slam. His effort to reach the door as quickly as possible, he said, was impeded by "as many as five persons, ladies and gentlemen," supposedly members of the cast, who came into the passage.

When he reached the door, Stewart hit the hinged side first, then changed to the correct side, opened the door, and went out. Stewart claimed that, despite the delays he had encountered, he got outside almost in time to catch Booth's horse by the rein as the actor, seemingly imperfectly mounted, pulled the animal around in a half circle, first from right to left, then from left to right. Failing in this effort, he said, he pursued Booth for forty or fifty yards after the assassin touched a spur to his mount and swept off toward F Street.[22]

Testimony of others indicates that Stewart exaggerated his effort. Jacob Ritterspaugh, who ran after Booth from his post near Edmund Spangler behind the scenes and got to the back door just in time to see the assassin riding away, made in his testimony no mention of seeing Stewart.[23] He did claim that, on rejoining Spangler, the scene-shifter hit him in the face with the back of his hand, at the same time saying, "Don't say which way he went." When Ritterspaugh asked what he meant by the slap, Spangler allegedly replied, "For God's sake, shut up." Ritterspaugh's testimony at the conspiracy trial played a large part in bringing Spangler a six-year sentence to the Dry Tortugas as an accessory to the crime.[24]

In his testimony, W. R. Smith, superintendent of the Botanical Garden in Washington, said that Stewart was "amongst the first that got on the stage," but added, "My impression is that Booth was off the stage before Mr. Stewart got on it."[25] J. L. Debonay, Ford's "responsible utility," testified that Stewart was the first man to get on the stage after Booth left but also said "I think he [Booth] had time to get out the back door before any person was on the stage."[26]

Harry Hawk, who had fled to his dressing room up a short flight of stairs at the left of the passage to the back door, came back after Booth had exited. His report of what followed is interesting but can probably be regarded as exaggerated in the light of other testimony.

> As I came back, Col. Steward [sic] . . . jumped to the stage and grabbed me.
>
> "Where is that man?" he demanded.
>
> "What man?" I asked.
>
> "The man that shot the President!"
>
> "My God!" was all I could exclaim. Then I saw in the upper box the President leaning forward, unconscious, while Mrs. Lincoln supported his head. The members of the company surrounded me. "Who did it?" they were asking.
>
> "An actor," said I.
>
> "What's his name?"
>
> "I won't tell," I replied. "There'll be a terrible uproar, and I want to keep out of any trouble."
>
> H. B. Phillips, our "old man" [the actor who had written the words for "Honor to Our Soldiers"], turned to me and said: 'Don't be a fool! This man has shot the President, and you'll be hanged if you hesitate to give his name.'"
>
> "It was John Booth," I said.
>
> They were amazed. It afterward developed that only myself

> and a man named [James] Ferguson positively identified Booth that night.[27]

Although Hawk seems to have exaggerated no less than Stewart, it is true that members of the theatre company—Emerson, Jeannie Gourlay, William Ferguson, Helen Truman, Charles Francis Byrne, John Buckingham, William Withers, and Laura Keene—who felt certain Booth was the assassin after seeing him in flight, were loath to say he was the murderer. Police Superintendent A. C. Richards talked with Miss Keene later that night and her statement was: "I do not know who shot the President, but the man who leaped from the box was Wilkes Booth."[28]

Richards also expressed doubts about Stewart's testimony. The superintendent had rushed downstairs from his seat in the dress circle upon hearing Miss Harris say the President was shot. He said he was preceded by Stewart "and together we hastily searched the wings and stage and found no one about . . . Coming upon a small open door in the rear of the stage opening upon the alley we saw at once it had been used for the escape." Richards said they also quizzed Peanuts John, who told them Booth had just galloped away after having some difficulty in mounting.[29]

Even stronger were the statements Richards made in an 1898 letter to Louis J. Weichmann, Surratt boarder and a key figure in the conspiracy trial, who was thinking of recording his knowledge in a book.

> Stewart drew largely upon his imagination when he gave his testimony as to what transpired immediately after the shot was fired . . . When I got upon the stage I found Stewart already there and no other person then in sight on the stage or among the curtains. I must have been on the stage within two minutes from the time the shot was heard. Stewart had had no time to make any explorations of the stage when I reached him . . . Together we searched among the scenery and finally found the door from the stage leading into the alley open. It was quite dark among the scenery on the stage and in the alley. As we stepped out into the alley I saw a man (Peanuts John I think) standing there and heard the rattling of a horse's feet moving rapidly down the alley but not in sight. The man . . . explained that the footsteps of the horse we heard were those of one he had been holding for a man whom he claimed he did not know and said that the man had had some difficulty in mounting his horse . . . The gyrations Stewart describes as having participated in could not have taken place as there was no horse and rider then there and in sight.[30]

In the same letter Richards cast further doubt on Stewart's credibility by saying, "His career as a lawyer had been somewhat shady.

Months before the scene he de[s]cribes . . . I had caused his arrest in connection with a large amount of R. R. bonds—some $200,000 in W&T bonds. However, no serious charge in connection with said bonds was sustained. The transaction was somewhat shady that is all as I remember it."[31]

When patrons in the orchestra and parquet chairs began their surge toward the stage, Miss Keene, fearing some of them would be injured, or even that a riot might develop, stepped before the footlights and made a plea for order. Many reported her act in later interviews and letters but varied considerably in what they heard her say. Most often quoted was, "For God's sake have presence of mind, and keep your places, and all will be well," or words to that effect.[32]

Although somewhat abated, the shouting and clamor continued, and Clay Ford sent John Buckingham to get Mayor Richard Wallach, who was on the sidewalk outside. The Mayor reached the stage after some difficulty passing through the crowd, and from that vantage point reassured the audience and requested that the theatre be cleared as quickly and quietly as possible.[33] Although some of the people began moving out in an orderly manner, many remained, meanwhile talking "in frightened whispers." "It seemed like some malignant spector stalked through the audience," Mrs. Virginia Lucas, wife of a Washington merchant, recalled.[34]

When Major Rathbone reached the outer door of the passage to the dress circle, he found the remnant of the music stand, one end in the mortice in the plaster, the other against the door's molding, holding firm against the pounding from the outside. By exerting considerable force, the Major succeeded in removing the bar and tossed it aside.[35]

After the President had been carried out, Isaac Jaquette entered the box with several other individuals, found the bar, and carried it home spotted with Rathbone's blood. Shortened a bit because a piece had been sawed off as a souvenir for an officer stopping at Jaquette's boarding house, the bar was used as evidence at the conspiracy trial.[36]

Among those who had been pounding on the door were two men who represented themselves as doctors. They were allowed to enter, and a few other individuals also pushed past the Major. Rathbone then caught sight of Lieutenant Crawford, who had been seated nearby with Captain Theodore McGowan, and asked him to prevent any additional persons from entering the box.[37]

The first person to enter the box from the dress circle was Dr. Charles A. Leale, twenty-three-year-old surgeon in charge of the wounded commissioned officers' ward at the United States Army General Hospital in Armory Square, Washington. On his heels came Dr. Albert F. A. King, a Washington physician, and William Kent, a government employee. Dr. Leale, wearing civilian clothes that night to avoid frequent demands made on all soldiers to see their passes, informed Mrs. Lincoln, standing beside the President's chair, that he was an Army surgeon.

"Oh, Doctor, is he dead? Can he recover? Do what you can for him. Oh, my dear husband!" cried Mary, who soon began to weep bitterly. Dr. Leale assured her he would do all that could be done, then turned his attention to the President.[38]

Men were also trying to reach the box by getting up from the stage. The first to succeed was William Flood, the sailor friend of the President mentioned earlier. Using his sailor training, he grabbed the side of the proscenium arch and shinnied upward until he could get his hand on the railing. Only with the help of Miss Harris, however, was he able to complete his climb.[39]

The second man up from the stage was Dr. Charles Sabin Taft, a surgeon at the Army's Signal Camp of Instruction in Georgetown, who was in the fourth row of orchestra seats with his wife and Mrs. Wright, their hostess and wife of the theatre's stage manager. When men on the stage began calling for a doctor, Dr. Taft felt duty-bound to respond, but Mrs. Taft clung to his coat and declared, "You shan't go. They'll kill you, too. I know they will."[40]

When a man on the stage recognized Dr. Taft and called for him by name, the doctor left his wife to be quieted by Mrs. Wright and former Congressman James R. Morris,[41] and made his way to the stage where Thomas Bradford Sanders, a clerk in the office of the Provost Marshal, General Defenses North of the Potomac, lifted him up to the President's box with some assistance from others nearby.[42]

With the help of others on the stage Lieutenant Bolton followed Taft into the box. Detailed as a lieutenant in the city's Provost Guard with responsibility at Ford's Theatre that night, he shortly called for the many still in the theatre to leave. "This was practically a waste of breath," he reported. "The women as well as the men made no attempt to leave, but held their ground in their anxiety to learn whether it were a reality that such foul murder had been done."[43]

By the time Taft entered the box the men already there had lifted Lincoln to a recumbent position on the floor after Leale had been unable to find movement of the artery with a finger on the right radial pulse. While holding the head and shoulder in helping to move the President, Leale's hand came in contact with a clot of blood near the left shoulder. Remembering that the assassin had carried a knife, and had cut Rathbone, Leale supposed the President had been stabbed.[44]

With a knife borrowed from Kent, Leale cut Lincoln's coat and shirt from the neck to the elbow. This knife later led to the discovery of Booth's derringer. After leaving the theatre, Kent missed his night key and hurried back to Ford's thinking he had dropped it in pulling out his knife.

While he was searching around on the floor of the box, his foot came in contact with the little handgun. Holding it up, he cried, "I have found the pistol!" He turned the gun over to Lawrence Gobright, the Associated Press agent who was also in the box, and it was used as evidence in the conspiracy trial.[45]

When Leale found no stab wound, he lifted the eyelids and saw evidence of brain damage. The quick passing of separated fingers of both hands through Lincoln's hair then revealed the wound. An obstructing clot of blood was removed to relieve the pressure on the brain, but the President showed no signs of life.

Leale next knelt over Lincoln, a knee on each side of his pelvis. Opening the President's mouth, he introduced two fingers of his right hand as far back as possible and pressed the base of the tongue down and upward to open the larynx and permit the free passage of air into the lungs. He and two of his companions then used artificial respiration, each of the latter manipulating an arm while the doctor pressed the diaphragm to cause air to be drawn in, then forced out of the lungs. During intermissions, Leale also stimulated the apex of the heart by exerting sliding pressure under and beneath the ribs with the thumb and index finger of his right hand. After these exercises had been continued for a few minutes, a feeble action of the heart was noted and irregular breathing.[46]

Evidence of the great shock Lincoln had suffered nevertheless continued, and Leale decided that something more must be done to retain life. He leaned over the President, thorax to thorax, face to face, drew a deep breath and forcibly breathed into the mouth and nostrils. After this procedure had been continued for a brief time, Leale found that action of the heart had improved. He watched for a few moments and saw that the President could continue breathing independently. He nevertheless pronounced the situation hopeless: "His wound is mortal; it is impossible for him to recover."[47]

Soon after the words, "The President is shot," aroused the audience, someone called for water; most individuals thought it was Miss Harris.[48] James Maddox, the theatre's property man, said he heard the call while on stage, ran for water and gave it to an officer when he returned.[49] Thomas Sherman said it was Miss Keene who had sent for the water.[50] Everyone seemed to agree that it was Miss Keene who delivered the water, either after carrying a pitcher or glass up to the state box, or after taking the water from someone at the door to the passageway and going on in. J. A. Covel said "She [Miss Keene] obtained the water from some source and, as I was near at hand, I helped her down from the stage and she passed up to the box where the President was dying."[51] Dr. George Maynard wrote, "Laura Keene came quickly through the gallery with a pitcher of water, lending an odd note to the scene with her costume and makeup."[52]

*Dr. Charles Sabin Taft, who assisted in ministering to Lincoln, both at the theatre and later at the Petersen house. (Lloyd Ostendorf Collection.)*

Thomas Bradford Sanders claimed that, hearing the call for water, he ran to the barroom next door (Taltavull's), "seized a pitcher of water and glass, exclaiming that it was for the President who had been shot, and ran back with it . . . to the door of the box" where he gave it to Miss Keene.[53] Lieutenant Crawford said Miss Keene had come up, wished to enter and was told, "If you will get some water, I'll let you pass." She had, he said, returned in a few minutes and was allowed to pass.[54] Flood, in the box, said Miss Keene brought in a pitcher of water, after which he sprinkled some on Lincoln's face. Kent likewise reported that Miss Keene had brought water into the box.[55]

Brandy as well as water was brought to the box, and Leale slowly

*Dr. Charles A. Leale, the Army surgeon who revived Lincoln with artificial respiration but declared the President's wound mortal. (Lloyd Ostendorf Collection.)*

poured a small quantity into the President's mouth. Dr. Leale's report says that it was swallowed and retained.

A widely accepted version of what took place in the state box just before the President was removed maintains that Laura Keene was holding his head in her lap, blood from his wound staining her yellow satin dress. Three members of the cast—E. A. Emerson (Lord Dundreary), Helen Truman (Augusta Mountchessington), and Charles Francis Byrne (Captain DeBoots)—claimed that they saw this for themselves.[56] Jeannie Gourlay (Mary Meredith) also declared that this happened but did not claim to have seen it herself.[57] Dr. Leale can be considered the best authority for the statement that Miss Keene held Lincoln's head. "While we were waiting for Mr. Lincoln to gain strength," he said, "Laura Keene . . . appealed to me to allow her to hold the President's head. I granted the request, and she sat on the floor of the box and held his head in her lap."[58] Kent, who had been standing nearby, said, "Laura Keene came up in the meantime, and the President's head was raised to rest in her lap."[59]

Doubt that the stains seen on the actress' dress were made by the President's blood is created by observations made by Dr. Taft and Lieutenant Crawford. "At that time," Dr. Taft reported, "there was no blood oozing from it [the wound]."[60] Crawford said, "There was no bleeding from the wound and but little ooze."[61] William Ferguson, who said he had accompanied Miss Keene into the President's box, corroborated their statements with the firm assertion that "The President did not bleed [at this time]."

"It is true," he said, "that blood was found on Miss Keene's dress, but it came from Major Rathbone . . . His wound bled very profusely . . . [and] it was the blood from Major Rathbone's wound that, in the midst of the excitement . . . got on Miss Keene's dress."[62]

Mrs. John B. Wright, close friend of Dr. Taft, always doubted if Miss Keene had even been in the box because the doctor, in relating to her "all the incidents of the night," never mentioned Laura Keene even though he was one of the first in the box after the shooting and left it with the wounded President.

"Laura," she continued, "could easily have got blood on her dress . . . in a variety of ways and places, for Major Rathbone was so terribly slashed by Booth's knife in the box that his blood was smeared all over the woodwork and made a trail out of the theatre."[63]

Adding to the confusion over Miss Keene's role in the state box is a statement Miss Harris, by that time Mrs. Rathbone, made in an interview with Emily Edson Briggs in 1878. Asked if it was true that the actress had held the President's head in her lap as stated in some of the newspapers, Mrs. Rathbone asserted emphatically: "No! that was a falsehood; Laura Keene did not enter the box from first to last. She might have been with the crowd who were trying to get in at the door, but only a very few were admitted, and she was not among the number."[64] No statement from Miss Keene about the alleged occurrence has been seen.

Several persons in the box asked whether the President could now be moved to the White House, but the surgeons agreed that he should be taken to the nearest house. They felt certain the President would not survive the seven-block trip over the rough streets to the White House.[65] Ten or fifteen minutes had passed since the President was shot.[66] Lieutenant Crawford asked the "knot of people," thought to be about forty, near the door of the box to fall back, pulled some of the chairs out of the upper row of the dress circle to make more room, then stationed himself at the head of the stair.[67]

Lieutenant Bolton claimed that clearing the way from the box was accomplished with great difficulty. "Those in front of us were willing to give way," he said, "but those in the rear under the terrible excitement were pressing forward, and I had to threaten and actually use the flat of my sword before a passage way was opened."[68]

Statements of persons who witnessed the President's removal from the box to the house where he died vary greatly concerning the number of persons involved and also regarding the way in which he was carried.

Initially, four members of Thompson's Battery C, Independent Pennsylvania Artillery—Jacob J. Soles, William Sample, Jabes Griffiths, and John Corey—helped the doctors carry out the dying President. These men had rushed to the outer door of the passageway from their nearby seats after hearing the cry that the President had been shot.[69]

Starting from the box, Lincoln was carried head first, Dr. Leale supporting the head, Dr. Taft the right shoulder, Dr. King the left, and the soldiers supporting the torso and feet as the bearers moved slowly through the dress circle lobby.[70] At the stair they switched so the soldiers at the feet could descend first.[71] At the same time two other individuals stepped forward to join the bearers.[72] Later developments seem to indicate that one of the two was Captain Edwin E. Bedee of the 12th New Hampshire Infantry, who had stopped off in Washington en route to join his regiment after a leave at his home in Meredith, New Hampshire. Who the other new bearer was has never been established, although claimants to the honor have been many.[73]

Major Rathbone and Mrs. Lincoln walked immediately behind the bearers, the former leaving a trail of blood on the lobby floor and stair.[74] When they reached the head of the stair, Rathbone requested Major (Horatio) Potter, an Army paymaster with Captain Brinkerhoff and a New Yorker like himself, to aid in assisting Mrs. Lincoln.[75] He also asked Lieutenant Crawford to find Miss Harris and serve as her escort.[76]

The crowd pressing into the lobby from the street completely obstructed the theatre exits, and Lieutenant Bolton asked Leale for instructions. "Give me your commands and I will see that they are obeyed," he asserted. The surgeon asked that a passage be cleared to the nearest house, and the Lieutenant, with his sword and his stern commands, managed to force the crowd back.[77]

*The William Petersen house in which Lincoln died.* Frank Leslie's Illustrated Newspaper *described the house as "one of the highest of its class in Washington." (Lloyd Ostendorf Collection.)*

When the little group reached the theatre door, Leale was again asked if the President could be taken to the White House and answered, "No, the President would die on the way."[78] About five minutes passed before it was determined where to take him.[79] Initially the surgeons were inclined to take him into Taltavull's as the nearest place where he might be treated. It was the proprietor who discouraged this idea. "Don't bring him in here," he ordered. "It shouldn't be said that the President of the United States died in a saloon."[80]

By this time ten members of the Union Light Guard had arrived under the command of Lieutenant James B. Jameson. The Guard was a company raised by Governor David Tod of Ohio in 1863 for escort duty at the White House, but its members were now being used as mounted orderlies. Jameson and his men had been stationed only a few blocks away when someone came rushing up with word that the President had been shot.[81]

The Light Guard helped to make a lane across the crowded street, but the little procession had to stop several times to give Leale opportunity to remove the clot of blood from the opening of the wound.[82] A report came back that the house opposite the theatre was closed. On the stoop of the house diagonally opposite, however, stood a man with a lighted candle. "Bring him in here," he called, beckoning. Slowly the bearers carried the precious burden up the winding steps of 453 (now 516) Tenth Street, a three-story brick house belonging to William Petersen, a merchant-tailor.[83]

How the President was carried on his short last journey appeared differently to many of the witnesses. Leale and Taft in their reports merely said he was carried out. Many others said he was carried out by "several men." James Mills said he was carried on the shoulders of two men, an obvious impossibility.[84] Thomas H. Sherman and Charles L. Willis saw four men carrying the President.[85] Mrs. Virginia Lucas agreed with Jacob Soles that six men carried the President.[86] William Ferguson and Mrs. Nelson Armstrong—on April 14 Kitty Brink, helping to make up members of the cast in dressing rooms until the clamor drew her to the stage—claimed that the President was carried out in the rocking chair in which he had been sitting.[87] Flood, who was the first person to reach the box from the stage, said four soldiers and the doctors carried Lincoln out on a stretcher.[88] Two members of the cast, E. A. Emerson and Mrs. J. H. Evans, declared he was carried out on a shutter.[89] Several other persons claimed he was carried out on a stretcher, in most cases indicating that it was improvised from a shutter.[90] Considering the fact that the partition normally dividing Boxes 7 and 8 was seven feet high and three inches thick, this interesting question has been raised: Could the "stretcher" on which Lincoln was carried to the Petersen house have been a section of the partition?

# XI
# "Now He Belongs to the Ages"

The man who called for Lincoln's bearers to come to the house across from Ford's was not the owner. William Petersen, in fact, did not seem happy that his house at 453 Tenth Street (now 516) was to become a shelter for the dying President. Seeing the bearers winding their way toward his place, Petersen, standing in front of his stoop, is reported to have shouted, "The President is coming," then rushed into the house, disappeared, and was not seen again until morning.[1]

Petersen was also irritated by the fact that hundreds of people came to the house just after Lincoln's death asking to see the room where the President died. Irritation changed to anger when many of the visitors carried off souvenirs, including pieces cut from the carpet and furniture and almost any item they could take undetected. Petersen shortly decided to charge admission, declaring that anyone interested in seeing the room should be willing to pay for the privilege.[2]

Petersen was likewise offended when some of the reporters described his home as a tenement house. He consequently insisted that Albert Berghaus, who arrived to cover "The Murder of President Lincoln" for *Frank Leslie's Illustrated Newspaper*, include in his article the statement, " . . . Mr. Petersen's house, in which the President died, is one of the most respectable houses in Washington, and not a tenement home, as stated by some papers." For good measure, Berghaus added, "The house is one of the highest of its class in Washington."[3]

The young man who guided the Lincoln bearers to the Petersen house was Henry S. Safford, who occupied a second story apartment with Thomas Proctor, a seventeen-year-old government employee who was spending much of his time reading law and later practiced in Brooklyn for many years. Safford, in charge of the War Department's Property Returns Division at age twenty-five, had been celebrating Lee's surrender for several nights like thousands of others in Washington. Tired, he had decided to stay home this night and rest. While sitting in his parlor reading, he heard a commotion in the street, raised a window, and learned the President had been shot.[4]

*Left: William Petersen, merchant-tailor, in whose house Lincoln died.* (Frank Leslie's Illustrated Newspaper, *April 29, 1865.*) *Right: Henry Safford, whose call, "Bring him in here," led the bearers to take Lincoln into the Petersen house. (National Park Service.)*

"I was soon down at the door and across the street and edging my way through the crowd half way into the theatre," he recalled later. "Finding it impossible to go further, as everyone acted crazy or mad, I retreated to the steps of my house. Some five minutes later when the bearers of the President's body had brought him nearly across the street one of the leaders asked: 'Where can we take him?' As there was no response from any other house, I cried out: 'Bring him in here!'"[5]

More than an hour earlier Carl Bersch, who would become noted as an artist, had prepared to record on canvas the activity taking place on Tenth Street. "All Washington was celebrating," Bersch wrote to his family a few days later. "Parades marched through the streets, waving flags and carrying many transparencies. Women with wide skirts, and wearing large poke bonnets, were as numerous as men. President Lincoln was known to be at Ford's Theatre, so Tenth Street was on the line of march . . . The scene was so unusual and inspiring, that I stepped out upon the balcony in front of my windows, with my easel and sketch papers, determined to make a picture of the whole scene and transfer it to canvas."[6]

Little did Bersch realize that he had just prepared to preserve for posterity a never-to-be-forgotten scene of national tragedy.

"Shortly after 10 o'clock," Bersch's letter continued, "a silence fell upon the surging crowd of revelers. The marching line halted. A loud cry came from a window of the theatre. 'President Lincoln has been shot;

clear the street.' Soldiers and police attended to that. In the course of 10 or 15 minutes, out of the north door of the theatre appeared a group of men, carrying the prostrate form of an injured man on an improvised stretcher. They stopped a few moments at the curb, hastily debating where to take the injured man to give him the best attention most quickly."[7]

They then, according to Bersch, observed the lights in the Petersen house and the young man standing on the topmost step, beckoning to them to bring the injured man in there.

"This was done as quickly as the soldiers could make a pathway through the crowd," Bersch continued. "My balcony being twelve or fourteen feet above the sidewalk and street, I had a clear view of the scene, above the heads of the crowd. I recognized the lengthy form of the President by the flickering light of the torches, and one large gas lamp post on the sidewalk. The tarrying at the curb and the slow, careful manner in which he was carried across the street, gave me ample time to make an accurate sketch of that particular scene; make it the center and outstanding part of the large painting I shall make, using the sketches I made earlier in the evening, as an appropriate background. A fitting title for the picture would, I think, be 'Lincoln Borne by Loving Hands on the Fatal Night of April 14, 1865.' Altogether it was the most tragic and impressive scene I have ever witnessed."[8]

Willed to the White House by Bersch's granddaughter, Mrs. Gerda Vey, "Borne by Loving Hands" was turned over to the National Park Service in 1978 and is now displayed at Ford's Theatre National Historic Site. It should be noted that Bersch in his letter agreed with many of those quoted earlier—that Lincoln was being carried on an improvised stretcher. His painting also testifies to this observation.

Ordered by the physician leading Lincoln's bearers to "Take us to your best room,"[9] Henry Safford waited until the slow-moving group negotiated the nine curving steps which took them to the hallway of the first floor above the "light" basement that gave the building the appearance of having four stories. George Francis, who dealt in house furnishings at 490 Seventh Street, and his wife, Huldah, occupants of the two rooms on the left of the hallway, had been preparing for bed in the back room when the commotion on the street drew them to a front window. When they heard someone say, "The President is shot," Francis hurried into his clothes and ran across the street just as the President was being carried out of the theatre.[10]

The command to take Lincoln to the best available room apparently led Safford to think first of the Francises' bedroom. However, its door, opposite the foot of the stair that led to the second floor from the right-hand side of the hall, was fastened, so he continued on to the little room on the rear of the building at the end of the hall.[11]

The room into which they took Lincoln was only 9½ feet wide and 17½ feet long. Its floor was covered with a worn Brussels carpet, its walls by a brownish paper, figured with a white design. Three engravings by J. H. Herring—"Village Blacksmith," "The Stable," and "The Barnyard"—and a photograph of an engraving of Rosa Bonheur's "Horse Fair" hung on the walls. The furniture included a table, a bureau, several chairs, and a low walnut four-poster bed.[12] On the bureau was a photograph of three women, later identified as that of the two sisters and mother of William T. Clark, to whom the room was rented.[13] Clark, a twenty-three-year-old member of Company F, 2nd District of Columbia Infantry, and at that time detailed as a clerk at the headquarters of General Christopher C. Augur, commander of the Department of Washington, was gone and did not return until Sunday morning.[14] (He then spent a great deal of time working with Albert Berghaus, artist for *Leslie's*, at the same time protecting the contents of his room against souvenir hunters. "Everybody has a great desire to obtain some momento from my room," he wrote his sister, Ida, on April 19, "so that whoever comes in has to be closely watched for fear they will steal something."[15])

William Clark was a meticulous housekeeper, and his bed had clean sheets and a spotless Irish worsted coverlet of red, white, and blue.[16] Lincoln was laid down gently on his back in the longitudinal center of the bed, but his great height made it necessary to elevate his knees. Intending to get his giant patient into a more comfortable position, Dr. Leale asked that the foot of the bed be removed. When it was found to be a fixture, he requested that it be broken off but this could not be done satisfactorily. The President was consequently moved to a diagonal position, his head on two pillows on the side of the bed near the door, his feet still encased in his boots, stretching over the side near the wall.[17]

No one in the room knew it, but the bed on which Lincoln lay dying had more than once held the form of his assassin. Petersen often rented rooms to actors playing at Ford's, and first John Matthews and later Charles Warwick, the actors to whom Booth had talked a few hours before the assassination, had occupied the room at one time or another during the 1864–65 play season. While each was the occupant, Booth had made use of the bed when weary from rides in the area. Matthews, in fact, claimed that he was a Petersen-house renter on April 14 and in his room there had burned the letter Booth had asked him to deliver to the *National Intelligencer*.[18]

The little room and the hallway, too, had become crowded with people who had followed the bearers and doctors, eager to learn how

*Carl Bersch's painting of Lincoln being borne from the theatre on a stretcher ("Lincoln Borne by Loving Hands"). The painting is now on display at Ford's Theatre National Historic Site. (National Park Service.)*

badly the President was hurt. The windows and door on the court (south) side of the room were opened to permit the entrance of fresh air, and at the doctors' request the officer in command of the Provost Guard at the theatre cleared the room of all but the medical men.[19]

Mary, Miss Harris, and Major Rathbone, who had experienced some difficulty crossing the street because of the huge crowd, finally reached the hallway, and Mary rushed ahead crying, "Where is my dear husband? Where is he?"[20] When she reached the back room and saw Lincoln's unconscious form, she fell to her knees beside him, sobbing bitterly and begging him to speak to her. The doctors were about to examine the President thoroughly to determine if he had suffered a wound or wounds from Booth's dagger, and at their request Mary allowed herself to be led across the hall to the Francises' now opened parlor overlooking the theatre. There she spent most of the next eight hours on the black horsehair sofa, frequently giving way to spasms of sobbing. "I cannot recall a more pitiful picture than that of poor Mrs. Lincoln, almost insane with sudden agony, moaning and sobbing out that terrible night," General Thomas M. Vincent, Assistant Adjutant General, recalled.[21]

Rathbone, whose wounded left arm had been bleeding profusely for more than twenty minutes, began to feel faint as he reached the Petersen house. He seated himself in the hall but soon fainted and was laid on the floor.[22] At this moment Miss Harris may have saved the life of her fiancé, because it was she who wrapped a handkerchief tightly over the wound like a tourniquet, stanching the flow of blood.[23] Rathbone was then taken to the Harris home, seven blocks away, in a carriage, and Dr. G. W. Pope, an old friend of the family, was called. He found Rathbone "pale as a corpse, almost exsanguined," He then discovered that the Major had probably escaped death by about one-third of an inch. Booth's dagger had gone through the inner part of the left upper arm, close to the armpit, penetrating the biceps muscle and grazing the bone. "It [the wound] came," Dr. Pope reported later, "within about one-third of an inch of what is called in surgical language the bracial artery and deep basilic vein, which lie close together at that part. Had the blade of the dagger severed those vessels, the Colonel [sic] would have bled to death in about five minutes."[24]

While Booth was carrying out his part of the assassination plan, Lewis Paine was doing his best to dispose of Secretary of State William H. Seward. He gained entrance to the Seward house opposite Lafayette Park at about 10:15 on the pretext of delivering a prescription for the Secretary, who was recovering from the severe concussion, fractured right arm, and broken jaw suffered in his carriage accident. Paine then beat Acting Secretary of State Frederick W. Seward almost insensible with his revolver before bursting into the Secretary's room on the third floor, knife in hand. A steel brace supporting Seward's jaw deflected

*Lewis Paine, attempting to carry out his assignment to murder Secretary of State Seward, is confronted by Frederick Seward, whom he clubbed almost insensible before gaining access to the Secretary's room. (National Park Service.)*

*Paine as he appeared after being taken into custody at the Surratt house on April 17. (National Park Service.)*

Paine's first thrust, but the Secretary received three serious wounds before he could roll from his bed.

George Robinson, a male nurse, grabbed Paine and was joined by Major Augustus H. Seward, the Secretary's other son. While laying wildly about with his knife, Paine gashed the Major seven times, the nurse four. He then fled, crying, "I'm mad, I'm mad," and on the way out stabbed (almost fatally) Emrick Hansell, a State Department messenger who had heard the noise and was going for help.[25]

Meanwhile, Atzerodt, who had told Booth he would do no killing, made no effort to assassinate Vice President Johnson.[26] Herold, who had been charged with serving as Paine's guide, fled when he heard the commotion at Seward's, galloped madly away to join Booth, and surrendered at Garrett's barn on April 26, shortly before Booth was shot. Paine apparently wandered about Washington, then was arrested the following Monday when he appeared at the Surratt house posing as a laborer.[27]

Word that the President had been shot spread rapidly through the city. A special dispatch to the *New York Times* filed at 11:15 described the situation thus: "A stroke from Heaven laying the whole of the city in instant ruins could not have startled us as did the word that broke from Ford's Theatre a half hour ago that the President had been shot. It flew everywhere in five minutes and set five thousand people in swift and excited motion on the instant." At least one other paper, the *Boston Weekly Advertiser*, used the same dispatch with only a few words changed.[28]

Remembering those moments, Mrs. Lenora H. Freudenthal added, "Everybody seemed to be out . . . and the excitement was terrible to behold."[29] Occasionally someone said something interpreted as condoning Booth's act; reaction was instant and harsh. "I recall," said W. H. Roberts, a cavalryman from Findlay, Ohio, "a soldier shooting to death a man who said he was glad Booth had shot Lincoln."[30]

Soon excitement gave way to fear as word of the attack on Seward reached those in Tenth Street. Then fear developed into terror for many when a vedette rode up exclaiming, "A plot, a plot! Secretary Seward's throat is cut from ear to ear; Secretary Stanton is killed in his residence; General Grant is shot at Baltimore, and Vice President Johnson is killed at the Kirkwood House."[31]

"The excitement then was intense; words fail to describe it," Lieutenant Bolton recalled. "I have in mind now an army captain in the street who lost his reason, becoming raving mad, and I was compelled to place him in charge of two of my guards and send him to the central guard house. Finding it an impossible task to clear the street with the small force under my command, I asked the vidette [sic] . . . to ride with all speed to the 'Circle' and tell them there to send a squadron of cavalry."[32]

It took mighty efforts by Lieutenant Bolton's men and those of the Union Light Guard under Lieutenant Jameson, aided shortly by another squadron of Light Guards under Sergeant Smith Stimmel, to keep the crowd in hand until the cavalry arrived from the War Department. The block was then cleared and guards stationed across the street above and below the Petersen house.[33] To provide additional protective strength, Superintendent A. C. Richards of the Metropolitan Police Department ordered all precincts to put every available man on duty.[34]

Wild rumors continued to fly all night. "Among them," Thomas Bradford Sanders told Harvey C. Burke, private secretary to the Commissioner of Navigation in the Department of Navigation and Labor (and later people's court judge in Baltimore), "was one that the Confederate prisoners in the Old Capitol prison were breaking out and were about to burn the town."[35]

Early in the excitement over the assassination there had been some who called for burning the theatre. Now many urged that violence be directed against the Confederates in Old Capitol prison.

"About 2,000 went to the Old Capitol prison to burn it, and they called upon the people to come out and see the rebels burn," Mrs. Beekman DuBarry, wife of the Assistant to the Commissary General of Subsistence, wrote her mother on April 16. "The police and troops were out and put a stop to it or it would have been done."[36]

It was fortunate that General Montgomery C. Meigs, the Quartermaster General, had ordered General Christopher C. Augur, Commander of the Department of Washington, to turn out the troops with "special vigilance and guards about the Capitol Prison."[37]

Excitement nevertheless continued high throughout the city. "Ten thousand rumors are afloat, and the most intense and painful excitement pervades the city," the *New York Tribune* asserted in a late Friday night dispatch. The *Washington National Intelligencer* observed next morning, "Such a night of horror has seldom darkened any community. The definite dread which conspiracy inspires seized on the public mind, and suspicion, apprehension, and agony pervaded the people."[38]

Writing to his father on April 16, James Suydam Knox summarized the situation: "Despair was on every countenance and black horror brooded over the city."[39]

After Mary left the back bedroom at Petersen's, the doctors removed the President's clothing, taking care to safeguard contents of the pockets. These were later revealed as a pair of gold-rimmed spectacles with sliding temples and one bow mended with string; a leather case for the spectacles; a pair of folding spectacles in a silver case; an ivory pocket knife with silver mounting; a watch fob of gold-bearing quartz or a similar stone, mounted in gold; a large white Irish linen handkerchief with "A. Lincoln" embroidered in red cross-stitch; a sleeve button with a gold initial "L" on dark blue enamel, and a brown leather wallet (including a pencil), lined with purple silk, with compartments for notes, United States currency, and R. R. tickets. In one of these compartments the President was carrying a five-dollar Confederate note and nine newspaper clippings.[40]

The President's body was examined from head to foot by Dr. Leale and no additional injury found.[41] The wound was then examined by Dr. Taft, a finger being used as a probe, and it was found that the ball had passed beyond the reach of the finger. Taft put a teaspoonful of diluted brandy between the President's lips and it was swallowed with difficulty. Ten minutes later a half-teaspoonful was administered and this was retained in the throat with no apparent effort made to swallow it.[42]

Lincoln's lower extremities were found to be cold, and at the doctors' request Henry Safford hustled about, found some bottles and heated water in the basement kitchen so the bottles could be kept constantly warm.[43] A steward from Lincoln Hospital procured additional bottles, blankets, and a large mustard plaster, which was applied over the solar plexus and to the anterior surface of the patient's body. When symptoms indicated renewed brain compression, Leale cleared the opening of the wound of clots and brain tissue so blood could again ooze from it and relieve pressure on the brain.[44] This was done frequently, and it was discovered that respiration was easy when the wound was discharging freely, labored when the discharge was arrested. The pulse also became stronger when the wound was discharging freely.[45] The President's eyes were closed and the lids and surrounding parts so ingested with blood that they gave the appearance of being bruised.[46]

Leale had sent messengers to members of the President's Cabinet, to Dr. Robert King Stone, the Lincolns' family physician, and to Dr. Joseph K. Barnes, Surgeon General of the United States, soon after the Petersen house had been reached.[47] A little later he also sent for the Reverend Dr. Phineas D. Gurley, pastor of the New York Avenue Presbyterian Church, the church the Lincolns attended. Dr. Stone arrived about eleven o'clock, and because of his relations with the family the case was turned over to him. After carrying his finger into the wound as Taft had done earlier, he confirmed Leale's prognosis made in the box at Ford's: The case was a hopeless one; the President would die. He added, however, that Lincoln's "vital tenacity was very strong, and he would resist as long as any man could."[48] Hours later the doctors present at various times during the evening expressed amazement at the accuracy of this prediction. The average man, they agreed, would not have survived Lincoln's wounds more than two hours.[49]

Dr. Barnes, accompanied by Assistant Surgeon General Charles H. Crane, arrived a few minutes after eleven. The former had been called to the Seward home and there treated the Secretary of State before learning of the President's assassination. He had left Dr. T. S. Verdi, the Sewards' family physician, to care for the others hurt by Paine, and hurried to the White House under the impression Lincoln would be there.[50]

Barnes and Stone agreed that actions taken by Leale and Taft were correct but suggested that a few more drops of brandy be administered to see if they could be swallowed. They were not, and no further attempt was made.[51] Shortly thereafter, twitching of the muscles on the left side of the face set in for about twenty minutes and the mouth was drawn slightly to one side.[52]

As Mary was being led from Clark's bedroom she had expressed a desire for someone to go to the White House for Robert. Eighteen-year-old C. C. Bangs, on his second tour of duty with the United States Christian Commission from Clinton, New York, had just arrived at the Petersen house and volunteered to go. After he had convinced the officer stationed at the door that he knew the way, he ran four and a half blocks to Willard's Hotel and hailed a hack.[53] At the White House, Robert and John Hay, who had been gossiping in an upstairs room, were quickly ready for the trip to Petersen's. Senator Charles Sumner, who had been visiting with Senator John Conness of California when he heard of the assassination, arrived at the White House at this moment under the impression the President had been taken there. He accompanied Robert, Hay, and Bangs to the Petersen house with the hackman the young New Yorker had ordered to wait.[54] By this time guards had been posted at each end of the block, but occupants of the carriage were recognized and allowed to pass.[55]

Robert was met at the door by Dr. Stone, who informed him with grave tenderness that there was no hope for his father. When Robert saw his father lying unconscious on a bed all too small for him, his face swollen and discolored, he broke down. After a few minutes, he went to the Francises' parlor and tried to comfort his mother, who was again giving vent to her grief.[56] She had spied Sumner, a longtime friend, as he followed Robert and Hay down the hall and had rushed to ask him whether her husband was dead. Sumner told her he had just arrived and knew nothing, then passed into the room where Lincoln lay.[57] The Senator sat down at the head of the bed, took one of the President's hands in his, and spoke to him. "It's no use, Mr. Sumner," one of the doctors told him. "He can't hear you. He is dead."

"No, he isn't dead," Sumner replied indignantly. "Look at his face, he is breathing." Sumner remained at the President's side throughout the night, listening to his breathing, which he said often sounded almost like a melody.[58]

Bangs meanwhile had been requested by Quartermaster General Montgomery Meigs to accompany a lieutenant to the headquarters of the Department of Washington with an order to put a guard around the entire city to prevent Booth's escape should he still be hiding in Washington.[59] When he returned, he was requested by Robert to go to the home of Senator James Dixon of Connecticut at 407 New York Avenue and bring Mrs. Dixon (Elizabeth Lord Cogswell), one of Mary's close friends, to the Petersen house. Mrs. Dixon was awakened by the arrival of the carriage and inquired from her upstairs window what was wanted. "The President is dead," Bangs replied, "and Captain Lincoln wishes you to come to Mrs. Lincoln as quickly as possible."[60]

When dressed, Mrs. Dixon took time to send word to her sister, Mrs. Mary Kinney at 18th West NM North, before leaving. After arrival at Petersen's the carriage was sent for Mrs. Kinney and her daughter,

Constance, who came to the Tenth Street house to be with Mary and Mrs. Dixon the rest of the night.[61]

Writing of the scene upon her arrival, Mrs. Dixon said:

> . . . on a common bedstead covered with an army blanket and a colored woolen coverlid lay stretched the murdered President his life blood slowly ebbing away. The officers of the government were there & no lady except Miss Harris whose dress was spattered with blood as was Mrs. Lincoln's who was frantic with grief beside him calling him to take her with him, to speak one word to her . . . I held her & supported her as well as I could & twice we persuaded her to go into another room.[62]

The record kept by one of the doctors at the bedside shows that Mary was again by her husband's side at 1:45[63] "[T]he scene that then occurred beggars description," John P. Usher, Secretary of the Interior, wrote his wife on April 16:

> She implored him to speak to her [and] said she did not want to go to the theatre that night but that he thought he must go . . . She called for little Tad [and] said she knew he would speak to him because he loved him so well, and after indulging in dreadful incoherences for some time was finally persuaded to leave the room.[64]

Robert, almost overcome with grief himself, endeavored to soothe his mother and help her to bear her grief.[65]

Edwin M. Stanton, Secretary of War, and Gideon Welles, Secretary of the Navy, had arrived at the Petersen house shortly after eleven, the first Cabinet members on the scene. Both had been to Seward's after getting information of Paine's attack and there learned about the assassination. They then drove to Tenth Street with Chief Justice David Kellogg Cartter of the Supreme Court of the District of Columbia and General Meigs, who had been clearing the Seward residence of the curious. Welles sought information about the President upon their arrival and was told by one of the physicians that "the President was dead to all intents, although he might live three hours or perhaps longer."[66]

Stanton took over at once, set up headquarters in the back parlor (the Francises' bedroom) and began issuing orders. Frank Abial Flower, in his biography of Stanton, summarized thus the Secretary's activities of the next few hours:

> He sent for several army officers to act as aides, directed General Thomas M. Vincent (Assistant Adjutant General) to take charge of affairs in the Petersen building; telegraphed General Grant at Philadelphia that Lincoln had been shot and to return at once to

> Washington; issued orders, oral and written, to the police and military authorities of the District to be prepared for emergencies; telegraphed to Chief Kennedy of New York to send on his best detectives immediately; ordered General L. C. Baker to return from New York to search for the assassins; soothed and cheered Mrs. Lincoln; advised Grant (at 11:30) at Philadelphia to watch every person approaching him and have a detached locomotive precede his train on its way to Washington; ordered President Garrett to use the utmost speed of the Baltimore and Ohio Railway to bring Grant to the capital; wrote and dispatched a note to Chief Justice Chase, saying the President could not live and to be ready to administer the oath of office to Vice-President Johnson; notified the Vice-President that the President was dying; and sent to the people bulletin after bulletin concerning the tragedy and Lincoln's condition.[67]

Two of the War Department's telegraphers, Thomas A. Laird and George C. Maynard, had been in the audience at Ford's. Laird at once ran to the home of Major Thomas T. Eckert on Thirteenth Street to alert the General Superintendent of Military Telegraph, then to the War Department to carry out Eckert's command that David Homer Bates, manager of the telegraph office, summon for duty every available operator and see that every wire was manned. Maynard rushed to the War Department and with Laird, Bates, and the assembled telegraphers spent the night sending out reports and orders as supplied by a relay of messengers established between Eckert at Petersen's and the War Department.[68] Messages on Lincoln's condition, as dictated by Stanton to Charles A. Dana, Assistant Secretary of War and a good stenographic writer, went to General John A. Dix, Commanding General, New York City, for distribution to the press throughout the country.[69]

"As these bulletins were spelled out in Morse telegraph characters over the wires leading north," Bates declared, "it seemed to us . . . whose fingers manipulated the keys, that never sadder signals formed."[70]

Stanton's messages to Dix, crisp and comprehensive, would have done credit to most of the professional news writers of the day. He was criticized, however, for moving his messages too slowly. His first one, not filed until 1:30 A.M. and put on the wires at 2:15 read:

> This evening at about 9:30 [sic] o'clock at Ford's Theatre, the President, while sitting in his private box with Mrs. Lincoln, Miss Harris, and Major Rathbone, was shot by an assassin who suddenly entered the box and approached behind the President. The assassin then leaped upon the stage, brandishing a large dagger or knife, and made his escape in the rear of the theatre.
>
> The pistol ball entered the back of the President's head, and penetrated nearly through the head. The wound is mortal. The President has been insensible ever since it was inflicted, and is now dying.

> About the same hour an assassin, whether the same or not, entered Mr. Seward's apartments, and, under a pretense of having a prescription, was shown to the Secretary's sick chamber. The assassin immediately rushed to the bed and inflicted two or three stabs on the throat and two on the face. It is hoped the wounds may not be mortal. My apprehension is that they will prove fatal.
>
> The nurse alarmed Mr. Frederick Seward, who, from an adjoining room, hastened to the door of his father's where he met the assassin, who inflicted upon him one or more dangerous wounds. The recovery of Frederick is doubtful. It is not probable that the President will live through the night.
>
> General Grant and his wife were advertised to be at the theatre this evening, but he started to Burlington at 6 o'clock.
>
> At a Cabinet meeting at which General Grant was present, the subject of the state of the country and the prospect of a speedy peace was discussed. The President was very cheerful and hopeful, and spoke very kindly of General Lee and others of the Confederacy and of the establishment of the government in Virginia. All the members of the Cabinet, except Mr. Seward, are waiting upon the President.
>
> I have seen Mr. Seward but he and Frederick were both unconscious.

That is the way Stanton's first dispatch read as the column one lead in the *New York Times* and *New York Herald* appearing about 2:30 A.M. Saturday. It was later edited slightly for the official records, the opening words, for instance, being changed to "Last evening, about 10:30 P.M." Not until his second dispatch was filed at 3:00 A.M. did Stanton mention Booth. Then he did so in a single sentence—"Investigation strongly indicates J. Wilkes Booth as the assassin of the President"—buried in the middle of a long second paragraph.[71]

For about two hours during the night, telegraph service was interrupted over some lines out of Washington, and rumors spread that they had been cut by the conspirators or accomplices. Eckert, however, revealed that service from the War Department had not been interrupted. The stoppage had occurred over only a portion of the commercial lines, and this had been caused by the crossing of wires in main batteries.[72]

Responsibility for the stoppage was assumed by William H. Heiss, Sr., superintendent of the "People's Line of Telegraph," one of several commercial telegraph companies doing business in Washington. News of the assassination, Heiss feared, might lead to violence in the South, either by instigating a general uprising there or by leading Union troops still in the territory to retaliate against Southerners and their property. It would therefore be better, he reasoned, for telegraph communications to go only to military officers, who could take steps to prevent or control violence.[73]

Stanton was not the only person busy in the back parlor at Petersen's. At Stanton's request, Judge Cartter, who had accompanied Stanton and Welles to the Petersen house, began hearing testimony shortly before midnight, and the Secretary listened intently when not busy otherwise. After an unidentified person started to take statements in longhand, it became evident that someone proficient in shorthand was needed. When General Augur came out on the steps at Petersen's and called for someone able to take shorthand, Albert Daggett, a State Department clerk standing on the balcony of the house next door, mentioned James Tanner, a fellow boarder there.[74]

This farm boy from Richmondville, New York, then only ten days past his twenty-first birthday, had run away at seventeen to enlist in Company C, 87th New York Volunteer Infantry, in 1861. After going unscathed through six battles, he had lost both legs below the knees when struck by a fragment from a bursting shell at the second Battle of Bull Run. When he learned to use artificial legs, he attended a business school in Syracuse, New York, then returned to Washington and became a clerk in the Ordnance Bureau of the War Department.[75]

On the night of April 14, Tanner had taken the horsecars to Grover's Theatre to see *Aladdin; or, the Wonderful Lamp* and there learned of the assassination. He had returned to Tenth Street, and after some difficulty getting past the guards, reached his second floor rooms which, with the balcony, were crowded with other residents of the house.[76]

Escorted into the Petersen house by Augur, Tanner took a seat opposite Secretary Stanton about twelve o'clock and started to take down testimony with the pen and ink provided, his shorthand following immediately below the eleven lines of longhand written by his unidentified predecessor.[77]

During the next hour and a half, Tanner, who later was to serve as Commander-in-Chief of the Grand Army of the Republic and as Register of Wills for the District of Columbia under Presidents Theodore Roosevelt, Taft, Wilson, Harding, and Coolidge, took the statements of six individuals, starting with Alfred Cloughly, a clerk in the Second Auditor's office. The others whose statements were recorded were Lieutenant Alexander McL. Crawford of the Veteran Reserve Corps; Harry Hawk, the only actor on stage when the shot was fired; James P. Ferguson, keeper of the restaurant adjoining Ford's Theatre on the north; Henry B. Phillips, the actor-singer who had written the words for "Honor to Our Soldiers"; and Colonel George V. Rutherford of the Quartermaster's Department.[78]

Cloughly, walking in Lafayette Square with a lady from the Treasury Department Registrar's office, had heard the cries of "murder" after Paine's attack on Seward and seen the would-be assassin ride away, then had investigated to find the Secretary's home in an uproar. As he

*Corporal James Tanner, whose war wounds had led him to attend business school and take up shorthand, took down at Stanton's request the testimony of six individuals given before Judge Cartter.*

rushed toward Ford's intending to inform Lincoln of the attack on Seward, he learned that the President had been shot. Inasmuch as he was near Senator Conness's, he went there and gave Conness and his guest, Senator Sumner, the bad news.[79]

Much of the information from Crawford's statement has already been noted in Chapter X. The statement also emphasized that Crawford had seen Hanscom, the newspaper editor, take a dispatch in to the President about twenty minutes before the assassination.

Hawk at first said he was still not positive that the man who leapt from the box was Booth. Later in his statement he said, "In my mind I don't have any doubt but that it was Booth."[80]

Ferguson said that from his place in Seat 59 in the dress circle he had been looking at the President's box with an opera glass when the shot was heard. He had then seen Mary clutch her husband around the neck, the President throw up his right arm, and Booth go over the box pulling off part of a flag. "Booth," said Ferguson, "looked me right up in the face" as he crossed the stage. "It alarmed me," he asserted, "and I pulled the lady with me down behind the banister. I looked right down at him and he stopped as he said 'I have done it' and shook the knife."[81]

Phillips, who said he had been "a very dear friend of Mr. Booth almost from infancy," testified that he had on Monday met Booth at Fourteenth Street and Pennsylvania Avenue while with three gentlemen from the Attorney General's office and had invited the actor to have a drink with them.

"Yes, anything to drive away the blues," Booth was quoted as replying.

"What is giving you the blues?" Phillips had asked.

"This news is enough to give anybody the blues," Booth was said to have answered. Because he was acquainted with Booth's Southern sympathies and was with officers from the Attorney General's office, Phillips had pressed Booth no further. He had not seen Booth in the theatre that night, he stated, but had heard Hawk declare, "I could say it [that it was Booth who had rushed past him] if I was on my death bed."[82]

In his statement, Rutherford merely said that he had at about 7:00 P.M. seen Booth throw his key on the counter at the National Hotel.[83]

Taking the statements was not easy because of numerous distractions. Mary's weeping and frequent exclamations of horror and grief could be plainly heard through the folding doors between the two parlors. The work was also interrupted frequently as Stanton received reports or issued orders. Additionally, the Secretary left occasionally to go to the bedside of the President, whose stertorous breathing could be heard following periods of complete silence.[84]

Despite interruptions, the statements he had soon taken made Tanner believe there was no doubt about Booth's guilt. "In fifteen minutes," he wrote on April 17 to Hadley F. Walch, once a student with him in business school, "I had testimony enough to hang Wilkes Booth, the assassin, higher than ever Haman hung."[85]

When the final statement had been taken at 1:30, Tanner began transcribing the testimony. Excited over the job he had been called upon to do, he had feared he would be unable to read his shorthand and was relieved to find his fears ungrounded.[86]

Although Stanton had been listening much of the time while Tanner was taking statements that fingered Booth as the assassin, the Secretary for some unknown reason made no mention of Booth in his first message (1:30 A.M.) to General Dix for distribution to the press. In his message filed at 3:00 A.M. and moved at 3:20 he made his cautious mention of Booth[87] (see page 141), but meanwhile some New York and Washington papers were naming the actor as Lincoln's murderer.

The *New York Tribune* was the first paper on the streets with news of the tragedy, in part through the efforts of a thirteen-year-old messenger boy, James Boozang. The lad was sitting in the *Tribune*'s Washington office on Fourteenth Street between F Street and Pennsylvania Avenue when a friend of some men in the office rushed in breathless with news of the assassination. Paul McAllister, chief editor, detailed his son to write the story, and this was done in a few terse sentences. A shout for a messenger boy brought young Boozang, who grabbed the paper and rushed for the telegraph office. At Tenth and Pennsylvania a guard grabbed him by the scruff of the neck and declared he was under arrest. Quickly, he explained his haste, and with the guard's blessing completed his run to get the *Tribune* dispatch on the wire far ahead of any competitor.[88]

The *Tribune*'s first dispatch did not mention Booth, but the Washington bureau kept a stream of dispatches flowing to Horace Greeley's paper. Both the thirteenth and fourteenth, filed more than an hour and a half before Stanton's first message was cleared, mentioned Booth. The thirteenth, dated on Friday, said, "There is one universal acclaim resting upon J. Wilkes Booth as the assassin," while the fourteenth, the first cleared after midnight, said, "The mass of evidence tonight is that J. Wilkes Booth committed the crime." The *New York World*, well over an hour before Stanton's first file arrived, had received this dispatch: "Everybody who knows the man, say [sic] that J. Wilkes Booth, the actor is the assassin. The evidence is concurrent at this late excited hour to that effect."

In Washington the *National Intelligencer* and *Morning Chronicle* were also ahead of Stanton in naming Booth as the murderer, the latter doing so in its second edition, the former in its third when it said, "Developments have rendered it certain that the hand which deprived our President of life was that of *John Wilkes Booth*, an actor."

One source of the information about Booth in the early editions of the New York and the Washington papers was probably the Metropolitan Police Department, whose report for Friday night read: "11 P.M. At this hour the melancholy intelligence of the assassination of Mr. Lincoln, President of the United States, at Ford's Theatre was brought to this office and the information obtained from the following persons goes to show that the assassin is a man named J. Wilkes Booth. Secretary Seward and both his sons and servant were attacked at the same hour by a man supposed to be John Serrett [sic]." Then followed the names of seventeen witnesses, among them James S. Knox and Joseph B. Stewart, who had attempted to capture Booth; James Maddox, Ford's property man; J. L. Debonay, the theatre's "responsible utility"; John Devenay, who had said just after Booth's drop to the stage, "He is John Wilkes Booth, and he has shot the President"; John Fletcher, the stableman who had furnished the horse ridden by Davey Herold; and Harry Hawk.[89]

Later entries in the log listed eight articles found in the vicinity of the assassination — a pistol (the derringer), a slouch hat, an opera glass case, a spur, a brass button, an India rubber button, a cape, and a hat supposed to be the President's — and the fact that Edmund Spangler, Ford's assistant carpenter, and Joseph Boser, unidentified, had been brought to headquarters "as witnesses in the assassination." Finally, the log revealed that John Parker, the Lincoln guard who had disappeared after the assassination, had brought in a woman, Lizzie Wilson, on suspicion.[90]

The doctors meanwhile had continued their vigil back in Clark's room at the Petersen house. At one time or another during the night sixteen were in the room,[91] and starting at 10:55 Dr. Ezra W. Abbott and Dr. Albert F. A. King had recorded the first of fifty readings of Lincoln's pulse and twenty of his respiration.[92] Between the first reading and 12:15, the pulse and respiration were fairly steady, the former ranging from 42 to 48, the latter from a high of 29 at 11:20 to a low of 21 at 12:15. By 12:15 ecchymosis was setting in around the eyes, and the pulse rate began to climb until it reached 95 at 1:30. Only once had any part of the President's body more than twitched, that at 12:55, when there was a brief struggling motion of the arms.[93]

It was shortly after 1:30 when Vice President Johnson paid a brief visit to the death chamber. He had been asleep in his room, No. 68, at the Kirkwood House when Leonard J. Farwell, Inspector of Inventions in the Patent Office and former Governor of Wisconsin, rushed into the hotel with news of the assassination. Farwell had been at Ford's with a friend and, fearing that a plot to murder the nation's key officers was being carried out, had run the three-and-a-half blocks to the Kirkwood House to warn Johnson.

By the time he had awakened Johnson, news of the attack on Seward had arrived. The incredulous Johnson asked Farwell to check at the Petersen house and Seward's to determine whether the stories were merely rumors. When Farwell returned with news that Lincoln and Seward were near death, Johnson went to the President's side, accompanied only by Farwell and Major James O. O'Beirne, commander of the Provost Guard.[94]

According to Charles Sumner, the Vice President remained only two minutes because Mary wanted to visit her husband again. Knowing that Mary could not abide Johnson, whom she called a demagogue, Sumner urged him to leave. He did so, saying that the house was crowded and his space could be better used by the doctors and others who might do something for the President.[95]

Long ago the room had become crowded with all members of the Cabinet (except Seward), high ranking military men, several members of Congress, and a few friends who had managed to get past the guards.

After Robert took his mother to the back parlor again at 2:10, Surgeon General Barnes introduced an ordinary silver probe into the President's wound. About three inches from the external orifice, it met an obstruction which the doctors decided must be a plug of bone driven in from the skull. The probe passed the obstruction but was too short to follow the track of the ball its whole length. A long Nelaton probe was then passed into the track of the wound for two inches beyond the plug of bone and the ball definitely felt. Passed still farther, the probe came in contact with fragments of the orbital plate.[96] After these explorations, nothing more was done with the wound except to keep it free from coagula. If this was allowed to form and remain even a short time, signs of increased compression appeared, the breathing became extremely stertorous and intermittent, the pulse feeble and irregular.[97]

Dr. Abbott's record shows that Mary visited her husband again at three o'clock but does not indicate how long she remained. Presumably, it was not for long, because the visit brought on greater weeping and heartbroken exclamations. Hugh McCulloch, Secretary of the Treasury, described the scene during Mary's presence as one that "pierced every heart and brought tears to every eye."[98] The doctors knew, moreover, that any long stay would result in even more emotional stress for the suffering wife. Blood and brain matter were oozing from the wound onto the clean napkin that had been laid over the crimson stains on the pillow before she entered.[99]

The doctors made recordings on conditions thirteen times after Mary returned to the back parlor shortly after three o'clock. Until 5:40 the recordings varied only slightly, the pulse between 60 and 64, the respiration 24 to 27. By six o'clock the pulse was failing; respiration was 28. Ten minutes later Dr. Barnes found the pulse hardly perceptible but counted it at 60. Respiration was 26 and stertorous.[100]

Before the final entry of death, only five recordings were made by Dr. Abbott or Dr. King after 6:25 when the pulse was thready and not counted; respiration was 22 and inspiration jerky. These five were: "6:30 – still failing and labored breathing; 6:40 – inspirations short and feeble; expirations prolonged and groaning; a deep, softly sonorous, cooing sound at the end of each expiration, audible to bystanders; 6:45 – respiration uneasy, choking and grunting; lower jaw relaxed; mouth open; a minute without a breath; face getting dark, 6:59 – breathes again a little more at intervals; another long pause;

7:00 – still breathing at long pauses; symptoms of immediate dissolution."[101]

With Lincoln's death imminent, Mary was allowed to come to her husband's side once more shortly before seven. Mrs. Dixon and two others in the room later detailed the scene which followed.

Mrs. Dixon wrote in a letter to her sister, Louisa, on May 1:

> . . . just as the day was struggling with the dim candles in the room we went in again. Mrs. Lincoln must have noticed a change for the moment she looked at him she fainted and fell upon the floor. I caught her in my arms & held her to the window which was open . . . She again seated herself by the President, kissing him and calling him every endearing name – The surgeons counting every pulsation & noting every breath gradually growing less & less – They then asked her to go into the adjoining room, and in twenty minutes came in and said, "It is all over! The President is no more."[102]

Dr. Taft recalled:

> Her last visit was most painful. As she entered the chamber and saw how the beloved features were distorted, she fell fainting to the floor. Restoratives were applied, and she was supported to the bedside, where she frantically addressed the dying man. "Love," she exclaimed, "live but one moment to speak to me once – to speak to our children!"[103]

Dr. Leale expanded on Taft's version.

> As Mrs. Lincoln sat on a chair by the side of the bed with her face to her husband's, his breathing became very stertorous and the loud, unnatural noise frightened her in her exhausted, agonized condition. She sprang up suddenly with a piercing cry and fell fainting to the floor. Secretary Stanton, hearing her cry, came in from the adjoining room and with raised arms called out loudly, "Take that woman out and do not let her in again." Mrs. Lincoln was helped up kindly and assisted in a fainting condition from the room. Secretary Stanton's order was obeyed and Mrs. Lincoln did not see her husband again before he died.[104]

As the gentle Mrs. Dixon led Mary away from her husband's bedside and back to her place on the parlor sofa, James Tanner heard the distraught wife moan, "Oh, my God, and I have given my husband to die."[105]

Later she wrote to a good friend, "All that I wished then was to die, if it had been our Heavenly Father's will."[106]

Gideon Welles, who had been in the death chamber since a little past eleven, standing except for a couple of hours in a chair at the foot of the bed, had begun to feel faint about six o'clock and left the house for a short walk in the open air.[107]

All night long, even when rain fell or threatened, the street as close to the Petersen house as people were allowed to approach had been packed with men and women hoping and praying for some word of encouragement from the bedside.[108]

"Large groups of people were gathered every few rods, all anxious and solicitous," Welles wrote in his diary. "Some one or more from each group stepped forward as I passed, to inquire into the condition of the President, and to ask if there was no hope. Intense grief was on every countenance when I replied that the President could survive but a short time. The colored people especially—and there were at this time more of these persons than of whites—were overwhelmed with grief."[109]

Rain had set in before Welles returned to the Petersen house about fifteen minutes later and took a seat in the back parlor, where half a dozen persons could be found, among them John P. Usher, Secretary of the Interior, asleep on the bed. A little before seven Welles returned to Lincoln's bedside and witnessed the pitiful scene as Mary made her last visit.[110]

How many persons were in Clark's 9½ x 17½-foot room when Lincoln breathed his last will probably never be known. Possibly as many as sixty-five were in and out of the room during the night, and sketches and paintings of the death scene and listings made by more than a score of individuals show from eleven to forty-seven persons present during the last moments of Lincoln's life. James Tanner, who had transcribed the last of his notes and passed into the room before seven, said, "There was no crowd in the room."[111] In a later address he said that the group included "about twenty or twenty-five in all, I should judge."[112]

A print showing eleven persons present at the deathbed or either of two showing twelve might be accepted, considering the size of the room, but for the fact that they picture individuals such as Vice President Johnson, Mrs. Lincoln, and Tad Lincoln, who assuredly were not in the room.[113]

Most other sketches or paintings with identifiable figures also include persons known to have been absent or omit one or more who certainly were present. A painting including forty-seven figures was designed by John B. Bachelder and painted by Alonzo Chappel. Titled *The Last Hours of Lincoln*, it apparently was meant to show individuals known to have visited during the night.[114]

When *Frank Leslie's Illustrated Newspaper* ran in its edition for April 29, 1865, an engraving "of the scene at the deathbed of President Lincoln," it carried the following testimony of its accuracy, dated "Washington, D. C., 453 10th Street, April 16, 1865," the day Albert Berghaus made his sketch:

We, the undersigned, inmates of No. 453 10th Street, Washington, D. C., the house in which President Lincoln died, and being present at the time of his death, do hereby certify that the sketches taken by Mr. Albert Berghaus, Artist for Leslie's *Illustrated Newspaper*, are correct.

| | |
|---|---|
| Henry Ulke | Thos. Proctor |
| Julius Ulke | Wm. T. Clark |
| W. Petersen | H. S. Safford |

However, in its article on "The Murder of President Lincoln" in the same issue, the paper did not list Proctor, Clark, or Safford among those "present at his death." It gave special credit to the Ulke brothers "for much valuable assistance" to Berghaus in preparing his sketches. In a letter to his sister, Ida, four days after the assassination, Clark, while not claiming that he had been present at the deathbed, did claim that he had aided Berghaus "in making a complete drawing of the last moments of Mr. Lincoln, as I know the position of everyone present."[115]

Considering the size of the room, the most acceptable depiction of the deathbed scene seems at first thought to be the pen-and-ink sketch which can be seen in the Army Medical Museum in Washington. This drawing, showing fourteen persons, was made by Hermann Faber, a hospital steward, who was sent to the Petersen house by Surgeon General Barnes just after 9:00 A.M. on April 15. Dr. Barnes wanted for the war records an accurate diagram of Clark's room, including individuals present at the time of the President's death. To aid him in his job Faber was given a list of known attendants on a slip of paper along with information on their positions when death came. Unfortunately, only Secretaries Stanton and Welles, Senator Sumner, Robert Lincoln, John Hay, and Drs. Barnes, Stone, and Crane can be identified with certainty in the sketch.[116] The other figures could be those of the Reverend Dr. Gurley, Tanner, and Drs. Abbott, King, Leale, and Taft, who were surely present. However, in the light of all testimony, a few other individuals must have also been in the room when Lincoln breathed his last. Like most of the dozens of other sketches and paintings purportedly showing the death scene, the Faber sketch may also include individuals not actually present.

A diagram of the house in which Lincoln died, made by Major A. F. Rockwell, Assistant Adjutant General, has been published often. Rockwell's sketch, made on the morning of April 15 and used by Nicolay

*"Death of Abraham Lincoln." Identified, left to right, are "Mr. J. Ulke, Mr. Colfax, Postmaster General Dennison, Mr. Farnsworth, Young Petersen, Mr. G. Welles, Chief Justice Chase, Mr. Petersen, Charles Sumner, Robert Lincoln, Surgeon Stone, Rufus F. Andrews, Surgeon General Barnes, Gen. Meade, Surgeon Crane, Gen. Halleck, Mr. Stanton, Mr. Safford."*

# DIAGRAM OF THE HOUSE IN WHICH PRESIDENT LINCOLN DIED.

FROM THE ORIGINAL PREPARED BY
MAJOR A. F. ROCKWELL, APRIL 15, 1865.

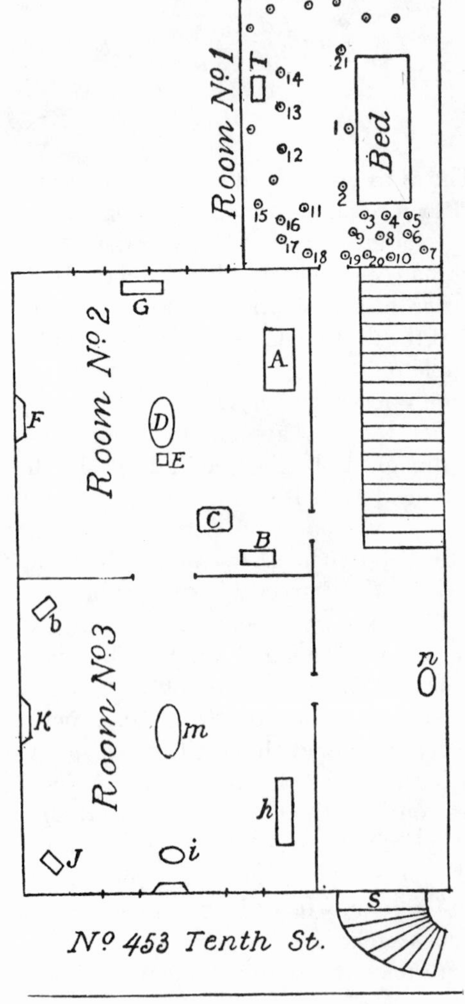


Tenth Street

S ——→ N

ROOM NO. 1 — The following indicates the position of persons present, when the Surgeon-General announced the death of the President at 7:22 A.M., April 15, 1865:

1. Surgeon-General Barnes (sitting on the side of the bed, holding the hand of the President).
2. Rev. Dr. Gurley.
3. Surgeon Crane (holding the President's head).
4. Robert Lincoln.
5. Senator Sumner.
6. Assistant Secretary M. B. Field.
7. Major John Hay, Private Secretary of the President.
8. Secretary Welles.
9. General Halleck.
10. Attorney-General Speed.
11. General Meigs (Quartermaster-General).
12. Secretary Usher.
13. Secretary Stanton.
14. Governor Dennison.
15. Major Thomas T. Eckert (Chief of Telegraph Corps at War Dep't).
16. Mrs. Kenney.
17. Miss Kenney.
18. Col. Thomas M. Vincent (War Dep't).
19. Col. L. H. Pelouze (War Dep't).
20. Major A. F. Rockwell (War Dep't).
21. Secretary Hugh McCulloch (occupied this position during the night, but was not present at the closing scene).

The few others noted were persons unknown to Colonel Rockwell. (Generals Augur, Farnsworth, and Todd, Drs. Stone, Leale, Taft, and Abbott were among them.)

ROOM NO. 2 — This room was used for the preliminary examination of witnesses. A stenographer was seated at the center table *(D)* from 12 to 8 in the morning. The Secretary (Stanton) wrote his dispatches to General Dix (with lead pencil) at the same table *(C)*.

*A*, Bed. *B*, Washstand. *C*, Table. *D*, Table. *E*, Chair. *F*, Fireplace. *G*, Dressing Case.

ROOM NO. 3 — This room was occupied by Mrs. Lincoln, Robert Lincoln, and two or three friends.

Mrs. Lincoln occupied the sofa *(H)* through the night.

*H*, Sofa. *I*, Table. *J* and *L*, Etageres. *K*, Fireplace.

HALL. — Carpet covered with oilcloth, stained with drops of blood.

*N*, Hat Rack. *S*, Large blood spot on doorstep.

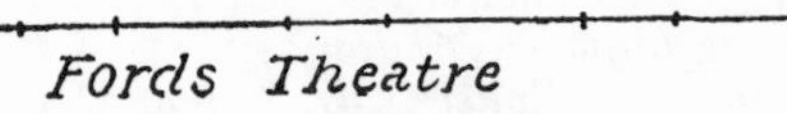

and Hay and other authors of Lincoln biographies, identified twenty-one persons and their positions in the room "at the time of death" and also indicates positions of eight persons he did not name. Those he listed were Dr. Joseph K. Barnes, Surgeon General; Dr. Charles H. Crane, Assistant Surgeon General; William Dennison, Postmaster General; Colonel Thomas T. Eckert, Superintendent of the War Telegraph Office; Maunsell B. Field, Assistant Treasurer of the United States; the Reverend Dr. Phineas D. Gurley, Pastor of the New York Avenue Presbyterian Church; General Henry W. Halleck, Union Chief of Staff; John Hay, Presidential Secretary; Mrs. Kenney [Mary Kinney]; Miss Kenney [Constance Kinney]; Robert Lincoln; General Montgomery C. Meigs, Quartermaster General; Colonel Louis H. Pelouze, Assistant Adjutant General; James Speed, Attorney General; Edwin M. Stanton, Secretary of War; Senator Charles Sumner; John P. Usher, Secretary of the Interior; General Thomas M. Vincent, Assistant Adjutant General; Gideon Welles, Secretary of the Navy; and Major Rockwell himself.[117]

Rockwell noted that the position he numbered 21 had been occupied by Hugh McCulloch, Secretary of the Treasury, who had been there during the night but "was not present at the closing scene."[118] After they had heard the Surgeon General say he thought the President might live for another six or seven hours, McCulloch and Schuyler Colfax, Speaker of the House, had left about five o'clock A.M., intending to return at eight.[119]

Among those certainly present but not identified by Rockwell were Tanner and Drs. Stone, King, Abbott, Leale, and Taft. Nor does Rockwell mention General Isham N. Haynie or Governor Richard J. Oglesby, both of Illinois, although in his diary for April 14–15 General Haynie wrote that he and Governor Oglesby at 11:00 P.M. "were admitted to the room where the President lay dying and remained until the President passed away."[120] Rockwell's diagram, like all the various sketches and paintings, also fails to show the position Dr. Leale claims that he maintained, "the only person between the bed and the wall where I stood, holding the President's hand."[121]

Other individuals who have been listed at the deathbed in articles, books, or pictures published since 1865 include Mrs. Dixon; Rufus Andrews, Surveyor of the Port of New York; William T. Otto, Assistant Secretary of the Interior; Alexander Williamson, Tad Lincoln's tutor; George V. Rutherford of the Quartermaster's Department; General John B. S. Todd, a delegate to Congress from Dakota Territory; Dr. Lyman Beecher Todd, Mrs. Lincoln's cousin; Drs. Neal Hall, Charles Lieberman, William Henry Ford, J. J. Woodward, and C. D. Gatch; Congressmen Isaac Arnold and John F. Farnsworth of Illinois, and Edward H. Rollins and Gilman Marston of New Hampshire; William Petersen's son; Miss Harris; the chief steward of the hospital, name not

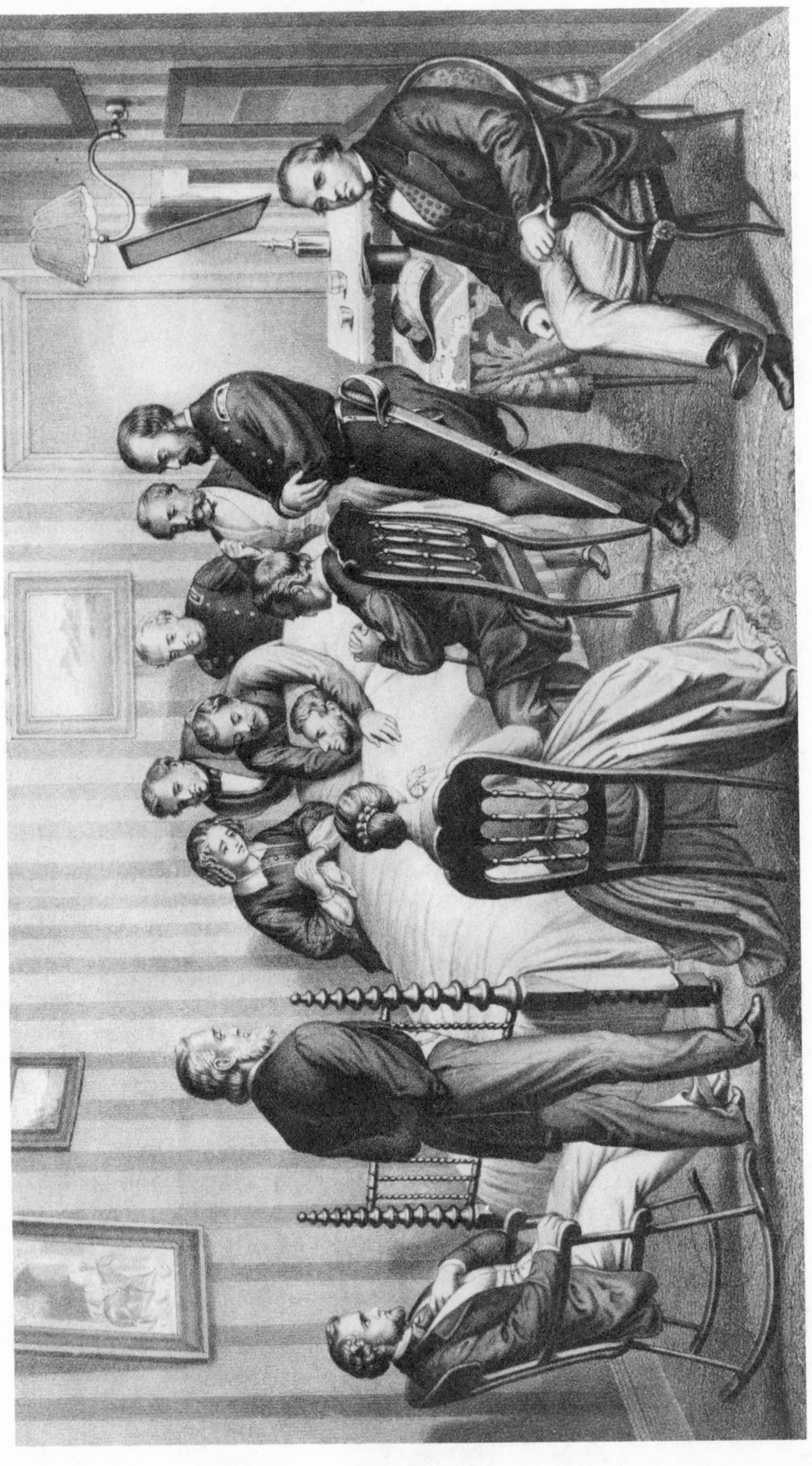

mentioned; General George G. Meade; Chief Justice David Kellogg Cartter of the Supreme Court of the District; former Governor Leonard J. Farwell of Wisconsin; a Major French; and Chief Justice Salmon P. Chase. (Chase in his diary indicated that he was not present.)

The death struggle for the President began shortly after seven. Even as his pulse began to fail, his face was scarcely more haggard than the faces of the sorrowing men and women around him.[122] General Vincent, who was in and out of the room, said of the scene, "As the sure approach of death was noticed, the deep sad gloom increased."[123]

Several times the President's pulse could not be counted. "Two or three feeble pulsations being noticed," Dr. Leale recalled, "[they were] followed by an intermission when not the slightest movements of the artery could be felt. The inspirations became very prolonged and labored, accompanied by a gutteral sound. The respirations ceased for some time and several anxiously looked at their watches until the profound silence was disturbed by a prolonged inspiration, which was followed by a sonorous expiration."[124] A few times when the intervals between inspirations and expirations were unusually long, Surgeon General Barnes applied his finger to the carotid artery, evidently to determine if death had come.[125]

To Stanton, standing near Dr. Barnes, Lincoln's breathing sounded like an aeolian harp, now rising, now falling and almost dying away, and then reviving. It reminded him of what he had noticed when one of his children had died in his arms years before.[126]

Robert Lincoln, who had thought "the interminable agony of the night would never end,"[127] twice gave way to overpowering grief and sobbed aloud during the minutes his father's respiration was becoming more and more suspended.[128] His grief was magnified by the thought that he might have saved his father's life if he had only accepted the invitation to be a member of the theatre party. As the youngest member of the group, his seat, he conjectured, would have been placed farthest from the front of the box. In this position, he would undoubtedly have seen Booth and grappled with him before he could have used his pistol.[129]

As death neared, Robert stood at the head of the bed, weeping on the shoulder of Senator Sumner. Tanner, writing a friend about that moment, said that "the utmost silence prevailed, broken only by the sound of strong men's sobs."[130] Surgeon General Barnes occupied a chair by the head of the bed, his finger still over the carotid artery seeking to detect pulsations. Dr. Stone sat on the edge of the foot of the bed, and Dr. Leale, standing by the wall, continued to hold the President's right

*"De letzten Augenblicke des Präsidenten Lincoln" ("The Last Moments of the President Lincoln").*

hand, his extended forefinger on its pulse. The young doctor, who had been by Lincoln's side for almost eight hours, hoped that his firm grasp on the dying man's hand would somehow "let him know that he was in touch with humanity and had a friend."[131]

When Dr. Barnes gently crossed the President's hands across his breast and said, "He is gone," Maunsell Field observed that there had been "no apparent suffering, no convulsion action, no rattling of the throat, none of the ordinary premonitory symptoms of death. Death in this case was a mere cessation of breathing."[132] The President had drawn his last breath at 21 minutes and 55 seconds past seven A.M. His great heart did not cease to beat until 22 minutes and 10 seconds past seven.[133]

At the moment Dr. Barnes made his announcement, Stanton, standing behind the Surgeon General and holding his hat, for some unknown reason raised his right arm fully extended and with slow and measured movement placed the hat on his head for a moment, then with the same deliberate movement removed it. Major Rockwell, who had observed this unusual action always wondered if it had been an involuntary movement or one intended by Stanton as a salute to his deceased chief.[134]

The Reverend Dr. Gurley, in a speech before the Presbyterian Synod of Baltimore at Carlisle, Pennsylvania, on October 16, 1866, related what happened next.

> Then I solemnly believe that for four or five minutes there was not the slightest noise or movement in that awful presence. We all stood transfixed in our positions, speechless, breathless, around the dead body of that great and good man.
>
> At length the Secretary of War, who was standing at my left, broke the silence and said, "Doctor, will you say anything?" I replied, "I will speak to God." Said he, "Do it just now."
>
> And there, by the side of our fallen chief, God put into my heart to utter this petition, that from that hour we and the whole nation might become more than ever united in our devotion to the cause of our beloved, imperiled country.
>
> When I ceased, there arose from the lips of the entire company a fervid and spontanious [sic] "Amen."[135]

As Dr. Gurley began, "Our Father and our God," Tanner had snatched pencil and notebook from his pocket to record the prayer, but

*"The Last Moments of Lincoln." Identified, left to right, are "P. M. Gen'l Dennison, John Hay [seated] . . . General Meigs, Attorney General Speed, Secretary Usher, Dr. Crane, Secretary Stanton, Surgeon General Barnes [seated], Hon. Charles Sumner, Robert Lincoln, Mrs. Lincoln, Rev. Dr. Gurley, Dr. Stone, Alex Williamson . . . Vice President Johnson, Secretary Welles, Secretary McCulloch, General Farnsworth [seated], General Augur, General Halleck." (Lloyd Ostendorf Collection.)*

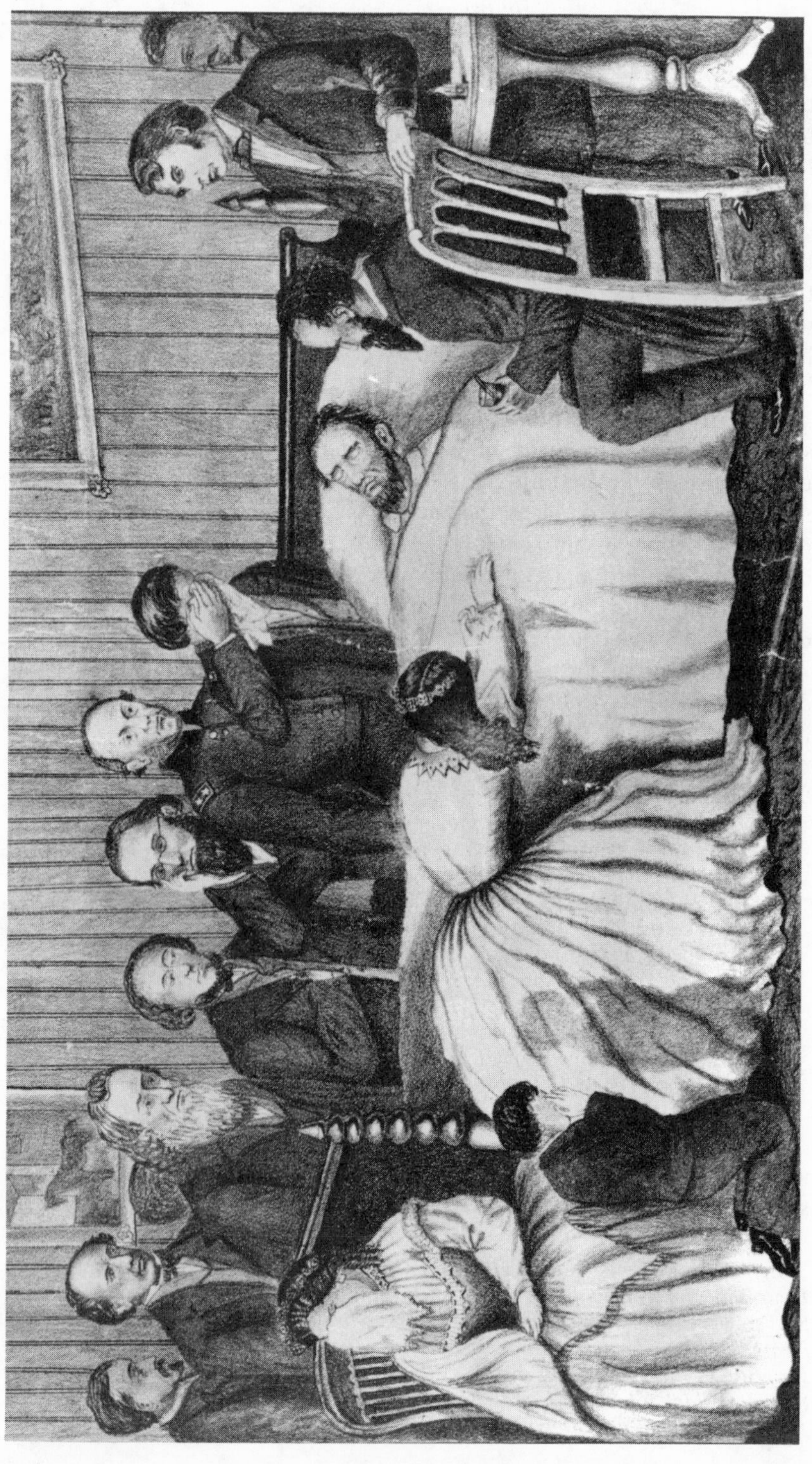

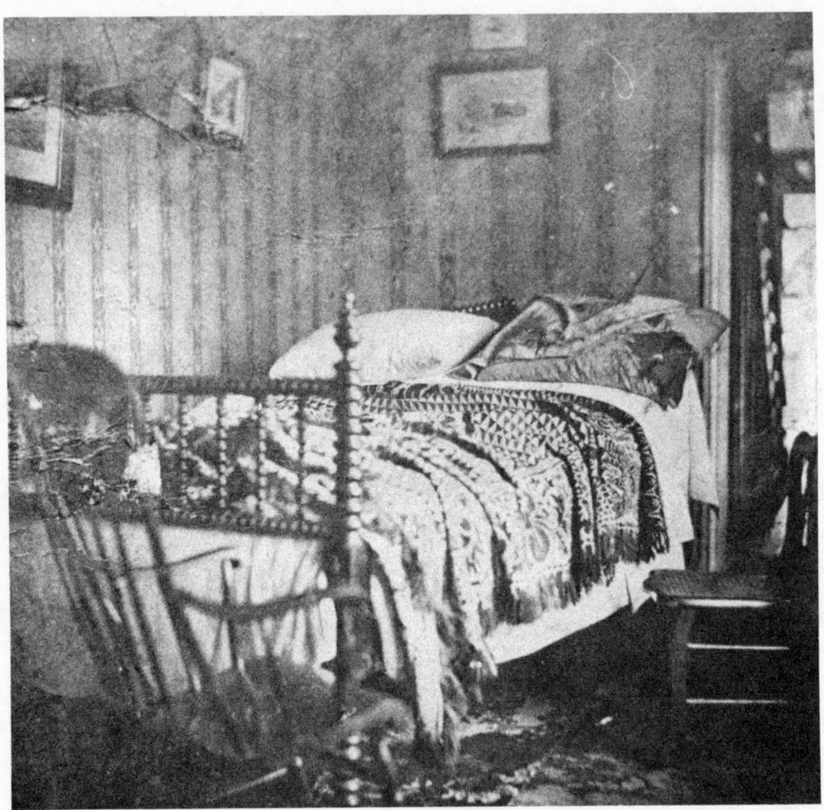

*Above: This picture, showing the deathbed of President Lincoln shortly after his body was removed to the White House, was taken by Julius Ulke, a Petersen house roomer who had been up all night to bring water for the doctors. It was acquired by the Louis A. Warren Lincoln Library and Museum in 1985.*

*Opposite: "Lincoln's Death Bed." Identified, left to right, are "Mr. Ulke, Mr. Chase, C. J., Miss Harris, Secretary Welles, Tad Lincoln, Secretary McCulloch, Secretary Stanton, General Halleck, Mrs. Lincoln, Robert Lincoln, President Lincoln, Surgeon General Barnes, Hon. Charles Sumner."*

his haste defeated his purpose. He had only one pencil, and its point caught in his coat and broke.[136]

As the pastor's "Thy will be done. Amen" was voiced in subdued and tremulous tones, Stanton, tears streaming down his cheeks, sobbed out words that were to become immortal: "Now he belongs to the ages."[137]

After completing his prayer by Lincoln's side, Dr. Gurley went into the front parlor, where Robert, Mrs. Dixon, the Kinneys, and Mary's cousin, Dr. Lyman Beecher Todd, were endeavoring to console the grieving widow. Here another prayer, interrupted frequently by Mary's sobs, was offered. Presently, her carriage arrived and she was led to it, fairly well composed until she reached the outer door and glanced across at the theatre. Then in her anguish she cried out several times, "That dreadful house—that dreadful house."[138]

In Clark's room immediately after the President's death, the expression on the face of the deceased was described by Field as being "purely negative." "But in fifteen minutes," he continued, "there came over the mouth, the nostrils, and the chin, a smile that seemed almost an effort of life."[139]

And over the entire countenance had come "a look of unspeakable peace." Abraham Lincoln's "happiest day" had also become his last.[140]

# Appendix
# Some Unsolved Mysteries

## 1. Eli K. Price and His $500 Check

A descendant of Welsh settlers, members of the Society of Friends who came to America about the time of William Penn (1682), Eli Kirk Price struggled to prepare for the law, was admitted to the Philadelphia bar at twenty-four, and became a noted chancery and real estate lawyer.[1]

Interested in law reform, he was three times elected to the state senate and was responsible for acts related to the sale and conveyance of real estate, the law of descent, the greater security of title, the statute of limitations, the protection of a wife's property from an improvident husband, and the aid of the deserted or neglected wife.[2] He was also responsible for a bill that united a dozen separate and distinct municipalities into the city of Philadelphia with an area of more than 130 square miles.[3] Price was the author of eight books, most of them related to the law, and his arguments before the Supreme Court over a fifty-nine year period fill some 150 volumes of reports.[4]

Although Price was one of Philadelphia's busiest lawyers, "this work did not prevent him from taking part in various organizations for intellectual and philanthropic ends." Through his efforts, Philadelphia's Fairmont Park was established in 1867 with him as chairman of its governing commission.[5] He was a trustee of the University of Pennsylvania, president of the University Hospital, Preston Retreat, Pennsylvania Colonization Society, and an officer of such other organizations as the American Philosophical Society, the Numismatical and Antiquarian Society and the Historical Society of Pennsylvania.[6]

From none of these activities is there a clue to the baffling question—"Why did Eli Kirk Price write that check?" How had he become obligated to Abraham Lincoln to the extent of $500—or was the money, as this author has theorized, meant to be a gift to some charity in which Abraham Lincoln was interested? In correspondence early in 1980, Philip Price, great-grandson of Eli K. Price and a counsel of the prestigious Philadelphia law firm of Dechert Price and Rhoades, wrote, "So far as I know there are no papers of any kind available that would throw any light on that particular check."[7]

Interesting is the fact that both banks related to the check were later liquidated. The First National Bank of Washington, Fifteenth Street West and F North, to which the check was endorsed, was being liquidated in 1874 with E. L. Stanton, son of Lincoln's Secretary of War, as receiver.[8] The Western Bank at 406–408 Chestnut Street, Philadelphia, in 1865, later became the Western National Bank and by 1914 was in liquidation.[9]

Today, its *raison d'etre* still a mystery—a fact which adds to its value—Eli Price's check is a prized possession of the Louis A. Warren Lincoln Library and Museum in Fort Wayne, Indiana.

## 2. The Guard with a Shoddy Record

Of the several mysteries still associated with the assassination of Abraham Lincoln, those related to John F. Parker, his guard on the night of April 14, are by far the most baffling—and no promise of their solution exists.

The plural pronoun "those" has been used here because the mystery of John Parker is many-faceted. Why was Parker, a member of the Metropolitan Police with the shoddiest of shoddy records, assigned to be a Presidential guard; in fact, why had he been retained on the force at all? Why was he not immediately reprimanded for leaving his post at the door of the President's box, placed on probation, or at least relieved of his assignment at the White House? And the mystery of Parker looms beyond comprehension when one ponders the fact that his name appears in no official record of Lincoln's death, that he was not called to testify at the conspiracy trial, and that the records related to his trial and its outcome before the Board of the Metropolitan Police have disappeared.

Parker, a carpenter and machinist before the war, served a three-month stint in the Union Army after the outbreak of hostilities, then became one of the city's first 150 patrolmen when the Metropolitan Police Force was organized in September, 1861. He became a Presidential guard on November 4, 1864, when four policemen were selected for that service.[1]

Metropolitan Police personnel records for Lincoln's day are among the records of the government of the District of Columbia in the custody of the General Archives Division of the National Archives. However, a letter from the office of James B. Rhoads, Archivist of the United States, said in June, 1979, "No file for the John Parker on duty the night of April 14, 1865, was found among these records." The letter further related that the Identification and Records Division of the Metropolitan Police had "confirmed that the personnel file for the John Parker in question was missing before the records were accessioned as part of the National Archives of the United States. The Metropolitan Police have tried a number of times to locate this file, but all attempts have been unsuccessful."[2]

Only two brief references to Parker have been found in the National Archives. The Register of Appointments of members of the police force, contained in Record Group 351 of the Metropolitan Police, has this entry: "*Name*: John F. Parker *Born*: May 19, 1830 *Place of Birth*: Frederick County, Va. *Age*: 31 *Occupation*: Carpenter *No. in Family*: 5 *Residence of Family*: 570 L St. N, Washington *Date of Appointment*: Sept. 11, 1861 *Date of Dismissal*: Aug. 13, 1868 *Cause of Dismissal*: gross neglect of duty.[3]

The other reference to Parker is found in the police log for April 14–15, stating that at 6 A.M. he had brought in Lizzie Williams on charges of suspicion. (She was not held.)

With a letter to the author dated January 30, 1980, Burtell M. Jefferson, Chief of Police in Washington, enclosed copies of the police log for April 14 and of the charge filed against Parker on May 1, 1865, and the call to trial for May 3. These, he said, "are all of the documents in our custody concerning Officer Parker."

Detailed reports of Parker's shoddy record as a policeman were, however, published before they disappeared. On October 14, 1862, he was charged with conduct unbecoming an officer and with the use of violent, coarse, and insolent language when a superior officer sought to explain that a groceryman had complained that officers loafing in front of his store were embarrassing him. Parker insisted that he had been jesting and had not meant to be disrespectful. Because this was his first offense he was merely reprimanded.[4]

On March 19, 1863, Parker was before the Police Board on charges that he had three days earlier been intoxicated, visited a house of prostitution, gone to bed with one of the inmates, fired a pistol through a window, and finally "used highly offensive language against an officer named Pumphrey." Witnesses, including employees of the house in question, came to Parker's defense with such strong testimony that the case was dropped.[5]

Less than two weeks later Parker was charged with being asleep in a streetcar when he should have been walking his beat. The charge was dropped the next day (April 2) after Parker testified that he and a fellow officer had heard ducks squawking and boarded the car to determine the cause of the commotion.[6]

Again on July 1, 1863, Parker was tried for neglect of duty and conduct unbecoming to an officer. This charge, dismissed eight days later, grew out of a complaint that he had refused to restrain some disorderly Negroes and had used insulting language to the lady complainant.[7]

Perhaps Parker's conduct during the next fourteen months was such that his superiors felt justified in selecting him as one of four newly appointed guards for the President. Except for occasional tardiness, his work as a guard between November, 1864, and April, 1865, seems to have been satisfactory. At any rate, it was sufficiently satisfactory to lead Mary Lincoln to issue to Provost Marshal James O'Beirne, in her husband's absence in Virginia on April 3, the letter needed to exempt Parker from the draft.[8]

Belief that Parker was actually related to Mary Lincoln and that this fact prompted her to write the letter to O'Beirne was expressed recently. This supposition is based on the fact that her mother's maiden name was Parker and that she had at least twice helped to secure government appointments for individuals bearing the name, one of them a man who may have been John F. Parker's father.[9]

That Parker continued on duty at the White House for some time after April 15 is indicated by the fact that Mary was reported to have given him a bitter tongue lashing one evening, accusing him of helping to murder her husband, and refusing to believe his denials.[10]

The copy of charges filed against Parker on May 1, 1865, and supplied by Police Chief Jefferson indicated that the guard was to be tried for neglect of duty. The specification as written by A. C. Richards, Superintendent of Police, read: "In this, that Said Parker was detailed to attend and protect the President, Mr. Lincoln, that while the President was at Ford's Theatre allowed a man to enter the President's box and shoot the President."

Only the fact that the complaint against Parker was dismissed on June 2 has been recorded.[11] No report of the trial has been found in Washington newspapers, a fact which makes one wonder why this central figure in the tragedy had received no mention in stories following the assassination.

Parker's bad conduct did not end with the assassination. Twice again he was tried: in November, 1865, for conduct unbecoming an officer, and in July, 1868, for gross neglect of duty. Finally fed up with the incorrigible officer, the board dismissed him on August 13, 1868.[12] After that until 1890 he was listed in city directories, sometimes as a carpenter, sometimes as a machinist. He died in Washington on June 28, 1890, of pneumonia, complicated by asthma.[13]

William H. Crook, who had escorted Lincoln on his last visit to the War Department, wrote bitterly of Parker's dereliction several times:

> Had he [Booth] found a man at the door of the President's box armed with a Colt's revolver, his alcohol courage might have

> evaporated. It makes me feel rather bitter when I remember that the President had said, just a few hours before, that he knew he could trust all his guards. And then to think that in that moment of test one of us should have failed him! Parker knew that he had failed in his duty. He looked like a convicted criminal the next day. He was never the same man afterward.[14]

## 3. Light on the Missing Dispatch

What happened to the dispatch that S. P. Hanscom, editor of the *National Republican*, said he delivered to the President shortly before the assassination? The answer to that question, never published, might be found in notes Lieutenant Alexander McL. Crawford sent to John Hay on January 13, 1887, presumably at Hay's request.[1]

In a lengthy account of his activities before and after the assassination, Crawford reminded Hay that he had received from the President's secretary on April 17, 1865, a note that read: "Do you know the name & address of the officer (a Captain in a New Hampshire regiment) who picked up the papers which fell from the President's pocket at the theatre . . . ? The papers are thought to be important & have not been returned as yet."

After talking with Hay, Crawford, according to his notes, had gone to the headquarters of the Department of Washington and got an endorsement on Hay's note: "Col. Long. Please find this officer if in your regiment as soon as possible. Give Lt. Crawford all facilities for finding what he desires."[2] A visit to Colonel Long had failed to lead Crawford to the Captain, a fact reported to Secretary of War Stanton with the comment, "I have no doubt about getting the papers but not from the Captain, he has had them too long for his own safety."

At the National Hotel later Crawford met Colonel George W. Gile of New Hampshire, then of the Veteran Reserve Corps, who was aware of Crawford's request. "There is a Congressman here I want you to know," Gile was reported as saying, leading Crawford to a large room on the first floor. There he was introduced to a gentleman whose name he did not catch perfectly, but he thought it was Martin or Marston.[3]

Upon hearing Crawford's name, the gentleman gave him a quick glance, indicated that he wanted a moment with him, and led him some distance from the ten or twelve other persons in the room.

"Will it be perfectly satisfactory and no other steps be taken if these papers are delivered at the White House tomorrow morning?" he asked Crawford in a low tone.

The Lieutenant wrote that he grasped the situation at once: The Captain had realized his imprudence in keeping the papers so long, could judge very nearly what the action of the Secretary of War would be—peremptory dismissal—and had gone to his Congressman.

"Yes," replied Crawford, "I guarantee that nothing more will be done if all the papers are returned . . . if the Secretary refuses to redeem my pledge I will be back here by midnight and tell you."

"I wish you had not given the pledge, why did you?" Stanton was quoted as saying when Crawford reported his conversation with the Congressman.

"Well, Mr. Secretary," had been the reply, "I knew you would dismiss him from the service for what was at the most imprudence or thoughtlessness and that stigma would rest on him for life whether he were reinstated or not . . . You will redeem my pledge, Mr. Secretary?"

"Yes, it will be respected," Stanton had replied.

The papers, according to Crawford's report, were left at the White House by nine o'clock the next day. "I have," Crawford wrote, "never learned who the Captain was . . ."

Although Lieutenant Crawford's notes seem to present a plausible solution to the mystery of the missing dispatch, there is another story which, while oddly resembling Crawford's in some details, appears even more plausible.

When Lincoln was carried from the theatre, the four Pennsylvania infantrymen who helped initially were joined at the stair by two other soldiers. One of them is believed to have been Captain Edwin E. Bedee, a member of the 12th New Hampshire Volunteer Infantry. Bedee enlisted as a sergeant major on September 20, 1862, became a lieutenant three months later and was wounded at Chancellorsville on May 3, 1863. He became a captain on September 10, 1863, and was wounded again during the Battle of Cold Harbor the following June.[4]

On November 29, 1864, a telegram from Brigadier General Charles K. Graham, commander of the Naval Brigade and flotilla of gunboats in the Army of the James, to Brevet Major General Alfred H. Terry, commanding the Army of the James, announced, "Col. Kaufman, 209th Pa. Vols. and Capt. Bedee of Col. [Joseph H.] Potter's staff, are missing and supposed to be captured."[5]

By order of James A. Seddon, the Confederacy's Secretary of War, to Brigadier General William M. Gardner, commander of the prison post at Salisbury, North Carolina, on December 29, 1864, Bedee was released "as the substitute of Capt. [Daniel R.] Boice of the Second New Jersey Cavalry now held in close confinement in retaliation for Lieutenant Gandy, C. S. A., at Wheeling, W. Va."[6]After an extended leave at his home in Meredith, New Hampshire, Bedee left to rejoin his regiment, and a stop in Washington enabled him to be present at Ford's Theàtre on April 14.[7]

As Lincoln was being carried across Tenth Street, some papers fell from his pocket, and Bedee picked them up. He tried to give them to John Hay and was instructed to deliver them later. Unable to locate Hay the following morning, Bedee turned the papers over to Stanton, then left Washington to join his regiment.[8]

When Hay had not received the papers by April 18, he notified Brevet Brigadier General James A. Hardie, Chief of the Inspector General's office. Hardie, over Stanton's name, telegraphed Brigadier General Marsena R. Patrick, Provost Marshal General of armies operating around Richmond, ordering Bedee's arrest and recovery of the papers.[9]

When Bedee was taken before General Charles Devens, commander of the 3rd Division, XXIV Corps, for questioning on April 19, he protested that he had turned the papers over to Stanton on April 15. General Devens sent this information to General Hardie, who learned the truth, and Bedee was released.[10]

His pride hurt, Bedee followed up with a letter to Stanton. "Doubting that your Honor would approve of the public disgrace of an officer who has endeavoured for the past three years to earn an honourable name in the defense of his country," Bedee wrote, "I take the liberty of laying this before you hoping your Honor's sense of justice will induce you to set the matter right with the Command with which I am connected."[11]

Stanton didn't reply, but General Hardie did with a letter of apology for his mistake, which he conceded "to have been an act of serious, tho unintentional injustice to yourself. In conclusion," General Hardie wrote, "I beg that you make such use of this letter as may in your opinion be necessary to repair as far as possible the evil occasioned by my action of the 18th of April."[12] Upon receipt of the letter Captain Bedee dropped the matter.

Whatever happened to the papers recovered through Bedee or Crawford—or maybe through both since it is possible that Lincoln had several papers in his pocket when assassinated—is still a mystery unsolved. Dr. Oliver Orr, authority on Lincoln at the Library of Congress, believes that they passed through several hands after their retrieval. It is his opinion that they are now mixed in with thousands of other pieces of paper in the library and could be found only by a researcher with a great deal of time and patience.

Also unanswered is another interesting question: Why did Nicolay and Hay, and especially the latter, never mention the missing paper or papers in writing about Lincoln?

## 4. Course of the Ball, Still Undetermined

Most individuals who have written about the wound that killed Lincoln have said that the ball passed through the head from near the left ear and came to rest behind the right eye. Normally, this tracing would seem unlikely inasmuch as Booth approached the President from the right side. James P. Ferguson gave the reason for the odd trace of the ball, however, when he said that he was watching the President at the moment Booth fired and that Lincoln then was peering into the orchestra, his head turned sharply to the left and downward.[1]

Whether Ferguson's observation was correct becomes a matter of doubt when testimony of surgeons present at the autopsy is examined. Seven were present when the autopsy was held in the President's bedroom at the White House at noon on April 15.[2]

In his brief report made to Brigadier General J. K. Barnes, Surgeon General of the Army, who had ordered the autopsy, Dr. J. J. Woodward, Assistant Surgeon, U.S.A., said: "The ball entered through the occipital bone about one inch to the left of the median line and just above the left lateral sinus, which it opened. It then penetrated the dura matter, passed through the left posterior lobe of the cerebrum, entered the left lateral ventricle and lodged in the white matter of the cerebrum just above the anterior portion of the left corpus striatum, where it was found."[3]

Three of the other doctors present described findings of the autopsy in trial testimony or journals later. Testifying at the trial of John Surratt in June, 1867, Dr. Barnes said: "The ball entered the scull [sic] to the left of the middle line, and below the line with the ear. It ranged forward and upward toward the right eye, lodging within half an inch of that organ."[4]

Dr. Robert King Stone, Lincoln's family physician, had given a different version of the autopsy finding when he testified at the trial of the conspirators two years earlier. "We traced the wound through the brain," he asserted, "and the ball was found in the anterior part of the same side of the brain, the left side."[5] In a handwritten description of the autopsy findings, Dr. Stone also said: "In orifice of wound, scale of lead 2½ inches in track of ball—entered the left ventricle, behind, followed the course of ventricle accurately, inclining upwards & inwards—plowing thro upper part of thalamus, nervi opticus & lodging in cerebral matter, just above the corpus striatum on left side."[6]

As if the statements of Dr. Woodward, Barnes, and Stone were not sufficiently confusing, Dr. Charles S. Taft, the second surgeon to enter Lincoln's box after the assassination and one of those present at the Petersen house throughout the night and also at the autopsy, made contradictory statements in an article published a week after the President's death. Telling of the probes made by Dr. Barnes shortly after two o'clock on Saturday morning, he wrote: "A long Nelaton probe was then procured and passed into the track of the wound for a distance of two inches beyond the plug of the bone, when the ball was distinctly felt; passing beyond this, the fragments of the orbital plate of the left orbit were felt."[7]

In describing procedures at the autopsy, however, Taft said: "The calvaria was removed, the brain exposed, and sliced down to the track of the ball, which was plainly indicated by a line of coagulated blood, extending from the external wound in the occipital bone, obliquely across from the left to right through the brain to the anterior lobe of the cerebrum, immediately behind the right orbit."[8]

Dr. George E. Curtis, Assistant Surgeon, U.S.A., who assisted Dr. Woodward in the autopsy, endorsed the latter's handwritten report to the Surgeon General as a "true copy," but at no time does he seem to have made a personal comment concerning the autopsy. The others present, Assistant Surgeon Notson, U.S.A., and Dr. Charles H. Crane, later Surgeon General, have not been quoted as far as is known.

But the failure of four surgeons to agree on the autopsy findings, two indicating one thing, another the opposite, and one making contradictory statements, leaves another question concerning Lincoln's assassination unanswered with certainty.

# Notes

*Key to abbreviations used for frequently mentioned sources:*

ALP Abraham Lincoln Papers
*CT The Conspiracy Trial for the Murder of the President* (Poore)
*CW The Collected Works of Abraham Lincoln* (Basler)
*DAB Dictionary of American Biography*
DLC Library of Congress
ISHL Illinois State Historical Library
*JHS The Trial of John H. Surratt*
LAWL Louis A. Warren Lincoln Library
LMU Lincoln Memorial University
NA National Archives
*NCAB National Cyclopedia of American Biography*
*OR The War of the Rebellion: A Compilation of the Official Records of the Union and Confederate Armies* (U.S. War Dept.)
*PIT The Assassination of President Lincoln and the Trial of the Conspirators* (Pitman)
*TBP The Trial of the Alleged Assassins and Conspirators* (Peterson)

## I. "He Was Full of Hope and Happiness"

1. Arnold, *Life of Abraham Lincoln*, p. 428; Boyd, *A Memorial Lincoln Bibliography*, p. 21; Brinkerhoff, *Recollections of a Lifetime*, p. 163; Poore, *Perley's Reminiscences*, 2:170; Justin G. Turner, "April 14, 1865: A Soldier's View," p. 179; Shephard, "Lincoln's Assassination Told by an Eye Witness," p. 918.
2. Stimmel, "Experiences as a Member of President Lincoln's Bodyguard," p. 30.
3. U. S. Naval Observatory, Weather Report, April 14–15, 1865.
4. Stephenson, *Lincoln*, p. 415; Laughlin, *Death of Lincoln*, p. 74; Bryan, *Great American Myth*, p. 145.
5. Bernard, "Glimpses of Lincoln in the White House," p. 176; Crook, "Lincoln As I Knew Him," p. 111.

6. Thomas D. Stewart, "An Anthropologist Looks at Lincoln," quotes J. W. Rogers, buyer for Julius Garfinckel & Co. of Washington, as saying that Lincoln's boots, according to present standards, were size 12B. Others have estimated his size as large as 14, Horatio Seymour once remarking that Lincoln wore "a No. 7 hat and a No. 14 boot" (Dana in "Lincoln and His Cabinet," lecture, p. 32).
7. Crook, "The Home Life of Abraham Lincoln," p. 4.
8. Arnold, *The Life of Abraham Lincoln*, p. 45; Randall and Currant, *Last Full Measure*, p. 377.
9. Brooks, "Personal Recollections," p. 226; idem, "Personal Reminiscences," March, p. 676.
10. Hay, *Addresses of John Hay*, pp. 339–40.
11. Brooks, "Personal Recollections," p. 226.
12. Ibid.; Curtis, *The True Abraham Lincoln*, p. 29; Carpenter, *Inner Life of Abraham Lincoln*, p. 217.
13. John Nicolay, "Lincoln's Personal Appearance," p. 932; Cottrell, *Anatomy of an Assassination*, p. 85; McMurtry, "The Health of Abraham Lincoln," pp. 7, 164.
14. Piatt, *Memories of Men Who Saved the Union*, p. 29.
15. Arnold, *History of Abraham Lincoln and the Overthrow of Slavery*, p. 661; idem, *Life of Abraham Lincoln*, p. 428.
16. Stoddard, *Inside the White House in War Times*, p. 24; Hay, *Addresses*, p. 322.
17. Stoddard, "Face to Face with Lincoln," p. 333.
18. Neill, "Abraham Lincoln and His Mailbag," p. 47.
19. Hay letter to Herndon, Sept. 5, 1866; Helen Nicolay, *Personal Traits of Abraham Lincoln*, p. 189.
20. Stoddard, "Face to Face," p. 333; idem, *Inside the White House*, p. 27.
21. *Lincoln Lore*, nos. 444 (Oct. 11, 1937), and 1485 (November 1961).
22. *CW*, 8:412.
23. Ibid., p. 411.
24. Ibid., p. 410.
25. Van Alen papers, DLC-ALP.
26. *CW*, 8:413; Nicolay and Hay, *Complete Works*, 11:94.
27. John Nicolay, *A Short Life of Abraham Lincoln*, p. 533.
28. Raymond, *Life and Public Services of Abraham Lincoln*, p. 779.
29. Ibid., pp. 693, 780–83.
30. John Nicolay notes for chap. 14, vol. 10, *Abraham Lincoln: A History*.
31. Barnes, "With Lincoln from Washington to Richmond," p. 40.
32. Brooks, *Washington in Lincoln's Time*, p. 44; idem, "Personal Reminiscences," March, p. 674; Daugherty, *Abraham Lincoln*, p. 187.

33. Carpenter, *Inner Life*, pp. 62–63.
34. Neill, “Lincoln and His Mailbag,” p. 16.
35. Neill, “Reminiscences of the Last Year of President Lincoln’s Life,” p. 42.
36. Lamon, *Recollections of Abraham Lincoln*, pp. 275–76; Hay, *Lincoln and the Civil War*, p. 236.
37. Carpenter, *Inner Life*, pp. 63–64; Herndon and Weik, *Herndon’s Life of Lincoln*, p. 454.
38. John Nicolay and John Hay, *Lincoln: A History*, 10:288: John Nicolay, *A Short Life*, p. 533.
39. John Nicolay, *A Short Life*, p. 534.
40. Carpenter, *Inner Life*, p. 65.
41. Hertz, *Hidden Lincoln*, p. 327.
42. *CW*, 8:412.
43. Ibid., pp. 410–13; Arnold, *History of Lincoln*, p. 675.
44. Angle, *Abraham Lincoln, by Some Men Who Knew Him*, p. 109.
45. Helm, *True Story of Mary, Wife of Lincoln*, p. 106.
46. Hay, *Lincoln and the Civil War*, pp. 43, 67, 74, 93, 105; Helen Nicolay, *Personal Traits of Abraham Lincoln*, pp. 290, 292, 306.
47. Neill, “Reminiscences,” p. 31.
48. Brooks, “Personal Recollections,” p. 222.
49. Hay, *Addresses*, p. 328.
50. Crook, “Lincoln As I Knew Him,” p. 111.
51. Keckley, *Behind the Scenes*, p. 138.
52. *CW*, 8:223.
53. Ibid.
54. Ibid., p. 224; Mearns, 1:12.
55. Porter, *Campaigning with Grant*, p. 389.
56. Keckley, pp. 137–38.
57. Oates, *With Malice Toward None*, p. 427.
58. Laughlin, “The Last Twenty-four Hours of Lincoln’s Life,” p. 12; Grant, *Personal Memoirs*, 2:489–90; Porter, *Campaigning*, pp. 473–74. Robert was misinformed or misquoted regarding General Lee’s spurs. Washington and Lee University received from Lee’s grandson, Dr. George Boling Lee, a pair of silver dress spurs purportedly worn by Lee when he surrendered. The Museum of the Confederacy in Richmond, which owns the handsome sword Lee wore at Appomattox, also has a pair of brass spurs owned by Lee but for which it has no specific history.
59. Keckley, p. 138.

## II. Visitors Note His “Exuberant Mood”

1. Colfax papers.

2. *NCAB*, 22:95.
3. Colfax, report of his speech in *Black Hawk Mining Journal.*
4. Barton, *President Lincoln*, 2:723; Rankin, *Intimate Character Sketches of Abraham Lincoln*, p. 283; Cole, *Memoirs of Cornelius Cole*, p. 229.
5. *OR*, 46 (3): 696–97; *CW*, 8:406n; Thomas and Hayman, *Stanton: The Life and Times of Lincoln's Secretary of War*, p. 354.
6. *CW*, 8:405.
7. Cole, *Memoirs*, p. 229; Rankin, *Character Sketches*, p. 283.
8. Colfax, report of his speech in *Black Hawk Mining Journal.*
9. Colfax papers.
10. Hollister, *Life of Schuyler Colfax*, p. 252.
11. Colfax, report of his speech in *Black Hawk Mining Journal; The Washington Evening Chronicle* became the first Capital City paper to publish the message when on Aug. 7, 1865, it reported Colfax's speech as given in Virginia City, Nevada, on June 26. Raymond became the first to publish it in a book when he included it in *Life and Public Services of Abraham Lincoln* late in 1865.
12. Hollister, *Life of Colfax*, p. 261.
13. Segal, *Conversations With Lincoln*, p. 392.
14. Colfax, report of his speech in *Black Hawk Mining Journal.*
15. Hollister, *Life of Colfax*, p. 257.
16. Ibid., p. 259.
17. Colfax, report of his speech in *Black Hawk Mining Journal.*
18. *OR*, 46 (3): 575; *CW*, 8:387n.
19. DLC–ALP; *CW*, 8:386.
20. Ibid., p.389.
21. Ibid., pp. 407–8n; *OR*, 46 (3): 657.
22. *CW*, 8:406–7.
23. Hollister, *Life of Colfax*, pp. 252–53.
24. Ibid., p. 253.
25. Colfax, report of his speech in *Black Hawk Mining Journal.*
26. Ibid.; Hollister, *Life of Colfax*, p. 253.
27. Hollister, *Life of Colfax*, p. 253.
28. Ibid.
29. Ibid., p. 252.
30. *NCAB*, 4:91.
31. *DAB*, 4:541.
32. Draper, "Lincoln's Parable," p. 1567.
33. Ibid.
34. *CW*, 8:412n.
35. Ibid.; Draper, "Parable," p. 1567.
36. Draper, "Parable," p. 1567; Stephenson, *Lincoln*, p. 419 (with story phrased a bit differently).

37. Brooks, "Personal Recollections," p. 228.
38. Ibid., p. 229.
39. Neill, "Reminiscences," p. 47; Rufus Wilson, *Intimate Memories*, p. 610.
40. *DAB*, 8:105–6; *CW*, 4:248, 516; 5:103, 127n, 316n, 320n; 6:133, 479.
41. Greenbie, *Anna Ella Carroll and Abraham Lincoln*, p. 292; 44th Congress, *Miscellaneous Document No. 179*.
42. Moss, "Lincoln and John Wilkes Booth," p. 951.
43. Crook, "Home Life of Abraham Lincoln," p. 5; Bates, *Lincoln in the Telegraph Office*, p. 7.
44. Grant, *Personal Memoirs*, 2:496, 508.
45. Bates, *Telegraph Office*, pp. 366–67.
46–47. Ibid., p. 367.
48. Ibid., p. 368.

## III. "There Must Be No Bloody Work"

1. Welles, *Diary*, 1:127.
2. John Nicolay, *A Short Life of Abraham Lincoln*, pp. 438–39.
3. Welles, *Diary*, 1:136.
4. Ibid., p. 131, quoting Caleb B. Smith, former Secretary of the Interior.
5. Ibid., *Diary*, 2:58.
6. Ibid., 1:131.
7. Ibid., 1:25.
8. Dana, "Lincoln and His Cabinet," *McClure's Magazine*, p. 562.
9. Seward, *Reminiscences of a War-Time Statesman and Diplomat*, p. 254.
10. Seward, *Seward at Washington*, p. 274.
11. John Nicolay and Hay, *Lincoln: A History*, 10:278–80; Swanberg, *First Blood*, pp. 333–38.
12. Seward, *Seward at Washington*, p. 274.
13. Seward, *Reminiscences*, p. 255.
14. Seward, *Seward at Washington*, p. 274; idem, *Reminiscences*, pp. 255–56.
15. Welles, *Diary*, 2:282–83; Macartney, *Abraham Lincoln and His Cabinet*, pp. 199–200.
16. Seward, *Reminiscences*, p. 255.
17. Ibid., pp. 255, 256.
18. Welles, *Diary*, 2:280–81.
19. Welles, "Lincoln and Johnson," p. 526; Seward, *Seward at Washington*, p. 275.
20. Seward, *Reminiscences*, pp. 256–57; Thomas and Hyman, *Stanton*, pp. 357–58.

21. Welles, "Lincoln and Johnson," p. 526.
22. Ibid.
23. Seward, *Reminiscences*, p. 256.
24. Welles, "Lincoln and Johnson," p. 526.
25. Ibid., pp. 526–27; Thomas and Hyman, *Stanton*, p. 358.
26. Welles, "Lincoln and Johnson," p. 527.
27. Ibid.
28. Ibid.
29. McCulloch, *Men and Measures of Half a Century*, p. 222.
30. Ibid., p. 242.
31. Simon, *Personal Memoirs of Julia Dent Grant*, pp. 154–55.
32. Porter, *Campaigning with Grant*, p. 498.
33. Simon, *Memoirs of Julia Grant*, p. 155.
34. Seward, *Reminiscences*, p. 257.
35. Hertz, *Abraham Lincoln, a New Portrait*, pp. 968–69.
36. Barrett, *Abraham Lincoln and His Presidency*, 2:355.
37. Usher, letter to his wife, April 16, 1865.

## IV. Urgent Business but Time for Good Deeds

1. Neill, "Reminiscences," p. 47; Rufus Wilson, *Intimate Memories of Lincoln*, p. 610.
2. Lomask, *Andrew Johnson*, p. 344; Milton, *Age of Hate*, p. 104; Stimmel, "Experiences," p. 29.
3. Rufus Wilson, *Intimate Memories*, p. 604; Neill, "Lincoln and His Mailbag," p. 13.
4. Chittenden, *Personal Reminiscences*, p. 241.
5. DLC–ALP; *CW*, 8:348.
6. *CW*, 8:369.
7. Ibid., 8:411.
8. Starr, *Further Light on Lincoln's Last Day*, pp. 45–47.
9. Ibid., p. 47.
10. *Library of Congress Information Bulletin*, Feb. 27, 1976, pp. 124–25.
11. Rufus Wilson, *Intimate Memories*, p. 603.
12. Chittenden, *Recollections of President Lincoln*, p. 445.
13. Barton, *The Great Good Man*, pp. 278–79; Starr, *Further Light*, p. 68.
14. Starr, *Further Light*, p. 67.
15. Browne, *Everyday Life of Abraham Lincoln*, p. 704; Starr, *Further Light*, p. 66.
16. *CW*, 8:411.
17. Herndon and Weik, *True Story of a Great Life*, p. 138.

18. *DAB*, 17:191.
19. Ibid.; Andrews, "Singleton Emerges as Lincoln's Lost Friend"; Starr, *Further Light*, p. 74.
20. *CW*, 8:200, 267, 343–44; Starr, *Further Light*, pp. 78–84; Andrews, "Singleton Emerges."
21. *DAB*, 17:191.
22. *CW*, 8:410.
23. Dana, *Recollections of the Civil War*, pp. 273–74.
24. *CW*, 8:413; Lyford, *Life of Edward Henry Rollins*, pp. 187–88.
25. Koch, *Colonel Coggeshall—the Man Who Saved Lincoln*, pp. 35, 55, 84.
26. Ward, Introduction to *Tributes to Abraham Lincoln From His Associates*, p. 148; Bryan, *Great American Myth*, p. 157; Chittenden, "Hour of His Thanksgiving," p. 5.

## V. "I Never Saw Him So Supremely Cheerful"

1. U. S. Naval Observatory, Weather Report.
2. Turner and Turner, *Mary Todd Lincoln, Her Life and Letters*, p. 257: letter to Mary Jane Welles, July 11, 1865.
3. Ibid., p. 284: letter to F. B. Carpenter, Nov. 15, 1865; Arnold, *Life of Abraham Lincoln*, p. 429; Helm, *True Story of Mary*, p. 255.
4. Turner and Turner, *Mary Todd Lincoln*, pp. 284–85: letter to Carpenter, Nov. 15, 1865.
5. Arnold, *Life of Lincoln*, pp. 429–30; Helm, p. 255.
6. Herndon and Weik, *Herndon's Life of Lincoln*, p. 390; Seitz, *Lincoln, the Politician*, p. 216.
7. Turner and Turner, *Mary Todd Lincoln*, p. 400: letter to the Reverend James Smith, Dec. 17, 1866.
8. Herndon and Weik, *True Story of a Great Life*, p. 221.
9. Brooks, *Abraham Lincoln, the Nation's Leader in the Great Struggle*, p. 452.
10. Arnold, *Life of Lincoln*, pp. 429–30.
11. Crook, *Through Five Administrations*, p. 65.
12. *New York Times*, Feb. 28, 1909.
13. Todd, letter to his brother, April 15, 1865.
14. *Worcester Telegram*, July 17, 1934.
15. Helm, *True Story of Mary*, p. 255; Tarbell, "Death of Lincoln," p. 378.
16. Haynie, "At the Deathbed of Lincoln," p. 954.
17. Rice, *Reminiscences of Abraham Lincoln*, pp. 447–48; Hay, *Lincoln and the Civil War*, p. 228.

18. Rice, *Reminiscences of Abraham Lincoln*, pp. 447–48.
19. Ibid., p. 448.
20. Ibid., p. 637.
21. Ibid., p. 448.
22. Ibid., pp. 449–50.
23. Tarbell, "Death of Lincoln," p. 378; Helm, *True Story of Mary*, p. 256.
24. Laughlin, "Last Twenty-four Hours," p. 12.

## VI. Reluctantly He Starts for the Theatre

1. Henry, letter to Mrs. Henry, April 19, 1865.
2. Ibid.
3. Crook, "Home Life of Abraham Lincoln," p. 56.
4. *DAB*, 3:82.
5. Brooks, *Washington in Lincoln's Time*, p. 257.
6. Ibid., p. 258.
7. Crook, *Through Five Administrations*, p. 1.
8. Ibid., p. 66.
9. Rice, *Reminiscences of Abraham Lincoln*, p. 404.
10. Crook, *Through Five Administrations*, p. 67.
11. Crook, *Memories of the White House*, p. 40.
12. Crook, *Through Five Administrations*, pp. 67–68, 74–75.
13. Angle, "Recollections of William Pitt Kellogg," pp. 332–36.
14. Starr, *Further Light*, pp. 105–6.
15. Grover, "Lincoln's Interest in the Theatre," p. 949.
16. Starr, *Further Light*, pp. 122–24.
17. Pendel, "What Tom Pendel Saw," p. 17.
18. Scrapbook of newspaper clippings, New York Public Library; Oldroyd, *Assassination of Abraham Lincoln*, p. 5.
19. Pendel, *Thirty-six Years in the White House*, p. 39.
20. Laughlin, "Last Twenty-four Hours," p. 12; idem, *Death of Lincoln*, p. 76; *Danville Commercial News*, Dec. 9, 1921.
21. B. F. Morris, *Memorial Record of the Nation's Tribute to Abraham Lincoln*, pp. 19–20.
22. Carpenter, *Inner Life*, p. 285; Luthin, *Real Abraham Lincoln*, p. 633; Browne, *Everday Life*, p. 705; Shea, *Lincoln Memorial*, p. 60.
23. *CW*, 8:410.
24. Pendel, *Thirty-six Years*, p. 39.
25. Colfax papers.
26. Pendel, *Thirty-six Years*, p. 39.
27. Colfax papers.

28. *DAB*, 1:394.
29. Bullard, "Abraham Lincoln and George Ashmun," p. 210; Carpenter, *Inner Life*, pp. 285–86; Shea, *Lincoln Memorial*, p. 60.
30. Stewart, "A Senator of the Sixties," p. 6; idem, *Reminiscences*, p. 190.
31. DLC; *CW*, 8:413.
32. *DAB*, 5:42; *Encyclopedia Americana*, International Edition © 1973, s.v. "Trent Affair."
33. Hammond, *Diary of a Union Lady*, pp. 353–54.
34. Ibid., p. 363; *DAB*, p. 216.
35. Stewart, "A Senator of the Sixties," p. 6; idem, *Reminiscences*, p. 190.
36. Arnold, *Life of Lincoln*, p. 431.
37. Browning diary, 2:18.
38. Pendel, *Thirty-six Years*, p. 40.
39. Stimmel, "Experiences," p. 32; Perley, "The Last of the Bodyguard," p. 409.
40. Pendel, *Thirty-six Years*, p. 40.
41. Lamon, *Recollections*, pp. 275–76.

## VII. The Stage Is Set for Murder

1. Kimmel, *Mad Booths of Maryland*, pp. 31, 65.
2. *DAB*, 2:448.
3. Clarke, *Unlocked Book*, pp. 45–46, 59.
4. Ibid., p. 202.
5. Ibid., pp. 67, 73.
6. Ibid., pp. 103–4.
7. *DAB*, 2:448.
8. Clarke, *Unlocked Book*, p. 73.
9. Roscoe, *Web of Conspiracy*, p. 31; Kimmel, *Mad Booths*, p. 65.
10. Clarke, *Unlocked Book*, pp. 56–57, 91.
11. Ibid., p. 152.
12. Ibid., p. 155.
13. Ibid., p. 157.
14. *DAB*, 2:448; *JHS*, 1:547.
15. *DAB*, 2:448–49.
16. *Madison Courier*, May 10, 1861; Kimmel, *Mad Booths*, p. 161; Bryan, *Great American Myth*, p. 88.
17. Clarke, *Unlocked Book*, p. 199; Bryan, *Great American Myth*, pp. 105–6.
18. *DAB*, 2:448.
19. Ibid., 2:449.

20. Ibid.; Booth, letter to his brother-in-law, John Sleeper Clarke, apparently written in November 1864, in Laughlin, *Death of Lincoln*, p. 21; Roscoe, p. 534; Bryan, p. 241.
21. Cate, "Ford, the Booths and Lincoln's Assassination," p. 18; Kimmel, *Mad Booths*, pp. 155–56; Bryan, *Great American Myth*, p. 86.
22. *DAB*, 2:449; Clarke, *Unlocked Book*, p. 203; Mahoney, *Sketches of Tudor Hall and the Booth Family*, p. 38.
23. Clarke, *Unlocked Book*, p. 117.
24. *DAB*, 2:449–50; Moore, *Case of Mrs. Surratt*, p. 11.
25. Arnold, *Defence and Prison Experiences of a Lincoln Conspirator*, pp. 47–48.
26. *JHS*, 1:330–31.
27. U. S. Congress, *Impeachment Investigation*, p. 674; Roscoe, *Web of Conspiracy*, p. 95.
28. Brooks, *Abraham Lincoln and the Downfall of American Slavery*, p. 455.
29. *CT*, 2:539; *PIT*, p. 99.
30. Grover, "Lincoln's Interest in the Theatre," p. 949.
31. *New York Tribune*, April 17, 1865; Bryan, *Great American Myth*, p. 148; Clark, *Abraham Lincoln in the National Capital*, p. 95n.
32. Clark, *Lincoln in the National Capital*, p. 95; Bryan, *Great American Myth*, p. 148; *New York Tribune*, May 1, 1865.
33. *JHS*, 1:495–96.
34. Moss, "Lincoln and John Wilkes Booth," p. 951.
35. *PIT*, p. 70; Kimmel, *Mad Booths*, p. 216; Bryan, *Great American Myth*, p. 156, quoting Browning's statement in the archives of the Judge Advocate General.
36. *Daily Constitutional Union*, April 15, 1865; *New York Sun* in special from Washington, April 19, 1865; Bryan, *Great American Myth*, p. 153.
37. Roscoe, *Web of Conspiracy*, p. 98.
38. *New York Tribune*, April 17, 1865.
39. Kimmel, *Mad Booths*, p. 216.
40. *PIT*, p. 75.
41. John T. Ford, "Behind the Curtain of Conspiracy," p. 488; Kimmel, *Mad Booths*, p. 215; Roscoe, *Web of Conspiracy*, p. 99.
42. *PIT*, pp. 74, 104, 110; *JHS*, 1:176; *CT*, 1:219.
43. *New York Evening Post*, July 8, 1884; John T. Ford, "Behind the Curtain," p. 489.
44. *New York Evening Post*, July 8, 1884; Bryan, *Great American Myth*, p. 152.
45. *New York Evening Post*, July 8, 1884; John T. Ford, "Behind the Curtain," p. 488.

46. *PIT*, p. 72; *JHS*, 1:226.
47. Simon, *Memoirs of Julia Grant*, p. 155.
48. Kimmel, *Mad Booths*, p. 217.
49. *PIT*, p. 113; *JHS*, 1:391.
50. *PIT*, p. 75; *CT*, 1:234.
51. *CT*, 1:198; Clark, *Lincoln in the National Capital*, p. 95; *Washington Star*, Sept. 10, 1901.
52. Ferguson, *I Saw Booth Shoot Lincoln*, p. 45.
53. Ibid. Patrons usually spoke of the Star as "Taltavull's." Actually, it was Taltavull and Grillo's, Scipiano Grillo being a partner in charge of the restaurant area. Peter Taltavull's name has usually been misspelled "Taltavul" by writers, although city directories of the time consistently gave it with two l's.
54. Ferguson, "The Story of the Assassination," p. 2; Ward, Introduction to *Tributes to Lincoln*, p. 15.
55. *PIT*, p. 101; *CT*, 3:15, 17.
56. *JHS*, 1:613.
57. Clark, *Lincoln in the National Capital*, pp. 95–96; Olszewski, *Restoration of Ford's Theatre*, p. 53.
58. *CT*, 3:12.
59. Olszewski, *Restoration*, p. 43.
60. Ibid., pp. 43, 45.
61. Ibid., pp. 5, 7, 9.
62. Ibid., pp. 21, 53, 107.
63. Ibid., p. 37.
64. Ibid., p. 39.
65. Spangler was known as Edward (or Ned) to fellow workers at Ford's Theatre and to lawyers and recorders during the conspiracy trial. On April 15, 1865, he signed himself as "Edman Spangler" in a statement made to Judge A. B. Olin (LAS File, M–599, Reel 6, frames 0201–0204, NA) and was so referred to in several newspaper articles following his release from prison in 1869. However, records of the First Reformed Church in York, Pa., his birthplace, show that he was baptized Edmund on Aug. 10, 1825, and those of St. Peter's Church, Waldorf, Md., indicate that he was buried there as Edmund following his death on Feb. 7, 1875. Spangler was a son of Sheriff William Spangler, and York's records of that man's family give the stagehand's Christian name as Edmund, followed by Edward in brackets.
66. *CT*, 1:227, 2:550; *PIT*, 74; *JHS*, 1:326.
67. *CT*, 1:227–28; *PIT*, 74.
68. *PIT*, p. 99; *CT*, 2:551.
69. *CT*, 1:416, 2:106; *PIT*, p. 76.
70. *CT*, 3:33; Olszewski, *Restoration*, p. 55; *PIT*, p. 110.

71. *PIT*, p. 110.
72. *CT*, 2:549, 3:32.
73. Ibid., 2:105–6.
74. Ibid., 1:415; *PIT*, p. 73.
75. *JHS*, 1:257.
76. *CT*, 3:39.
77. Olszewski, *Restoration*, p. 55; *CT*, 2:549–51.
78. *CT*, 2:550.
79. Ibid.
80. *PIT*, p. 82.
81. Ibid., p. 112.
82. *JHS*, 1:327–28.
83. Olszewski, *Restoration*, p. 124.
84. Ford, letter to the author, Dec. 2, 1965.
85. *CT*, 1:461; *JHS*, 1:328.
86. *CT*, 3:38.
87. *JHS*, 1:328. For a time during the trial of John Surratt it seemed that Theodore Benjamin Rhodes, a clock and watch repairman, had provided answers concerning the mysterious bar and mortice. Rhodes testified that he had entered the theatre about 11:45 A.M. on April 14 and gone down into the state box for about half an hour. There, Rhodes said, he observed a man who claimed to be connected with the theatre gouge out the mortice and fit a bar from it to the corridor door. "The President is going to be here tonight . . . and we are going to endeavor to arrange it so he won't be disturbed," Rhodes quoted the man as saying. "The crowd may be so immense as to push the door open, and we want to fasten it so this cannot be the case" (*JHS*, 1:501–2). Rhodes' testimony was discredited when he was cross-examined. Among other things, it was shown that Rhodes could not have entered the theatre in the manner described, that there was no back door to the box as he claimed, that decorating of the box did not take place during the time he said he was present, and that his description of the bar was inaccurate (*JHS*, 1:540–41).
88. *CT*, 1:460.
89. *JHS*, 1:328.
90. Ibid., 1:547.
91. Ibid., 1:614–15; *CT*, 3:182; *PIT*, p. 111.
92. Judge Abram B. Olin, Associate Justice of the Supreme Court of the District of Columbia, testified during the conspiracy trial (*PIT*, p. 82; *CT*, 1:409–10) that he had, during a visit to Ford's with Senator Harris and Clara Harris on Sunday, April 16, seen on the passageway floor neither shavings from the hole in the door of Box 7 nor plaster cut from the wall to provide a seat for the bar to the corridor door. During the trial of John Surratt two years later he

presented testimony which left the truth in doubt. First he testified that he had seen both shavings and plaster on the passageway floor on April 16 (*JHS*, 1:519–20). A few days later, after seeing a copy of the testimony he had given at the conspiracy trial, he asked to be heard again and testified in part as follows: "If I were called to testify today again . . . I would testify as I did a few days ago, and yet I ought to say, perhaps, that after such a lapse of time as has occurred between the transaction and the present hour, if what was shown me be a correct report of my testimony before the military commission, it is more likely to be accurate than testimony recently given by me, because all the circumstances were then fresh in my recollection, and the transaction was a recent one" (*JHS*, 2:785–86).

93. *PIT*, pp. 109, 111; *JHS*, 1:613–14; *CT*, 3:30.
94. MacCulloch, "This Man Saw Lincoln Shot," pp. 115–16.
95. Special to the *New York Tribune*, filed at 4:50 P.M. April 15, 1865, published April 17.
96. Kimmel, *Mad Booths*, p. 217.
97. Clarke, *Unlocked Book*, pp. 168–69.
98. *CT*, 1:190.
99. U. S. Congress, *Impeachment Investigation*, p. 783; Roscoe, p. 102.
100. U. S. Congress, *Impeachment Investigation*, p. 783; *National Intelligencer*, July 18, 1867.
101. U. S. Congress, *Impeachment Investigation*, p. 783.
102. Porter, *Campaigning*, pp. 498–99.
103. Roscoe, *Web of Conspiracy*, p. 103.
104. U. S. Congress, *Impeachment Investigation*, p. 783; *National Intelligencer*, July 18, 1867.
105. *PIT*, p. 39; *TBP*, p. 44.
106. *TBP*, p. 74; Spangler's statement in Mudd, *Life of Samuel A. Mudd*, p. 325.
107. Spangler's statement in Mudd, *Life of Mudd*, p. 325.
108. *New York Tribune*, April 17, 1865.
109. *JHS*, 1:329.
110. Withers' statement prepared for the government; American Press Association article by John W. Lawrence, distributed 1912, LAWL.
111. *PIT*, p. 307; Moore, p. 15.

## VIII. Lincoln's Guard Leaves His Post

1. Turner and Turner, *Mary Todd Lincoln*, p. 697: letter to J. B. Gould, April 22, 1880; Harris, letter to "My Dear M—," April 29, 1865.

2. Harris, letter to "My Dear M__"; Briggs, "Assassination Night."
3. Moore, *Case of Mrs. Surratt*, p. 16.
4. Olszewski, *Restoration*, p. 56.
5. Richards, *Story of Abraham Lincoln's Assassination*, unpaginated; John Davenport in *National Republican*, April 22, 1922.
6. *CT*, 3:224.
7. *Boston Herald*, April 11, 1897; *New York Times*, Feb. 14, 1926; *New York World*, Feb. 17, 1924; *Sioux City Journal*, April 26, 1914.
8. Ferguson, *American Magazine*, August, 1920, p. 80.
9. *Journal of the Illinois State Historical Society*, October, 1927, p. 424; Wilgus, "The Lincoln Tragedy."
10. MacCulloch, "This Man Saw Lincoln Shot," p. 116.
11. *Boston Herald*, April 11, 1897.
12. Laughlin, "Our American Cousin," p. 192.
13. *National Republican*, undated, LAWL.
14. Olszewski, *Restoration*, p. 57.
15. Brooks, "Personal Recollections," p. 224.
16. Leale, "Lincoln's Last Hours,"*Harper's Weekly*, Feb. 13, 1909, p. 7.
17. *American Magazine*, August, 1920, p. 82.
18. Rathbone in *JHS*, 1:124; Leale, "Lincoln's Last Hours," *Harper's Weekly*, p. 7; Hazelton in *Good Housekeeping*, February, 1927, p. 116; Sanford, letter to sister, April 16, 1865, in Pratt, *Concerning Mr. Lincoln*, p. 122; DuBarry, letter to mother, April 16, 1865, in *Journal of the Illinois State Historical Society*, September, 1946, p. 366; James Suydam Knox, letter to father, April 15, 1865, in *Saturday Review*, Feb. 11, 1956, p. 11.
19. Withers' account prepared for the government.
20. *New York World*, April ? 1909.
21. *Boston Globe*, April 11, 1915.
22. *Baltimore Sun* and *New York World*, Feb. 12, 1926; *Saturday Evening Post*, Feb. 12, 1927, p. 40.
23. *Associated Press*, April 14, 1936.
24. *CT*, 2:544.
25. Rathbone affidavit.
26. *CT*, 2:551, 3:32.
27. *Sioux City Journal*, April 26, 1914; *Oakland Tribune*, Feb. 11, 1923; *Kansas City Star*, Feb. 8, 1925.
28. *Boston Globe*, April 11, 1915.
29. Ibid.
30. Crook, "Lincoln's Last Day," p. 527.

## IX. Tragedy Strikes, Mary's Hand in His

1. *CW*, 6:392.

2. Carpenter, *Inner Life*, p. 49.
3. *CW*, 6:392.
4. Carpenter, *Inner Life*, p. 52.
5. Brooks, "Personal Reminiscences," March, p. 675; Randall and Currant, *Last Full Measure*, p. 379.
6. *Oakland Tribune*, Feb. 11, 1923; *New York World*, Feb. 7, 1924.
7. *CT*, 2:531.
8. Laughlin, "Our American Cousin," pp. 186–88.
9. Olszewski, *Restoration*, pp. 112, 114–16, 122.
10. *DAB*, 10:283–84; Creahan, *Life of Laura Keene*, pp. 15, 18, 25, 70, 77, 92, 100, 128, 142, 167.
11. Deering, letter to "My Dear Friend," April 26, 1865; *Century Magazine*, February, 1893, p. 634; *Boston Globe*, Nov. 30, 1915; Helm, *True Story of Mary*, p. 257.
12. Olszewski, *Restoration*, p. 79; *JHS*, 1:124; Rathbone affidavit; *Lincoln Lore*, no. 1569 (November 1968).
13. Briggs, "Assassination Night."
14. *National Republican*, June 8, 1865; Eisenschiml, *Why Was Lincoln Murdered?* p. 24.
15. *CT*, 1:190; *PIT*, p. 76; *JHS*, 1:129; Todd, letter to his brother.
16. *New York Evening Post*, July 8, 1884.
17. Although it has invariably been given as Jennie on programs and posters and in books and articles, the first name of Jeannie Gourlay Struthers as it appears in this book is spelled correctly according to her signed writings at Georgetown University and in the Louis A. Warren Lincoln Library and Museum.
18. Jeannie Gourlay Struthers ms., "A Voice From the Past," in papers of the Rev. Patrick J. Cormican, S. J., Georgetown University.
19. *CT*, 3:18; *PIT*, p. 105.
20. *CT*, 1:226; *PIT*, p. 74; *TBP*, p. 48.
21. MacCulloch, "This Man Saw Lincoln Shot," p. 116.
22. Buckingham, *Reminiscences and Souvenirs of the Assassination of Abraham Lincoln*, p. 13; *CT*, p. 73.
23. *CT*, 1:181–86; *PIT*, pp. 72–73; *JHS*, 1:131–33, 146–47, 184–85.
24. *Richmond Whig*, April 25, 1865; Clark, *Lincoln in the National Capital*, p. 98.
25. *JHS*, 1:131–57, 183–85.
26. Ibid., 558–76.
27. Ibid., 556.
28. Ibid., 566–71.
29. Ibid., pp. 556, 559, 571.
30. Ibid., pp. 556, 569.
31. International News story in *Richmond Times-Dispatch*, May 9, 1929; special correspondence, *Brooklyn Eagle*, May 22, 1929.

32. Jeannie Gourlay Struthers, letter to M. J. Boyer, Feb. 15, 1923; *Minneapolis Journal*, April 27, 1914; newspaper interview with Mrs. Struthers from Montclair, N. J., Feb. 5, 1915, LMU.
33. *CT*, 1:179; *PIT*, p. 72; *JHS*, 1:157.
34. Buckingham, *Reminiscences*, p. 13.
35. *CT*, 1:194; *PIT*, p. 78; McGowan statement in Shea, *Lincoln Memorial*, pp. 65–66.
36. Todd, letter to his brother.
37. Stoddard, *True Story of a Great Life*, p. 459; Nicolay, *A Short Life*, p. 537.
38. Trefousse, "Belated Revelations of the Assassination Committee," p. 14.
39. Brinkerhoff, *Recollections*, p. 167; Justin G. Turner, "Tragedy of an Age," p. 208.
40. Oldroyd, *Assassination*, pp. 20–21.
41. Shaw, *McClure's Magazine*, December, 1908, pp. 183–84.
42. *CT*, 1:190; *PIT*, p. 76; *TBP*, p. 38.
43. *JHS*, 1:129.
44. Wright, *Magazine of History*, February, 1909, p. 113.
45. *CT*, 3:182; Rathbone affidavit.
46. Helm, p. 257.
47. Turner and Turner, *Mary Todd Lincoln:* letter to Edwin Lewis Baker, Jr., April 11, 1877, p. 632.
48. Henry, letter to Mrs. Henry, April 19, 1865, ISHL; Shutes, *Lincoln and the Doctors*, p. 133.
49. Hawk interview, *Boston Herald*, April 11, 1897.
50. *CT*, 1:190; *PIT*, p. 76; *TBP*, p. 38.
51. Lattimer, "The Wound That Killed Lincoln," p. 487.
52. *CT*, 1:196; *PIT*, p. 78.
53. Albert W. Boggs, *Chicago Daily News*, Feb. 11, 1926; Lt. John T. Bolton, *Magazine of History*, extra no. 34, p. 7 (135); Boyd, *A Memorial Lincoln Bibliography*, p. 21; Brinkerhoff, *Recollections of a Lifetime*, p. 168; Lenora H. Freudenthal, *Washington Star*, Feb. 13, 1928; Capt. Oliver L. Gatch, *McClure's Magazine*, December, 1908, p. 184; Charles H. Johnson, *Boston Globe*, April 11, 1915; William T. Kent, *St. Louis Globe-Democrat*, Dec. 3, 1891; J. K. Kleinhen, *San Diego Union*, Feb. 10, 1935; Mrs. Caleb Milligan (Anne S. Brown), *Cleveland Plain Dealer*, April 15, 1928; A. C. Richards, *Ravenna Republican*, April 19, 1906; Frederick Sawyer, *Civil War Magazine*, March, 1976, p. 65; Julia Adelaide Shephard, *Century Magazine*, April, 1909, p. 917; Thomas H. Sherman, *New York World*, Feb. 12, 1926; Dr. Charles Sabin Taft, *Century Magazine*, February, 1893, p. 634; William Hershey, Lt. John B. Rivard, and Daniel H. Veader, Assassination File, LAWL.

54. Thomas Bradford Sanders, *Reading Eagle*, April 2, 1911.
55. J. F. Troutner, *Sioux City Journal*, June 10, 1915.
56. Francis Wilson, *John Wilkes Booth*, p. 115.
57. *New York Times*, Feb. 14, 1926.
58. *Boston Herald*, April 11, 1897.
59. *Sioux City Journal*, Apr. 26, 1914; *Chicago Daily News*, Feb. 11, 1926.
60. *The Independent*, April 4, 1895, p. 2 (430).
61. *New York Evening Post*, July 8, 1884.
62. Booth diary.
63. Weik, "A New Story of the Lincoln Assassination," p. 561.
64. Gobright, *Recollections of Men and Things in Washington During the Third of a Century*, p. 351.
65. *Boston Herald*, April 11, 1897; Hawk letter to father, April 16, 1865, in Clark, *Lincoln in the National Capital*, p. 100; *Elgin Courier News*, April 14, 1931; *PIT*, p. 39.
66. *CT*, 1:192; Harris, *Assassination of Abraham Lincoln*, p. 39.
67. *Ohio Archaeological and Historical Publications*, vol. 30, 1921, p. 3.
68. *JHS*, 1:125.
69. *Reading Eagle*, April 2, 1911.
70. Raymond, *Life and Public Services*, p. 697.
71. *New York Times*, Feb. 28, 1909.
72. *Winchester Star*, Dec. 30, 1925.
73. Shea, *Lincoln Memorial*, p. 66.
74. Assassination File, LAWL.
75. Bolton, *Magazine of History*, extra no. 34, p. 7 (135).
76. *Journal of the Illinois State Historical Society*, October, 1927, p. 425.
77. *National Republican*, n. d., in LAWL.
78. Brinkerhoff, *Reminiscences*, p. 168.
79. Ruth Reynolds, "Seventy-five Years Ago Tonight"; Bates, *Lincoln in the Telegraph Office*, p. 369.
80. Browne, *Everyday Life*, p. 706; Francis Wilson, *John Wilkes Booth*, p. 114.
81. Olszewski, *Restoration*, p. 96, plate xv.
82. *PIT*, p. 100.
83. Oldroyd, *Assassination*, p. 19.
84. *CT*, 2:532.
85. *PIT*, p. 76; *Ohio Archaeological and Historical Publications*, vol. 30, 1921, p. 3; Harris, p. 39; William Hershey, Assassination File, LAWL; Capt. Isaac Hull, 87th Pennsylvania Volunteer Infantry, Assassination File, ISHL.
86. Rathbone affidavit.
87. *CT*, 1:192–93; *PIT*, p. 76; Harris, *Assassination*, p. 40; Leale, "Lincoln's Last Hours," *Harper's Weekly*, p. 7; Capt. Henry W. Mason, *New Bedford Sunday Standard*, April 13, 1919.

88. Harris, *Assassination*, p. 40; Ferguson, *I Saw Booth Shoot Lincoln*, p. 37; Oldroyd, *Assassination*, p. 19; Bryan, *Great American Myth*, p. 181.
89. Leale, "Lincoln's Last Hours," *Harper's Weekly*, p. 7.
90. *Boston Sunday Globe*, April 12, 1914.
91. *Boston Globe*, April 11, 1915.
92. Ibid.
93. Baker, *History of the United States Secret Service*, p. 465; John Davenport, *National Republican*, April 22, 1922; Capt. Henry W. Mason, *New Bedford Sunday Standard*, April 13, 1919; Rietveld, "An Eyewitness Account of the Assassination of Abraham Lincoln," p. 64; Shephard, "Lincoln's Assassination," p. 917; Samuel R. Ward, *Elgin Courier News*, April 14, 1931.
94. James Suydam Knox, "A Son Writes of the Supreme Tragedy," p. 11; Arnold, *Life of Lincoln*, p. 432; Boyd, p. 21; Brooks, *Lincoln and the Downfall of Slavery*, p. 456; Raymond, p. 697; Shephard, p. 917.
95. George A. Townsend, *The Life, Crime and Capture of John Wilkes Booth*, p. 9.
96. Capt. Isaac Hull, Assassination File, ISHL; Mrs. Caleb Milligan, *Boston Globe*, Feb. 12, 1928; James Mills, *New York Sun*, n.d., LAWL; Henry Polkinhorn, *Boston Post*, Feb. 11, 1923; W. H. Roberts, *Cleveland Plain Dealer*, Feb. 12, 1927; Charles L. Willis, *Brooklyn Eagle*, April 22, 1929.
97. Leale, "Lincoln's Last Hours," *Harper's Weekly*, p. 7; Frederick A. Sawyer, *Civil War History*, March, 1976, p. 65; Dr. Octavius K. Yates, West Paris, Me., Assassination File, LAWL.
98. *Washington Sunday Star*, Nov. 5, 1911; *The Independent*, April 4, 1895, p. 2 (430).
99. *National Republican*, Jan. 27, 1923, p. 7.
100. *New York Times*, Feb. 28, 1909; Wilgus, "The Lincoln Tragedy."
101. Ferguson testimony in Whiteman Introduction to *While Lincoln Lay Dying*, unnumbered page.
102. John Lindsey, *Philadelphia Public Ledger*, Feb. 11, 1931.
103. Hawk, letter to father, in Clark, *Lincoln in the National Capital*, p. 100; *Boston Herald*, April 11, 1897.
104. Clark, *Lincoln in the National Capital*, pp. 108, 109; *Saturday Evening Post*, Feb. 12, 1927, p. 42.
105. *CT*, 1:198–99; *PIT*, p. 79.
106. Withers' statement prepared for the government.
107. *PIT*, p. 97.
108. *CT*, 1:227; *PIT*, p. 74.
109. Chittenden, *Personal Reminiscences*, p. 244, quoting letter of Francis P. Blair, April 17, 1865.

## X. "It Is Impossible for Him to Recover"

1. Bolton, "The Assassination of President Lincoln," p. 7 (135); *Harrisburg Evening News*, April 13, 1929.
2. *PIT*, p. 78; Harris affidavit, in Morris, *Memorial Record*, p. 44.
3. Ferguson, *I Saw Booth Shoot Lincoln*, p. 51; Helm, *True Story of Mary*, p. 258; Mrs. J. H. Evans, *Sioux City Journal*, April 26, 1914.
4. *CT*, 1:196; *PIT*, p. 78; John Nicolay, *A Short Life*, p. 539.
5. Ward, Introduction to *Tributes to Lincoln*, pp. 12–13.
6. *New Bedford Sunday Standard*, April 13, 1919.
7. Harris affidavit in Morris, *Memorial Record*.
8. *Sioux City Journal*, April 26, 1914.
9. *New York Times*, Feb. 14, 1926.
10. *McClure's Magazine*, December, 1908, p. 184.
11. *North American Review*, April, 1896, p. 424.
12. *Oakland Tribune*, Feb. 11, 1923; *New York World*, Feb. 17, 1924.
13. *National Republican*, Jan. 27, 1923, p. 7.
14. *Ohio Archaeological and Historical Publications*, January, 1921, p. 3.
15. DeMotte, "The Assassination of Abraham Lincoln," p. 425; John T. Hutchinson, *New York Times*, n.d., Assassination File, LAWL.
16. Ward, p. 13.
17. *CT*, 2:463; Leale, "Lincoln's Last Hours," *Harper's Weekly*, p. 7; Henry W. Mason, *New Bedford Sunday Standard*, April 13, 1919; Thomas Bradford Sanders, *Reading Eagle*, April 2, 1911; Shaw, "The Assassination of Lincoln," p. 184; Sherman, "Saw Assassin Leap from Box to Stage," *New York World*, Feb. 12, 1926; Taft, "Abraham Lincoln's Last Hours," p. 635.
18. Ward, Introduction to *Tributes to Lincoln*, p. 13.
19. Weik, "A New Story," p. 562.
20. *Boston Post*, Feb. 11, 1923.
21. James Suydam Knox, letter to his father, April 15, 1865.
22. *CT*, 2:70–72; *PIT*, pp. 79–80; *JHS*, 1:125–27.
23. *CT*, 2:460–61; *PIT*, p. 97.
24. *CT*, 2:461; *PIT*, pp. 97, 107.
25. *CT*, 3:49; *PIT*, p. 106.
26. *CT*, 3:19; *PIT*, p. 105.
27. *Boston Herald*, April 11, 1897.
28. Wilgus, "The Lincoln Tragedy."
29. Ibid.
30. Weichmann, *A True History*, p. 418.
31. Ibid.
32. Clark, *Lincoln in the National Capital*, p. 109; Creahan, *Life of Laura Keene*, p. 27; Helm, *True Story of Mary*, p. 258; Charles H.

Johnson, *Boston Globe*, April 11, 1915; Rietveld, "An Eyewitness Account," p. 64; John Rivard, Assassination File, LMU; Thomas Bradford Sanders, *Reading Eagle*, April 2, 1911; Sherman, "Saw Assassin Leap."

33. Buckingham, *Reminiscences*, p. 15; Bryan, *Great American Myth*, p. 183; Rietveld, "An Eyewitness Account," p. 64.
34. *Los Angeles Times*, Feb. 12, 1930.
35. *PIT*, p. 78; Rathbone affidavit.
36. *CT*, 1:413; *PIT*, p. 82; *TBP*, p. 67.
37. *PIT*, p. 78; Crawford statement in Nicolay and Hay notes for chap. 14, vol. 10, *Abraham Lincoln: A History*.
38. Leale, "Lincoln's Last Hours,"*Harper's Weekly*, p. 7.
39. *New York Times*, Feb. 28, 1909.
40. *Boston Globe*, April 11, 1915.
41. Ibid.; *Ohio Archaeological and Historical Publications*, January, 1921, p. 5.
42. *Reading Eagle*, April 2, 1911, *Baltimore Sun*, May 29, 1967; Taft, "Abraham Lincoln's Last Hours," p. 635.
43. *Magazine of History*, extra no. 34, p. 8 (136).
44. Leale, "Lincoln's Last Hours," *Harper's Weekly*, p. 8.
45. *CT*, 1:257; *PIT*, p. 82; *TBP*, p. 52; *St. Louis Globe-Democrat*, Dec. 3, 1891.
46. Leale, "Lincoln's Last Hours," *Harper's Weekly*, p. 8.
47. Ibid.
48. *CT*, 2:537; Clark, *Lincoln in the National Capital*, p. 109; Shepard, "Lincoln's Assassination," p. 917.
49. *CT*, 2:109; *PIT*, p. 76.
50. *New York World*, Feb. 12, 1926.
51. J. A. Covel, letter from Chicago, June 16, 1893, to the editor of an unnamed paper, Assassination File, LAWL.
52. *National Republican*, n.d., LAWL.
53. *Reading Eagle*, April 2, 1911.
54. Crawford statement.
55. *New York Times*, Feb. 28, 1909; *St. Louis Globe-Democrat*, Dec. 3, 1891.
56. *New York Times*, Feb. 14, 1926; *Kansas City Star*, Feb. 8, 1925; *Philadelphia Bulletin*, March 10, 1931.
57. *Minneapolis Journal*, April 27, 1914.
58. Leale, "Lincoln's Last Hours," *Harper's Weekly*, p. 8.
59. *St. Louis Globe-Democrat*, Dec. 3, 1891.
60. *Century Magazine*, February, 1893, p. 635.
61. Crawford statement.
62. Ward, Introduction to *Tributes to Lincoln*, p. 14.
63. *Boston Globe*, April 11, 1915.

64. *Philadelphia Weekly Times*, Dec. 29, 1878.
65. Leale, "Lincoln's Last Hours," *Harper's Weekly*, p. 8; Taft, "Abraham Lincoln's Last Hours," p. 635.
66. Carl Bersch account in Lewis Gardner Reynolds, "Lincoln's Last Night," *Washington Star*, April 16, 1933; George Maynard, *National Republican*, n.d., LAWL.
67. Crawford statement.
68. *Magazine of History*, extra no. 34, pp. 8–9 (136–37).
69. *New York Times*, Feb. 8, 1931.
70. Ibid.; Leale, "Lincoln's Last Hours,"*Harper's Weekly*, p. 8.
71. Ibid., p. 10.
72. *New York Times*, Feb. 8, 1931; Mrs. Virginia Lucas, *California Daily Register*, Feb. 11, 1933.
73. Jeannie Gurley Struthers always persisted in interviews and in letters to Congressman T. C. McFadden and others that her actor father, T. C. Gourlay (Sir Edward Trenchard in *Our American Cousin*), helped carry the President out. Others by whom or for whom the claim was made: Col. Otto Dowling of Dixon, Ill. (in Clark, *Lincoln in the National Capital*, p. 104); Albert Daggett, a clerk in the State Department, in letters to his mother and sister, April 15 and 16, 1865 (*Lincoln Lore*, no. 1478, April, 1961, and LAWL); Capt. Edwin E. Bedee, 12th New Hampshire Volunteer Infantry (*Lincoln Herald*, Spring, 1979, p. 18); Augustus "Gussie" Clark, formerly a private in the 1st Massachusetts Volunteer Heavy Artillery and in April, 1865, an employee of the War Department, in a letter to his uncle, S. M. Allen, April 16, 1865 (Massachusetts Historical Society); Capt. Oliver C. Gatch and Dr. Charles D. Gatch (*McClure's Magazine*, December, 1908, p. 184); the Reverend William James, member of the Christian Commission (*Abraham Lincoln Supplement Magazine*, vol. 3, and newspaper articles, LAWL); John H. McCormick, employee of the Government Printing Office (*St. Louis Globe-Democrat*, May 18 [or 19], 1892); Lt. ________ Sear, 187th Ohio Infantry (*Burrell's Washington Press*, n.d., 1894, LAWL); Charles H. Estes, thrice-wounded member of the Veteran Reserve Corps (*Portsmouth Herald*, Feb. 13, 1928).
74. *CT*, 1:197; *PIT*, p. 78.
75. *CT*, 1:197; *PIT*, p. 78; Brinkerhoff, *Reminiscences*, p. 169.
76. Crawford statement.
77. Leale, "Lincoln's Last Hours,"*Harper's Weekly*, p. 10.
78. Ibid.
79. *New York Times*, Feb. 8, 1931.
80. *Philadelphia Times*, date obscured, 1893, LAWL.
81. Ibid.
82. Leale, "Lincoln's Last Hours," *Harper's Weekly*, p. 10.

83. *Boyd's Washington and Georgetown Directory*, 1864.
84. *Boston Globe*, April 12, 1914.
85. *New York World*, Feb. 12, 1926; *Brooklyn Eagle*, April 22, 1929; *Richmond Times-Dispatch*, May 19, 1929.
86. *California Daily Register*, Feb. 11, 1933.
87. *Saturday Evening Post*, Feb. 12, 1927, p. 44; *Pensacola Journal*, Feb. 12, 1935; *Elizabethtown News*, Feb. 15, 1935.
88. *New York Times*, Feb. 28, 1909.
89. *New York Times*, Feb. 14, 1926; *Sioux City Journal*, April 26, 1914.
90. Mrs. Sarah H. Eastman (Sarah Russell), *Washington Star*, Feb. 12, 1936; Carl Bersch, letter to his family after the assassination and quoted in *Washington Star*, April 16, 1933; J. F. Troutner, *Sioux City Journal*, June 10, 1915; Whipple, *Story Life of Lincoln*, p. 649; Laughlin, *Death of Lincoln*, p. 99; *Leslie's Weekly*, March 26, 1908.

## XI. "Now He Belongs to the Ages"

1. *Washington Sunday Star*, Jan. 24, 1909.
2. Henry Safford account, Gov. Henry Horner scrapbook, ISHL.
3. *Frank Leslie's Illustrated Newspaper*, April 29, 1865; *Lincoln Lore*, no. 523 (April 17, 1939).
4. Safford account; *Springfield Republican*, Feb. 18, 1917.
5. Safford account.
6. Lewis Gardner Reynolds, "Lincoln's Last Night," including Carl Bersch account.
7. Ibid.
8. Ibid.
9. Leale, "Lincoln's Last Hours," *Harper's Weekly*, p. 10.
10. Craig, "Historic Furnishings," unpublished document, p. 14; Francis, letter to niece, Josephine; Van Ark, "New Light on Lincoln's Death," p. 82.
11. Craig, "Historic Furnishings," unpublished document, p. 13; Van Ark, "New Light," p. 82.
12. *Frank Leslie's Illustrated Newspaper*, April 29, 1865; Oldroyd, *Assassination*, pp. 35–37; Craig, "Historic Furnishings," unpublished document, pp. 22–23; *Washington Sunday Star*, April 11, 1937; *Lincoln Lore*, no. 523 (April 17, 1939).
13. William T. Clark, letter to sister, Ida, April 19, 1865.
14. Safford account.
15. William T. Clark, letter to sister, Ida.
16. Kundhardt and Kundhardt, *Twenty Days*, p. 47.
17. Leale, "Lincoln's Last Hours," *Harper's Weekly*, p. 10.
18. Ward, Introduction to *Tributes to Lincoln*, p. 15; *Saturday Evening Post*, Feb. 12, 1927, p. 46; *The Independent*, April 4, 1895, p. 3

(431); Clarke, *Unlocked Book*, p. 175; Forrester, *This One Mad Act*, p. 227.

19. Leale,"Lincoln's Last Hours," *Harper's Weekly*, p. 10; *Century Magazine*, February, 1893, p. 635.
20. Kundhardt and Kundhardt, "Twenty Days," p. 48.
21. Flower, *Edwin McMasters Stanton*, p. 282n.
22. *PIT*, p. 79; Rathbone affidavit; Shea, *Lincoln Memorial*, p. 63.
23. Pope, letter to editor, *Washington Star*, Nov. 13, 1896.
24. Ibid.
25. *JHS*, 1:251–52, 254, 262–63; *PIT*, pp. 156–57.
26. See chap. 7, note 111.
27. Weichmann, *True History*, p. 185.
28. Quoted in King, "Assassination of President Lincoln"; *Blumhaven Digest*, August, 1938, pp. 5, 7.
29. *Washington Evening Star*, Feb. 13, 1928.
30. *Cleveland Plain Dealer*, Feb. 12, 1927.
31. *Magazine of History*, extra no. 34, p. 9 (137).
32. Ibid.
33. Ibid.; Stimmel, "Experiences," p. 31; Perley, "The Last of the Bodyguard," p. 409.
34. Searcher, *Farewell to Lincoln*, p. 32.
35. *Baltimore Sun*, May 27, 1967.
36. *Journal of the Illinois State Historical Society*, September, 1946, p. 368.
37. *OR*, 46 (3): 736.
38. Bryan, *Great American Myth*, p. 196.
39. *Saturday Review*, Feb. 11, 1956, p. 11.
40. *Library of Congress Information Bulletin*, Feb. 27, 1976, pp. 124–25.
41. Leale, "Lincoln's Last Hours," *Harper's Weekly*, p. 10.
42. Parker, "Assassination and Gunshot Wound of President Lincoln," p. 147.
43. Safford account; Kundhardt and Kundhardt, *Twenty Days*, p. 49.
44. Leale, "Lincoln's Last Hours," *Harper's Weekly*, p. 10.
45. Parker, "Assassination and Gunshot Wound," p. 148; Taft, "Last Hours of Abraham Lincoln," p. 453.
46. Taft, "Abraham Lincoln's Last Hours," p. 635.
47. Leale, "Lincoln's Last Hours," *Harper's Weekly*, p. 10.
48. *PIT*, p. 81.
49. Parker, "Assassination and Gunshot Wound," p. 148; Taft, "Last Hours of Abraham Lincoln," p. 453.
50. *PIT*, p. 157; Leale, "Lincoln's Last Hours,"*Harper's Weekly*, p. 10.
51. Taft, "Last Hours of Abraham Lincoln," p. 453; idem, "Abraham Lincoln's Last Hours," p. 635.

52. Taft, "Last Hours of Abraham Lincoln," p. 453; Parker, "Assassination and Gunshot Wound," p. 148.
53. *Washington Post*, April 12, 1896.
54. Storey, "Dickens, Stanton, Sumner and Storey," p. 463.
55. *Washington Post*, April 12, 1896.
56. John Nicolay and Hay, *Abraham Lincoln: A History*, 10:301.
57. Storey, p. 463.
58. Ibid.
59. *Washington Star*, April 12, 1896.
60. Ibid.; *The Collector*, March, 1950, p. 49; Mrs. Elizabeth Dixon, letter to her nephew, Othaniel Charles Marsh, April 14, 1866.
61. *The Collector*, p. 50; *New York Times*, Feb. 12, 1950; Mrs. Elizabeth Dixon, letter to her sister, Mrs. Louisa Wood, May 1, 1865, in *Lincoln Lore*, no. 1587 (May 1970); Mary Dixon, letter to Ralph Borreson, Aug. 29, 1967.
62. *The Collector*, p. 50; *New York Times*, Feb. 12, 1950.
63. Raymond, *Life and Public Services*, p. 785.
64. Usher, letter to his wife; *North American Newspaper Alliance*, Feb. 11, 1931.
65. Arnold, *Sketch of the Life of Abraham Lincoln*, p. 52.
66. Welles, *Diary*, 2:286.
67. Flower, *Edwin McMasters Stanton*, p. 281.
68. Bates, *Lincoln in the Telegraph Office*, pp. 371–72; Laird and Maynard accounts, Assassination File, LAWL.
69. Flower, *Edwin McMasters Stanton*, p. 280; *OR*, 46 (3): 780–81.
70. Bates, "Recollections of Abraham Lincoln," p. 636.
71. *OR*, 46 (3): 780–81.
72. U.S. Congress, *Impeachment Investigation*, p. 673.
73. *Sioux Falls Argus*, March 11, 1908; Loux, "Mystery of the Telegraph Interruption," pp. 235–36.
74. Whiteman, Introduction to *While Lincoln Lay Dying*, p. 4; Tanner, "At the Deathbed of Abraham Lincoln," p. 34.
75. Whiteman, Introduction to *While Lincoln Lay Dying*, pp. 1–3; *DAB*, 18:298; Tanner, "At the Deathbed," p. 34.
76. Barton, *Life of Lincoln*, 2:470.
77. Whiteman, Introduction to *While Lincoln Lay Dying*, p. 4.
78. Ibid., pp. 5–6.
79. Ibid., unnumbered pages.
80. Ibid.
81. Ibid.
82. Ibid.
83. Ibid.
84. *American Historical Review*, April, 1924, p. 515; Barton, *Life of Lincoln*, 2:471; *National Republic*, August, 1926, p. 34.

85. *American Historical Review*, April, 1924, p. 516; Barton, *Life of Lincoln*, 2:472.
86. Whiteman, Introduction to *While Lincoln Lay Dying*, pp. 5–6.
87. *OR*, 46 (3): 781.
88. *New York Herald Tribune*, Feb. 15, 1925.
89. Log of Metropolitan Police Department, April 14–15, 1865, NA.
90. Ibid.
91. *Lincoln Lore*, no. 627, April 14, 1941.
92. Raymond, *Life and Public Services*, pp. 785–86; Baker, *History of the Secret Service*, p. 467; Shea, pp. 70–71; Parker, p. 148; Oldroyd, pp. 32, 35; Taft, "Last Hours," pp. 453–54.
93. Shea, *Lincoln Memorial*, pp. 70–71; Oldroyd, *Assassination*, pp. 32, 35; Baker, *History of the Secret Service*, p. 467.
94. Farwell, letter to Sen. James R. Doolittle, Feb. 8, 1866; Lomask, *Andrew Johnson*, p. 9.
95. Sumner, letter to John Bright, the English liberal, May 1, 1865, in Pierce, *Memoirs and Letters of Charles Sumner*, 4:241; Milton, *Age of Hate*, p. 161; Lomask, *Andrew Johnson*, p. 9. Milton and Lomask, however, say that Johnson stayed half an hour.
96. Taft, "Last Hours of Abraham Lincoln," p. 453; Parker, "Assassination and Gunshot Wound," p. 148.
97. Leale, "Lincoln's Last Hours," *Harper's Weekly*, p. 10.
98. McCulloch, *Men and Measures*, p. 224.
99. Taft, "Abraham Lincoln's Last Hours," p. 635.
100. Shea, *Lincoln Memorial*, p. 71; Parker, "Assassination and Gunshot Wound," p. 148.
101. Taft, "Last Hours of Abraham Lincoln," p. 454; Parker, "Assassination and Gunshot Wound," p. 148; Shea, *Lincoln Memorial*, p. 71; *New York Times*, April 17, 1865.
102. *The Collector*, p. 50.
103. Taft, "Abraham Lincoln's Last Hours," p. 635.
104. Lattimer, "Wound That Killed Lincoln," p. 482; Leale, "Lincoln's Last Hours," address, p. 11.
105. *American Historical Review*, April, 1924, p. 516.
106. Turner and Turner, *Mary Todd Lincoln*, p. 562: letter to James H. Orne, May 8, 1870.
107. Welles, *Diary*, 2:287.
108. DeMotte, "Assassination of Abraham Lincoln," p. 426.
109. Welles, *Diary*, 2:287–88; idem, "Death of Lincoln," pp. 589–90.
110. Welles, "Death of Lincoln," p. 590.
111. *American Historical Review*, April, 1924, p. 516.
112. Barton, *Life of Lincoln*, 2:479.
113. *Lincoln Lore*, no. 1517, July, 1964.
114. Ibid.

115. *Lincoln Lore*, no. 523, April 17, 1939; William T. Clark, letter to his sister, Ida.
116. Blum, "Mystery of the Dying President's Attendants," pp. 22, 24.
117. *Century Magazine*, June, 1890, p. 310.
118. Ibid.
119. Hollister, *Life of Colfax*, p. 254.
120. Haynie, "At the Deathbed of Lincoln," p. 954.
121. Leale, "Lincoln's Last Hours," address, pp. 11–12.
122. John Nicolay, *A Short Life*, p. 540.
123. *Magazine of History*, extra no. 61, 1917, p. 27.
124. Leale, "Lincoln's Last Hours," address, p. 11.
125. Field, "Last Moments of the President."
126. Storey, "Dickens, Stanton, Sumner, and Storey," p. 465.
127. Helm, *True Story of Mary*, p. 260.
128. Welles, *Diary*, 2:288.
129. *Danville (Ill.) Commercial News*, Dec. 9, 1921; Stevens, *A Reporter's Lincoln*, p. 72.
130. *American Historical Review*, April, 1924, p. 516.
131. Leale, "Lincoln's Last Hours,"*Harper's Weekly*, p. 27.
132. *New York Times*, April 17, 1865.
133. Taft, "Last Hours of Abraham Lincoln," p. 453.
134. *Century Magazine*, June, 1890, p. 311.
135. *The Presbyterian*, Nov. 3, 1866.
136. Tanner, "At the Deathbed," p. 35.
137. John Nicolay and Hay, *Abraham Lincoln*, 10:302.
138. Field, "Last Moments of the President."
139. Ibid.
140. John Nicolay and Hay, *Abraham Lincoln*, 10:302.

## Appendix

### *1. Eli K. Price and His $500 Check*

1. *NCAB*, 10:412–13.
2. *DAB*, 15:212.
3. *NCAB*, 10:413.
4. Ibid.
5. *DAB*, 5:212.
6. *NCAB*, 10:413.
7. Price, letters to Francis L. Gowen, Vice President, Western Savings Bank, Philadelphia, Jan. 9 and Feb. 15, 1980, and to author, March 17 and April 30, 1980.
8. *Boyd's Washington and Georgetown Directory*, 1874.
9. *McElroy's Philadelphia Directory*, 1865, 1914.

### 2. *The Guard with a Shoddy Record*

1. *Boyd's Washington and Georgetown Directory*, 1860; Eisenschiml, *Why Was Lincoln Murdered?* p. 12; Crook, *Through Five Administrations*, p. 1.
2. Rhoads office, letter to Congressman Clarence J. Brown, dated June 8, 1979, answering a query on behalf of the author.
3. Dorothy Provine, Civil Archives Division of NA, letter to the author, June 12, 1979.
4. Eisenschiml, *Why Was Lincoln Murdered?* p. 12; Kimmel, "Fatal Remissness of Lincoln's Guard Unpunished."
5. Eisenschiml, *Why Was Lincoln Murdered?* pp. 12–13; Kimmel, "Fatal Remissness."
6. Eisenschiml, *Why Was Lincoln Murdered?* p. 13.
7. Ibid.; Kimmel, "Fatal Remissness."
8. Eisenschiml, *Why Was Lincoln Murdered?* pp. 14–15.
9. Sprague, "Mary Lincoln—Accessory to Murder," pp. 241–42.
10. Keckley, *Behind the Scenes*, pp. 193–95.
11. Eisenschiml, *Why Was Lincoln Murdered?* p. 16; Kimmel, "Fatal Remissness."
12. Kimmel, "Fatal Remissness."
13. *Boyd's Washington and Georgetown Directory*; Hall, "The Mystery of Lincoln's Guard."
14. Crook, "Lincoln's Last Day," p. 528.

### 3. *Light on the Missing Dispatch*

1. Crawford's story concerning the dispatch is taken from the Lieutenant's notes, which, when typed, cover ten pages, in John Nicolay and Hay notes for chap. 14, vol. 10, of *Abraham Lincoln: A History*, ISHL.
2. The only Long listed as a colonel by Heitman (*Historical Register and Dictionary of the United States Army*) on the date mentioned was William Hale Long from New York, who had been advanced to the rank of colonel on April 2 for gallantry and meritorious service in the assault on Petersburg.
3. Presumably Gilman Marston, who had just resigned his commission as brigadier general attached to the Army of the James to become a Congressman.
4. Cooney, "Lincoln's Lost Letters," p. 17.
5. *OR*, 42 (3): 655.
6. Ibid., ser. II, vol. 7, p. 1296.
7. Cooney, "Lincoln's Lost Letters," p. 18.
8. Capt. Bedee, letter to Secretary Stanton from Headquarters, 2nd

Brig., 3rd Div., 24th Army Corps in the field, April 26, 1865, James A. Hardie papers, DLC; Cooney, "Lincoln's Lost Letters," p. 18.
9. Ibid.
10. Ibid.
11. Bedee letter to Stanton.
12. Hardie, letter to Capt. Bedee, May 5, 1865, James A. Hardie papers, DLC.

### 4. *Course of the Ball, Still Undetermined*

1. *PIT*, p. 76; *CT*, 1:190–91.
2. Taft, "Last Hours of Abraham Lincoln," p. 454.
3. Report of autopsy on President Lincoln, Surgeon General's Office, NA.
4. *JHS*, 1:121.
5. *PIT*, p. 82.
6. Stone autopsy statement.
7. Taft, "Last Hours of Abraham Lincoln," p. 453; Parker, "Assassination and Gunshot Wound," p. 148.
8. Taft, "Last Hours of Abraham Lincoln," p. 454; Parker, "Assassination and Gunshot Wound," p. 149.

# Bibliography

## I. Resources

This section gives grateful acknowledgment and recognition to the many individuals, organizations, and institutions who gave aid over more than a quarter of a century during which information was being collected for this book. Persons listed, some of them now deceased, are those who were associated with the institutions or organizations at the time visits were made or with whom correspondence was carried on to secure information. Also listed are institutions by whom books, microfilm, or photo copies were made available.

Abbot Public Library, Marblehead, Mass.: Christine Evans.
Abraham Lincoln Book Shop, Chicago: Ralph G. Newman.
Antioch College Library, Yellow Springs, Ohio: Bruce Thomas.
Blumhaven Library and Museum, Philadelphia: Herman Blum.
Brown University Library, Providence, R. I.: Virginia M. Trescott.
Case Western Reserve University Library, Cleveland, Ohio.
Clark University, Robert Hutchings Goddard Library, Worcester, Mass.: Marion Henderson.
Cleveland Public Library, Cleveland, Ohio: Jean Davenport.
College of Physicians of Philadelphia: Christine A. Ruggers.
Colorado Historical Society, Denver: Catherine T. Engel.
Essex Institute, Salem, Mass.: Irene R. Norton.
Ford's Theatre National Historic Site, Washington, D.C.: Gail Glicksman, park technician; Frank Hebblethwaite, museum technician.
Georgetown University Library, Washington, D.C.: Nicholas B. Scheetz.
Historical Society of Pennsylvania, Philadelphia: Helen Smolen, Michele Voge.
Historical Society of York County, Pa.: Landon Chas. Reisinger.
Illinois State Historical Library, Springfield: Harry E. Pratt, Marion Dolores Pratt, James T. Hickey, Mildred V. Schultz, Roger D. Bridges, Mary Michals, George Herman.
Indiana State Library, Indianapolis: Jean E. Singleton.

IOOF, Grand Lodge of Ohio, Springfield: Charles R. Carter, Richard Crull, J. G. Honefanger, Sr., Harry Schaeperklaus.

Kent State University Libraries, Kent, Ohio: Rosemary Harrick, Ruth E. Main.

Lebanon Historical Society, Lebanon, N. H.: Robert H. Leavitt.

Library of Congress, Washington, D. C.: Oliver Orr, Gilbert Gude, John C. Broderick, Frances Reynolds, Frank J. Carroll, William Sartain, Katherine Gould, Norman Beckman, Susan Manakul, Gary Kohn, Charles Kelley, Grace Hallett.

Lincoln Memorial University Library, Harrogate, Tenn.: James D. Taylor, Stewart L. Watson, Edgar G. Archer, Marjorie Del-pan, Margie Brooks Bradley, Ann Beatty, Eva Mallicoat.

Louis A. Warren Lincoln Library and Museum, Fort Wayne, Ind.: Mark E. Neely, Jr., Mary Jane Hubler, John David Smith, Sara Melvin, Ruth E. Cook.

Marblehead Historical Society, Marblehead, Mass.: Marion Gosling.

Martin Luther King Memorial Library, Washington, D. C.: G. R. F. Kay, Roxanna Deane.

Massachusetts Historical Society, Boston: Louis L. Tucker.

Metropolitan Police Department, Washington, D. C.: Burtell M. Jefferson, Chief.

Museum of the Confederacy, Richmond, Va.: Les Jensen.

National Archives, Washington, D.C.: James E. O'Neill, Dale Floyd, Dorothy Provine, Michael Musick, Howard Wehmann, Gibson Smith, and others.

Naval Historical Center, Washington Navy Yard: Mary F. Loughlin.

New Britain Public Library, New Britain, Conn.: Barbara Hubbard.

New York Public Library: Robert E. Kingery.

New York State Historical Association, Cooperstown: Amy Barnum.

Newport Historical Society Library, Newport, R. I.: Madelene E. Wordell.

Newport Public Library, Newport, R. I.: Maureen Rooney.

Omaha Public Library, Omaha, Neb.: Thomas Heenan.

Presbyterian Historical Society, Philadelphia, Pa.: Gerald W. Gillette.

Princeton University, Princeton, N. J.: Earle E. Coleman.

Reading Public Library, Reading, Pa.: Patricia Weiherer.

Reed Memorial Library, Ravenna, Ohio: Phyllis Cettomai.

Rochester Historical Society, Rochester, N. H.: Jean W. Martin.

St. Louis Public Library, St. Louis, Mo.: Marlene F. Coleman.

Saint Peter's Church, Waldorf, Md.: Mary Ann Wilson.

Sioux Falls Public Library, Sioux Falls, S. D.: Judy Murphy.

Springfield Library and Museum Association, Springfield, Mass.: Anne Williamson.

State Historical Society of Wisconsin, Madison: John A. Peters.

State Library of Ohio, Columbus: Clyde Hordusky.
Toledo–Lucas County Public Library, Toledo, Ohio: Ruth M. Anderson.
Union College, Schaffer Library, Schenectady, N. Y.: Loretta Walker.
Union League of Philadelphia: Maxwell Whiteman, Patricia McLaughlin.
University of Cincinnati Library, Cincinnati, Ohio.
University of Michigan, Clements Library: Howard H. Peckham.
U. S. Naval Observatory, Washington, D. C.
Virginia Historical Society, Richmond: Edward L. Dooley, Jr.
Warder Public Library, Springfield, Ohio: Edward Byers, Lucie Osborn, Carol Maiorano, Gary Williams, Joan Holder, Linda Davis, Christine Snow.
Washington and Lee University, Cyrus Hall McCormack Library, Lexington, Va.: Betty Kondayan.
Wittenberg University Library, Springfield, Ohio: Bob Lee Mowery, Luella Eutsler, Rita Harnish, Albert LaRose, Regina Entorf, Kathy Schulz.
Yale University, New Haven, Conn.: Patricia L. Bodak.

To this list the author happily adds the names of the following individuals, some now deceased, who undertook research projects, provided information or materials, or gave sound advice:

John C. Brennan, Laurel, Md., friend.
Former Congressman Clarence J. Brown, Ohio, and members of his staff, Virginia Gano and Margaret Harpster.
Frank Ford, New York City, son of Harry Clay Ford.
Francis I. Gowen, Vice President, Western Savings Bank, Philadelphia.
Harold Hammond, Francestown, N. H., author and friend.
Michael W. Kauffman, Alexandria, Va., friend.
W. C. Langston, M. D., York, Pa., Lincoln historian and collector.
Dr. Arthur L. Lutz, Professor Emeritus of Physics, Wittenberg University.
Stewart W. McClelland, Indianapolis, former president of Lincoln Memorial University and lecturer on Lincoln.
R. Gerald McMurtry, Fort Wayne, Ind., Lincoln historian.
Robert C. Marcotte, Peabody, Mass., friend.
Lynne Nickell, Director of Publications, Wittenberg University.
Martha J. Peters, Fremont, Neb., former editorial staff member.
Jack Pickering, Editorial Director, Pennsylvania State University Press.
Philip Price, Philadelphia, great-grandson of Eli K. Price.
Mrs. Esther Starr, Millersburg, Pa., widow of author John W. Starr, Jr.
Louis A. Warren, Fort Wayne, Ind., author and director emeritus, Lincoln National Life Foundation.

Donald Welch, Wood River, Neb., and Washington, D. C., grandson and research assistant.

## II. Manuscripts, Documents, Collections

Assassination File (newspaper stories, articles, and papers), Illinois State Historical Library, Springfield.

Assassination File (newspaper stories, articles, and papers), Lincoln Memorial University Library, Harrogate, Tenn.

Assassination File (newspaper stories, articles, and papers), Louis A. Warren Lincoln Library and Museum, Fort Wayne, Ind.

Bates, Edward. Diary. Library of Congress, Washington, D. C.

Bedee, Capt. Edwin E. Letter to Edwin M. Stanton, April 26, 1865. James A. Hardie Papers. Library of Congress, Washington, D. C.

Booth, John Wilkes. Diary. Ford's Theatre National Historic Site, Washington, D. C.

Browning, Orville. Diary. Illinois State Historical Society, Springfield.

Clark, Augustus "Gussie." Letter to S. M. Allen, April 16, 1865. Massachusetts Historical Society, Boston.

Clark, William T. Letter to sister, Ida, April 19, 1865 (copy), Ford's Theatre National Historic Site, Washington, D. C.

Colfax, Schuyler. Papers. Indiana State Library, Indianapolis.

Craig, Vera. "Historic Furnishings Plan for Petersen House (House Where Lincoln Died)," unpublished document. National Park Service, Harper's Ferry, W. Va., Harper's Ferry Center.

Crawford, Lt. Alexander McL. Statement. Illinois State Historical Library, Springfield.

Daggett, Alfred. Letter to his mother, Mrs. Joseph Daggett, April 15, 1865. Louis A. Warren Lincoln Library and Museum, Fort Wayne, Ind.

Deering, John, Jr. Letter to "My Dear Friend," April 26, 1865. Louis A. Warren Lincoln Library and Museum, Fort Wayne, Ind.

Dixon, Mrs. Elizabeth Lord Cogswell. Letter to her nephew, Othaniel C. Marsh, April 14, 1866. Yale University Library, New Haven, Conn.

Dixon, Mary. Letter to Ralph Borreson, April 29, 1967. Illinois State Historical Library, Springfield.

Farwell, Leonard J. Letter to Senator James R. Doolittle, Feb. 8, 1866. State Historical Society of Wisconsin, Madison.

Ford, Frank. Letter to author, Dec. 2, 1965.

Francis, George. Letter to niece, Josephine, n.d., Chicago Historical Society.

Gourlay, William. Letter to Lincoln Life Insurance Co., March 6, 1968. Louis A. Warren Lincoln Library and Museum, Fort Wayne, Ind.

Hardie, General James A. Letter to Capt. Edwin E. Bedee, May 5, 1865. James A. Hardie Papers. Library of Congress, Washington, D. C.

Harris, Clara. Letter to "My Dear M__," April 29, 1865. Louis A. Warren Lincoln Library and Museum, Fort Wayne, Ind.

Hay, John. Letter to William H. Herndon, Sept. 6, 1866. New York Public Library.

Henry, Dr. Anson G. Letter to Mrs. Henry, April 19, 1865. Illinois State Historical Library, Springfield.

Horner, Gov. Henry. Scrapbook. Illinois State Historical Library, Springfield.

Knox, James Suydam. Letter to his father, April 15, 1865. Papers and biographical material of James Suydam Knox. Princeton University Archives, Princeton, N.J.

Lee, General Robert E. Information on his sword and spurs. Virginia Historical Society, Richmond; and Washington and Lee University, Lexington, Virginia.

Lyman–Lincoln Collection. IOOF Grand Lodge of Ohio, Springfield.

Metropolitan Police Dept., Washington, D. C. Log for April 14–15, 1865. National Archives.

*Montauk*, Navy and Old Army Branch. Log. National Archives.

Nicolay, John, and Hay, John. Notes for use in writing *Abraham Lincoln: A History*. Illinois State Historical Library, Springfield.

Rathbone, Major Henry R. Affadavit sworn to before Justice Abram B. Olin of the Supreme Court, District of Columbia, April 17, 1865. National Archives, War Dept. Records, File "R," R. B., JAO, p. 74.

Safford, Henry S. Letter to Osborn H. Oldroyd, June 26, 1903. Ford's Theatre National Historic Site, Washington, D. C.

Sanford, Charles. Letter to Edward Payson Goodrich, April 15, 1865. Clements Library, University of Michigan, Ann Arbor.

Scrapbook of Newspaper Clippings. New York Public Library.

Service and Pension Records of Civil War Veterans. National Archives.

Stone, Dr. Robert King. Autopsy statement. New York State Historical Association, Cooperstown.

Struthers, Jeannie Gourlay. Letter to Congressman L. T. McFadden, April 28, 1923. Louis A. Warren Lincoln Library and Museum, Fort Wayne, Ind.

_______. Letters to M. J. Boyer, Feb. 13 and Dec. 11, 1923, and Jan. 3, 1924 (copies). Louis A. Warren Lincoln Library and Museum, Fort Wayne, Ind.

_______. "A Voice From the Past." Article written for the Georgetown University Archives at the request of the Rev. Patrick J. Cormican, S. J., Librarian. Cormican Papers, Georgetown University, Washington, D. C.

Tanner, James. Letter to Henry F. Walch, April 17, 1865. Clements Library, University of Michigan, Ann Arbor.

Todd, George B. Letter to his brother, Henry, April 15, 1865. State Historical Society of Wisconsin, Madison.

U. S. Congress. House. *Miscellaneous Document no. 179*. 44th Cong., 1st sess. State Library of Ohio, Columbus.

U. S. Naval Observatory. Weather report for April 14–15, 1865, Washington, D. C.

Usher, John P. Letter to his wife April 16, 1865 (copy). Library of Congress, Washington, D. C.

Van Alen, Gen. James H. Letters. Abraham Lincoln Papers. Library of Congress, Washington, D. C.

Woodward, Dr. J. J. Lincoln autopsy report to Surgeon General Joseph K. Barnes, April 15, 1865. National Archives.

## III. Articles, Papers, Addresses

Andrews, Matthew Page. "Singleton Emerges as Lincoln's Lost Friend." *New York Times* (Feb. 12, 1928).

Angle, Paul M. "The Recollections of William Pitt Kellogg." *Abraham Lincoln Quarterly* (September 1945).

Arnold, Isaac. "Abraham Lincoln." Paper read before the Royal Historical Society, London, June 16, 1881. Chicago: Fergus Printing, 1881.

"The Assassination of President Lincoln, 1865." Letter of James Tanner to Henry F. Walch, April 17, 1865. *American Historical Review* (April 1924).

Bangs, C. C. "News of Booth's Shot." *Washington Post* (April 12, 1896).

Barnes, Capt. James, U.S.N. "With Lincoln from Washington to Richmond." *Magazine of History*, extra no. 161 (1930).

Bates, David Homer. "Lincoln and Charles A. Dana." *The Independent* (April 4, 1895).

————. "Recollections of Abraham Lincoln." In *History of the Ohio Society of New York*. New York: Grafton Press, 1906.

Bernard, Kenneth A. "Glimpses of Lincoln in the White House." *Abraham Lincoln Quarterly* (December 1952).

Blum, Herman. "The Mystery of the Dying President's Attendants." *Lincoln Herald* (Spring 1967).

Bolton, John T. "The Assassination of President Lincoln." *Magazine of History*, extra no. 34 (1914).

Bradford, Gamaliel. "The Wife of Abraham Lincoln." *Harper's Monthly Magazine* (September 1925).

Briggs, Emily Wilson. "Assassination Night, How Lincoln Met His Death." *Philadelphia Weekly Times* (Dec. 29, 1878).

Brinkerhoff, Roeliff. "Tragedy of an Age: An Eyewitness of Lincoln's Assassination," edited by Arthur M. Markowitz. *Journal of the Illinois State Historical Society*, Summer, 1973.

Brooks, Noah. "The Character and Religion of President Lincoln." Letter, May 10, 1865. Privately printed, 1919.

———. "The Close of Lincoln's Career." *Century Magazine* (May 1895).

———. "Personal Recollections of Abraham Lincoln." *Harper's New Monthly Magazine* (July 1895).

———. "Personal Reminiscences of Abraham Lincoln." *Scribner's Monthly* (February and March 1878).

Bullard, F. Lauriston. "Abraham Lincoln and George Ashmun." *New England Quarterly* (June 1946).

Carpenter, Francis B. "Mrs. Lincoln's Letter of Nov. 15, 1865." *Hearst's International Cosmopolitan* (February 1930).

Cate, Wirt Armistead. "Ford, the Booths and Lincoln's Assassination." *Emory University Quarterly* (March 1949).

Chamberlin, Earl T. "Four Men Who Bore Lincoln from Ford's Theatre Named." *New York Times* (Feb. 8, 1931).

Chandler, William E. Address in presenting statue of John P. Hale to the State of New Hampshire in front of Capitol. Concord, N. H.: Republican Press Assoc., 1892.

Chittenden, L. E. "The Hour of His Thanksgiving." *The Independent* (April 4, 1895).

Christian, Joseph. "The Lincoln I Knew." *McClure's Magazine* (January 1908).

Cole, Cornelius. "The Lincoln I Knew." *Collier's Weekly* (Feb. 10, 1923).

Colfax, Schuyler. "Life and Principles of Abraham Lincoln." Address given at South Bend, Ind., April 24, 1865. Philadelphia: J. B. Rodgers, 1865.

———. Report of his speech delivered in Central City, Colorado Territory, May 29, 1865. *Black Hawk Mining Journal* of Black Hawk, Colorado Territory (May 30, 1865).

Collins, Charles William. "Lincoln's Last Day." *Chicago Tribune Magazine* (Feb. 6, 1955).

Cooney, Charles F. "Lincoln's Lost Letters." *Lincoln Herald* (Spring 1970).

Corbett, Alexander. "She Saw Lincoln Shot." *Boston Sunday Globe* (April 11, 1915).

Crook, William H. "The Home Life of Abraham Lincoln." *Saturday Evening Post* (June 4, 1910).

———. "Lincoln As I Knew Him." Compiled and written down by Margarita Spalding Gerry. *Harper's Monthly Magazine* (December 1906 and June 1907).

________. "Lincoln's Last Day." *Harper's Monthly Magazine* (Sept. 1907).

Cuyler, John. "The Assassination of Abraham Lincoln." *Magazine of History* (March 1916).

Dana, Charles A. "Lincoln and His Cabinet." Lecture delivered before the New Haven Historical Society, March 10, 1896. Cleveland and New York: DeVinne Press, 1896.

________. "Lincoln and His Cabinet." *McClure's Magazine* (April 1898).

________. "Reminiscences of Abraham Lincoln." In Rice's *Reminiscences of Abraham Lincoln by Distinguished Men of His Time*. New York: North American Review, 1888.

DeMotte, William H. "The Assassination of Abraham Lincoln." *Journal of the Illinois State Historical Society* (October 1927).

Doherty, E. P. "Pursuit and Death of John Wilkes Booth." *Century Magazine* (January 1890).

Draper, Andrew Sloan. "Lincoln's Parable." *Harper's Weekly* (Oct. 26, 1907).

DuBarry, Helen A. "Eyewitness Account of Lincoln's Assassination." *Journal of the Illinois State Historical Society* (September 1946).

Dunn, Linda. "Restored Ford's Stirs Lincoln Memories." *Baltimore Sun* (May 29, 1967).

Faust, A. B. "Carl Bersch – Artist and Portrait Painter." *The American-German Review* (August 1944).

Ferguson, William J. "His Eyewitness Account." *Saturday Evening Post* (Feb. 12, 1927).

________. "I Saw Lincoln Shot!" *American Magazine* (August 1920).

________. "The Story of the Assassination." *The Independent* (April 4, 1895).

Field, Maunsell. "Last Moments of the President." *New York Times* (April 17, 1865).

Ford, John T. "Behind the Curtain of Conspiracy." *North American Review* (April, 1889).

Frear, James Archibald. "The Passing of Lincoln As Pictured by Corporal James Tanner." Remarks of the Hon. James A. Frear, Wisconsin, in the House of Representatives, June 1, 1926. Washington: Government Printing Office, 1926.

Fry, James B. "Reminiscences of Abraham Lincoln." In Rice's *Reminiscences of Abraham Lincoln by Distinguished Men of His Time*. New York: North American Review, 1888.

Gardner, Virginia. "A Girl of 1865 Tells of Seeing Lincoln Shot." *Chicago Tribune* (Feb. 12, 1936).

Gillette, Daniel. "The Last Days of Payne." *New York World* (April 3, 1892).

Gleason, D. H. L. "Conspiracy Against Lincoln." *Magazine of History* 13 (1914).

Gonzales, John Edward. "William Pitt Kellogg, Reconstruction Governor of Louisiana." *Louisiana Historical Quarterly* (April 1946).

Grover, Leonard. "Lincoln's Interest in the Theatre." *Century Magazine* (April 1909).

Hall, James O. "The Mystery of Lincoln's Guard." *Surratt Society News* (May 1982).

Harper, Helen Leale. "Lincoln's Last Night." *Daughters of the American Revolution Magazine* (February 1953).

Hay, John. "Life in the White House in Time of Lincoln." *Century Magazine* (November 1890).

Haynie, Edwin C. "At the Deathbed of Lincoln." *Century Magazine* (April 1896).

"He Saw the Tragedy of April, 1865." *National Republican* (Jan. 27, 1923).

Horton, H. Leavitt. "Mrs. Dixon's Letter to Her Sister, Mrs. Louisa Woods." *New England Chronicle*, no. 1 (1950).

"How Newspapers Reported the Assassination of President Lincoln." *Blumhaven Digest* (August 1957).

James, William. "The Night on Which Lincoln Died." *Lewis S. Hayden Abraham Lincoln Supplement*, 3 (1903).

Johnson, Arnold Burgess. "Recollections of Charles Sumner—Assassination of Abraham Lincoln." *Scribner's Monthly* (June 1875).

Kimmel, Stanley P. "Fatal Remissness of Lincoln's Guard Unpunished." *Washington Sunday Star* (Feb. 9, 1936).

King, Horatio. "Assassination of President Lincoln." *New England Magazine* (December 1893).

Knox, James Suydam. "A Son Writes of the Supreme Tragedy." *Saturday Review* (Feb. 11, 1956).

Kundhardt, Dorothy Meserve, and Kundhardt, Philip B., Jr. "Assassination!" *American Heritage* (April 1965).

Laird, Thomas A. "Booth Flourishes Dagger, Asserts This Eyewitness." Unidentified newspaper article. Assassination File, Louis A. Warren Lincoln Library, Fort Wayne, Ind.

Lattimer, John K. "Autopsy on Abraham Lincoln." *Journal of the American Medical Association* (Aug. 2, 1965).

________. "The Wound That Killed Lincoln." *Journal of the American Medical Association* (Feb. 15, 1964).

Laughlin, Clara E. "The Last Twenty-four Hours of Lincoln's Life." *Ladies' Home Journal* (February 1909).

________. "Our American Cousin." *McClure's Magazine* (December 1908).

Lawrence, John W. "An Unsung Song Prevented Panic When Lincoln Was Shot." American Press Association, 1912.

Leale, Charles A. "Lincoln's Last Hours." *Harper's Weekly* (Feb. 13, 1909).

———. "Lincoln's Last Hours." Address given before the Commandery of the State of New York, Military Order of the Loyal Legion of the U. S., New York City, at its February meeting, 1909.

*Library of Congress Information Bulletin*, Feb. 27 and June 18, 1976. "Lincoln Relics Examined."

*Lincoln Lore*. Published by the Lincoln National Life Insurance Co., Fort Wayne, Ind., as Bulletin of the Lincoln National Life Foundation, April 15, 1929–June, 1977; as Bulletin of the Louis A. Warren Lincoln Library and Museum July, 1977—. Published weekly through June, 1956; monthly since July, 1956.

"April 14, 1865." No. 105 (April 13, 1931).
"The New York Herald." No. 159 (April 25, 1932).
"Lincoln's Apparel, Head to Foot." No. 162 (May 16, 1932).
"A Personal Description of Abraham Lincoln." No. 270 (June 11, 1934).
"The White House—1861 to 1865." No. 335 (Sept. 9, 1935).
"Lincoln's Last Writing." No. 444 (Oct. 11, 1937).
"The Petersen House." No. 523 (April 17, 1939).
"The President's Office." No. 531 (June 12, 1939).
"Stanton at Lincoln's Bedside." No. 575 (April 15, 1940).
"Physicians at Lincoln's Bedside." No. 627 (April 14, 1941).
"Lincoln's Attitude Toward the Bible." No. 974 (Dec. 8, 1949).
"Assassination Directory." No. 1126 (Nov. 6, 1950).
"Lincoln's Last Recorded Words." No. 1299 (Feb. 1, 1954).
"The New York Herald, April 15, 1865." No. 1425 (November 1956).
"Schuyler Colfax—Lincoln Lecturer." No. 1475 (January 1961).
"Lincoln's Bank Checks." No. 1485 (November 1961).
"Was Andrew Johnson Present at Lincoln's Bedside?" No. 1517 (July 1964).
"The Clothing Worn by President Lincoln on the Night of His Assassination," No. 1569 (November 1968) and No. 1570 (December 1968).
"Mrs. Dixon's Letter to Her Sister, Mrs. Louisa Wood." No. 1587 (May 1970).
"Major Rathbone and Miss Harris Guests of the Lincoln's in the Ford's Theatre Box." No. 1602 (August 1971).
"The Contents of Lincoln's Pockets at Ford's Theatre." No. 1669 (March 1977).
"The Last Book Lincoln Read." No. 1704 (February 1980).

"Lincoln Relics Examined." *Library of Congress Information Bulletin* (Feb. 27 and June 18, 1976).

"Lincoln's Death—Eyewitness Account." *The Collector* (April 1950).

Loux, Arthur F. "The Mystery of the Telegraph Interruption." *Lincoln Herald* (Winter 1979).

McBride, Robert. "Lincoln's Bodyguard." *Indiana Historical Society Publication*, no. 1 (1911).

MacCulloch, Campbell. "This Man Saw Lincoln Shot." *Good Housekeeping* (February 1927).

McMurtry, R. Gerald. "The Health of Abraham Lincoln." *Everybody's Health* (February 1933).

________. "A Memento of Lincoln's Assassination." *Lincoln Herald* (June 1947).

Maynard, George C. "That Evening at Ford's." *National Republican* (n.d.).

Morris, James R. "Assassination of Abraham Lincoln." *Ohio Archaeological and Historical Publications* (January 1921).

Morrow, Honore Willisie. "Lincoln's Last Day Described in Letters of His Wife."*Hearst's International-Cosmopolitan* (February 1930).

Moss, M. Helen Palmer. "Lincoln and John Wilkes Booth As Seen on the Day of the Assassination." *Century Magazine* (April 1909).

Munroe, Seaton. "Recollections of Lincoln's Assassination." *North American Review* (April 1896).

*National Republican*, Jan. 27, 1923. "He Saw the Tragedy of April, 1865."

Neill, Edward D. "Abraham Lincoln and His Mailbag." Documents of Chaplain Neill, edited by T. Blegen. Minnesota Historical Society.

________."Reminiscences of the Last Year of President Lincoln's Life." In *Glimpses of the Nation's Struggle*, a series of papers read before the Minnesota Commandery of the Military Order of the Loyal Legion of the U. S., ser. 1, St. Paul Book and Stationery Co., 1887.

Nicolay, John G. "Lincoln's Personal Appearance." *Century Magazine* (October 1891).

Parker, Owen W. "The Assassination and Gunshot Wound of President Abraham Lincoln." *Minnesota Medicine* (February 1948).

Parsons, Lewis B. "General Parsons Writes of Lincoln's Death in Letters to His Mother." *Journal of the Illinois State Historical Society* (Winter 1951).

Peckham, Howard. "James Tanner's Account of Lincoln's Death." *Abraham Lincoln Quarterly* (December 1924).

________. "Rare Letter on Lincoln Given Library." *Michigan Alumnus* (Jan. 16, 1937).

Pendel, Thomas. "What Tom Pendel Saw, April 14, 1865." *Magazine of History*, extra no. 133 (1927).

Perley, M. Elizabeth. "The Last of the Bodyguard." *The Christian Advocate* (May 2, 1935).

———. "Lincoln's Death Laid to Absence of Guard." *Chicago Daily News* (Feb. 5, 1924).

Phillips, Charlotte A. "A Local Man Saw Lincoln Killed; Retells Story." *San Diego Union* (Feb. 10, 1935).

Pratt, Harry E. "Lincolniana in the Illinois State Historical Library." *Journal of the Illinois State Historical Society* (1933).

Read, Harry. "A Hand to Hold While Dying." *Lincoln Herald* (Spring 1977).

Reynolds, Lewis Gardner. "Lincoln's Last Night." *Washington Star* (April 16, 1933).

Reynolds, Ruth. "Seventy-five Years Ago Tonight, Lincoln Was Shot." *New York Sunday News* (April 14, 1940).

Rietveld, Ronald D. "An Eyewitness Account of the Assassination of Abraham Lincoln." *Civil War History* (March 1976).

Rockwell, A. E. "At the Deathbed of Abraham Lincoln." *Century Magazine* (June 1890).

Ruggles, M. B. "Pursuit and Death of John Wilkes Booth." *Century Magazine* (January 1890).

Sanford, Albert B. "A New and True Story of Lincoln." *Municipal Facts* (January-February 1927).

Seward, Frederick W. "Recollections of Lincoln's Last Hours." *Leslie's Weekly* (Feb. 4, 1909).

Seymour, Samuel J. "I Saw Lincoln Shot." *Amer. Weekly* (Feb. 7, 1954).

Shaw, E. R. "The Assassination of Lincoln." *McClure's* (Dec. 1908).

Shephard, Julia Adelaide. "Lincoln's Assassination Told by an Eye Witness." Letter, April 16, 1865. *Century Magazine* (April 1909).

Sherman, Thomas H. "Saw Assassin Leap From Box to Stage." *New York World* (Feb. 12, 1926).

Smith, Goodwin. "The Death of President Lincoln." *Magazine of History*, no. 185 (1933).

Sprague, Ver Lynn. "Mary Lincoln—Accessory to Murder." *Lincoln Herald* (Winter 1979).

Stewart, Thomas Dole. "An Anthropologist Looks at Lincoln." *Annual Report of Smithsonian Institution* (1952).

Stewart, William M. "A Senator of the Sixties." Edited by George Rockwell Brown. *Saturday Evening Post* (Feb. 15, 1908).

Stimmel, Smith. "Experiences as a Member of President Lincoln's Bodyguard, 1863–1865." *North Dakota Historical Quarterly* (Jan. 1927).

Stoddard, William O. "Face to Face with Lincoln," ed. by William O. Stoddard, Jr. *Atlantic Monthly* (March 1925).

Storey, Moorfield. "Dickens, Stanton, Sumner and Storey." *Atlantic Monthly* (April 1930).

Taft, Charles Sabin. "Abraham Lincoln's Last Hours." *Century Magazine* (February 1895).

_______. "Last Hours of Abraham Lincoln." *Philadelphia Medical and Surgical Reporter* (April 22, 1865).

Tanner, James H. "At the Deathbed of Abraham Lincoln." *National Republic* (August 1926).

Tarbell, Ida M. "The Death of Abraham Lincoln." *McClure's* (Dec. 1896).

Taylor, W. H. "A New Story of the Assassination of Lincoln." *Leslie's Weekly* (March 26, 1908).

Todd, George. "Eyewitness Describes Lincoln's Assassination in Letter to Brother." *Baltimore and Ohio Magazine* (February 1926).

Trefousse, Hans L. "Belated Revelations of the Assassination Committee." *Lincoln Herald* (Spring–Summer 1956).

Tucker, Louis Leonard. "Eyewitness to Lincoln's Last Hours." *Yankee* (April 1979).

Turner, Justin G., ed. "April 14, 1865: A Soldier's View." *Lincoln Herald* (Winter 1964).

Van Ark, Dorothy Hemenway. "New Light on Lincoln's Death." *Saturday Evening Post* (Feb. 12, 1944).

Weik, Jesse W. "A New Story of Lincoln's Assassination." *Century Magazine* (February 1913).

Welles, Gideon. "The Death of Abraham Lincoln." *Atlantic Monthly* (November 1909).

_______. "Lincoln and Johnson." *The Galaxy* (April 1872).

Wilgus, C. W. S. "The Lincoln Tragedy." Interview with A. C. Richards, former Superintendent of Police, Washington, D. C. Ravenna, Ohio, *Republican* (April 19, 1906).

Woods, George B. "Assassination of President Lincoln." *Magazine of History*, extra no. 153 (1929).

Wright, Annie F. F. "The Assassination of Abraham Lincoln." *Magazine of History* (February 1909).

Yates, Richard. "Abraham Lincoln." Address delivered in the House of Representatives, Feb. 12, 1921. *Congressional Record-House* (1921).

## IV. Books

Abbott, Abbott A. *The Assassination and Death of Abraham Lincoln*. New York: American News, 1865.

Angle, Paul M., ed. *Abraham Lincoln, by Some Men Who Knew Him*. Chicago: American House, 1950.

_______, ed., with the assistance of Richard G. Case. *A Portrait of Abraham Lincoln in Letters of His Eldest Son*. Chicago Historical Society, 1968.

*Appleton's Cyclopedia of American Biography*, ed. by James Grant Wilson and John Fiske. 6 vols. New York: D. Appleton, 1888–1889.

Arnold, Isaac. *The History of Abraham Lincoln and the Overthrow of Slavery*. Chicago: Clarke & Co., 1866.

________. *The Life of Abraham Lincoln*. Chicago: Jensen, McClurg & Co., 1885.

________. *Sketch of the Life of Abraham Lincoln*. New York: J. B. Bachelder, 1869.

Arnold, Samuel Bland. *Defence and Prison Experiences of a Lincoln Conspirator*. Hattiesburg, Miss.: The Book Farm, 1943.

*Assassination and History of the Conspiracy*. Cincinnati: J. R. Hawley & Co., 1865.

Baker, Lafayette C. *History of the United States Secret Service*. Philadelphia: L. C. Baker, 1867.

Barrett, Joseph H. *Abraham Lincoln and His Presidency*. 2 vols. Cincinnati: Robert Clarke & Co., 1904.

Barton, William E. *The Great Good Man*. Indianapolis: Bobbs–Merrill, 1927.

________. *The Life of Abraham Lincoln*. 2 vols. Indianapolis: Bobbs–Merrill, 1925.

________. *President Lincoln*. 2 vols. Indianapolis: Bobbs–Merrill, 1933.

Basler, Roy P. Foreword for reprint edition of *Assassination and History of the Conspiracy*. New York: Hobbs, Dorman & Co., 1965.

________, ed., with Pratt, Marion Dolores, and Dunlap, Lloyd A., asst. eds. *The Collected Works of Abraham Lincoln*. For the Abraham Lincoln Assoc., Springfield, Ill. 8 vols and index. New Brunswick: Rutgers University Press, 1953–1955.

Bates, David Homer. *Lincoln in the Telegraph Office*. New York: Century, 1907.

Beale, Howard K., ed. *The Diary of Edward Bates*. Washington, D. C.: Government Printing Office, 1933.

Benjamin, Marcus, ed. *Washington During War Time*. Washington, D. C.: National Tribune, 1902.

Beveridge, Alfred J. *Abraham Lincoln*. Vol. 3. Boston and New York: Houghton Mifflin, 1928.

Binns, Henry Bryan. *Abraham Lincoln*. New York: E. P. Dutton, 1907.

Bishop, Jim. *The Day Lincoln Was Shot*. New York: Harper & Bros., 1955.

Boatner, Mark N., III. *The Civil War Dictionary*. New York: David McKay, 1959.

Borreson, Ralph. *When Lincoln Died*. New York: Appleton–Century, 1965.

Boyd, Andrew. *A Memorial Lincoln Bibliography*. Albany, N.Y.: Andrew Boyd, 1870.

Brinkerhoff, Roeliff. *Recollections of a Lifetime*. Cincinnati: Robert Clarke & Co., 1900.

Brooks, Noah. *Abraham Lincoln*. New York: G. P. Putnam's Sons, 1888.

________. *Abraham Lincoln and the Downfall of American Slavery.* New York: G. P. Putnam's Sons, 1894.

________. *Abraham Lincoln, the Nation's Leader in the Great Struggle.* New York: G. P. Putnam's Sons, 1909.

________. *Washington in Lincoln's Time.* New York: Century, 1896.

Browne, Francis F. *The Everyday Life of Abraham Lincoln.* New York and St. Louis: N. D. Thompson, 1886.

Bryan, George S. *The Great American Myth.* New York: Carrick & Evans, 1940.

Buckingham, John E. *Reminiscences and Souvenirs of the Assassination of Abraham Lincoln.* Washington: Press of R. H. Derby, 1894.

Carpenter, Francis B. *The Inner Life of Abraham Lincoln.* New York: Hurd and Houghton, 1868.

Chapman, Ervin. *Latest Light on Abraham Lincoln.* New York: Fleming H. Revell, 1917.

Chittenden, L. E. *Personal Reminiscences, 1840–1890.* New York: Richmond, Groscup, 1893.

________. *Recollections of President Lincoln and His Administration.* New York: Harper & Bros., 1892.

Clark, Allen G. *Abraham Lincoln in the National Capital.* Washington: W. F. Roberts, 1925.

Clarke, Asia Booth. *The Unlocked Book.* New York: G. P. Putnam's Sons, 1938.

Coggeshall, E. W. *The Assassination of Lincoln.* Chicago: Walter M. Hill, 1920.

Cole, Cornelius. *Memoirs of Cornelius Cole.* New York: McLoughlin Bros., 1908.

Cottrell, John. *Anatomy of an Assassination.* New York: Funk & Wagnalls, 1966.

Creahan, John. *The Life of Laura Keene.* Philadelphia: Rodgers Printing, 1897.

Crispin, William Frost. *Abraham Lincoln, the First American.* Akron, Ohio: 1911.

Crook, William H. *Memories of the White House.* Compiled and edited by Henry Rood. Boston: Little, Brown & Co., 1911.

________. *Through Five Administrations.* Compiled and edited by Margarita Spalding Gerry. New York: Harper & Bros., 1910.

Crosby, Frank. *Life of Abraham Lincoln.* New York: P. F. Collier & Son, 1900.

Curtis, William Elery. *The True Abraham Lincoln.* Philadelphia: J. B. Lippincott, 1903.

Dana, Charles A. *Recollections of the Civil War.* New York: D. Appleton & Co., 1898.

Daugherty, James. *Abraham Lincoln.* New York: Viking, 1943.

DeWitt, David M. *The Assassination of Abraham Lincoln and Its Expiation*. New York: Macmillan, 1909.

*Dictionary of American Biography*, ed. by Allen Johnson and Dumas Malone. Published under the auspices of the American Council of Learned Societies. Vols. 1–20. New York: Charles Scribner's Sons, 1928–1936.

Donald, David. *Charles Sumner and the Rights of Men*. New York: Alfred A. Knopf, 1970.

———. *Inside Lincoln's Cabinet*. New York: Longmans, Green & Co., 1954.

Eisenschiml, Otto. *Why Was Lincoln Murdered?* New York: Grosset & Dunlap; Boston: Little, Brown & Co., 1937.

*Encyclopedia Americana*, International Edition © 1973. "Trent Affair."

Farwell, Leonard J. *Western Pioneer Life*. Sketch of the career of the Hon. Leonard J. Farwell, ex-Governor of Wisconsin, by an old friend. Chicago: Alexander Duncan, 1871.

Ferguson, William J. *I Saw Booth Shoot Lincoln*. New York: Houghton Mifflin, 1930.

Field, Maunsell. *Memories of Many Men and Some Women*. New York: Harper & Bros., 1874.

Flower, Frank A. *Edwin McMasters Stanton, the Autocrat of the Rebellion, Emancipation and Reconstruction*. New York: W. W. Wilson, 1905.

Forrester, Izola. *This One Mad Act*. Boston: Hale, Cushman & Flint, 1937.

Gilmore, Hugh R., Jr. *Medical Aspects of the Assassination of Abraham Lincoln*. London: L. Staples, Ltd., 1954.

Gobright, Lawrence A. *Recollections of Men and Things in Washington During the Third of a Century*. Philadelphia: Claxton, Remsen & Haffelfinger, 1869.

Grant, Ulysses S. *Personal Memoirs of U. S. Grant*. Vol. 2. New York: Charles L. Webster & Co., 1886.

Greenbie, Sydney, and Barstow, Marjorie. *Anna Ella Carroll and Abraham Lincoln*. Manchester, Me.: Falmouth, 1952.

Hall, Daniel. *Addresses Commemorative of Abraham Lincoln and John P. Hale*. Concord, N. H.: Republican Press Assoc., 1892.

Hammond, Harold. *A Commoner's Judge*. Introduction by Allan Nevins. Boston: Christopher, 1954.

———, ed. *Diary of a Union Lady*. Foreword by Allan Nevins. New York: Funk & Wagnalls, 1962.

Harnsberger, Caroline Thomas. *The Lincoln Treasury*. Chicago: Wilcox & Follett, 1950.

Harris, Thomas Mealey. *Assassination of Lincoln*. Boston: American Citizen, 1892.

Hay, John. *Addresses of John Hay*. Essay Index Reprint Series. Freeport, N. Y.: Books for Libraries Press, 1970.

________. *Lincoln and the Civil War in the Diaries and Letters of John Hay*, selected and with an Introduction by Tyler Dennett. New York: Dodd, Mead & Co., 1939.

Heitman, Francis B. *Historical Register and Dictionary of the United States Army*. 2 vols. Government Printing Office, 1903.

Helm, Katherine. *The True Story of Mary, Wife of Lincoln*. New York: Harper & Bros., 1928.

Herndon, William H., and Weik, Jesse W. *Abraham Lincoln, the True Story of a Great Life*. 2 vols. New York: D. Appleton & Co., 1906.

________, and ________. *Herndon's Life of Lincoln*. Cleveland and New York: World Publishing, 1949.

Hertz, Emanuel. *Abraham Lincoln, a New Portrait*. New York: Horace Liveright, 1931.

________. *The Hidden Lincoln*. New York: Viking Press, 1938.

Hobson, J. T. *Footprints of Abraham Lincoln*. Dayton, Ohio: Otterbein, 1909.

Hollister, O. J. *Life of Schuyler Colfax*. New York: Funk & Wagnalls, 1888.

Keckley, Elizabeth. *Behind the Scenes*. New York: G. W. Carleton & Co., 1868.

Kimball, Ivory George. *Recollections from a Busy Life*. Washington: Carnaham Press, 1912.

Kimmel, Stanley F. *The Mad Booths of Maryland*. Indianapolis: Bobbs-Merrill, 1940.

________. *Mr. Lincoln's Washington*. New York: Coward-McCann, 1957.

Koch, Freda Postle. *Colonel Coggeshall – The Man Who Saved Lincoln*. Columbus, Ohio: PoKo, 1985.

Kundhardt, Dorothy Meserve, and Kundhardt, Philip B., Jr. *Twenty Days*. New York: Harper & Row, 1965.

Lamon, Ward Hill. *The Life of Abraham Lincoln*. Boston: James R. Osgood & Co., 1872.

________. *Recollections of Abraham Lincoln, 1847–1865*, ed. by Dorothy Lamon Teillard. Washington: Dorothy Lamon Teillard, 1911.

Lattimer, John. *Kennedy and Lincoln*. New York: Harcourt Brace Jovanovich, 1980.

Laughlin, Clara E. *The Death of Lincoln*. New York: Doubleday, Page & Co., 1909.

Leiber, Francis. *Martyr's Memorial*. New York: American News, 1865.

Lewis, Lloyd. *Myths After Lincoln*. New York: Harcourt, Brace & Co., 1929.

Lomask, Milton. *Andrew Johnson, President on Trial*. New York: Farrar, Straus & Cudahy, 1960.

Luthin, Richard H. *The Real Abraham Lincoln*. Englewood Cliffs, N.J.: Prentice Hall, 1960.

Lyford, James Otis. *Life of Edward Henry Rollins*. Boston: D. Estes & Co., 1906.

McBride, Robert N. *Lincoln's Body Guard, the Union Light Guard of Ohio*. Indianapolis: Robert N. McBride, 1908.

Macartney, Charles E. *Abraham Lincoln and His Cabinet*. New York: Scribner's, 1931.

McClure, Stanley W. *Ford's Theatre and the House Where Lincoln Died*. Washington, D. C.: U. S. National Park Service, 1969.

McCormack, Thomas J., ed. *Memoirs of Gustave Koerner*. Cedar Rapids, Ia.: Torch, 1909.

McCulloch, Hugh. *Men and Measures of Half a Century*. New York: Charles Scribner's Sons, 1888.

Mahoney, Ella V. *Sketches of Tudor Hall and the Booth Family*. Belair, Md.: 1925.

Martin, Edward W. *The Life and Public Services of Schuyler Colfax*. Chicago: P. Garrett & Co., 1868.

Mearns, David C. *The Lincoln Papers*. 2 vols. Garden City, N. Y.: Doubleday & Co., 1948.

Milton, George Fort. *The Age of Hate*. New York: Coward–McCann, 1930.

Moore, Guy W. *The Case of Mrs. Surratt*. Norman: University of Oklahoma Press, 1954.

Morris, B. F., comp. *Memorial Record of the Nation's Tribute to Abraham Lincoln*. Washington, D. C.: W. H. and O. H. Morrison, 1865.

Mudd, Nettie. *Life of Samuel A. Mudd*. New York: Neale, 1906.

*National Cyclopedia of American Biography*. Vols. 1–14. New York: James T. White, 1898–1917.

Neely, Mark E., Jr. *The Abraham Lincoln Encyclopedia*. New York: McGraw–Hill, 1982.

Nicolay, Helen. *Personal Traits of Abraham Lincoln*. New York: Century, 1912.

Nicolay, John G. *A Short Life of Abraham Lincoln*. New York: Century, 1902.

————, and Hay, John. *Abraham Lincoln: A History*. 10 vols. New York: Century, 1890.

————, and ————, eds. *Complete Works of Abraham Lincoln*. 12 vols. New York: Francis D. Tandy, 1905.

Oates, Stanley. *With Malice Toward None*. New York: Harper & Row, 1976.

Oldroyd, Osborn H. *The Assassination of Abraham Lincoln.* Washington, D. C.: O. H. Oldroyd, 1901.

_______. *The Lincoln Memorial.* Chicago: Gem, 1883.

Olszewski, George J. *Restoration of Ford's Theatre.* Washington, D. C.: U. S. Department of Interior, National Park Service, Government Printing Office, 1963.

Pendel, Thomas. *Thirty-six Years in the White House.* Washington: Neale, 1902.

Peterson, T. B. *The Trial of the Alleged Assassins and Conspirators at Washington City, D. C., in May and June, 1865.* Philadelphia: T. B. Peterson & Bros., 1865.

Piatt, Don. *Memories of Men Who Saved the Union.* Chicago: Belford, Clarke & Co., 1887.

Pierce, Edward Lillie. *Memoirs and Letters of Charles Sumner.* Boston: Roberts Bros., 1877, 1893.

Pitman, Benn, comp. *The Assassination of President Lincoln and the Trial of the Conspirators.* Cincinnati: Moore, Wilstach & Baldwin, 1865. Facsimile edition with introduction by Philip Van Dorn Stern. New York: Funk & Wagnalls, 1954.

Poore, Ben Perley. *The Conspiracy Trial for the Murder of the President.* 3 vols. Boston: J. E. Tilton, 1865–1866.

_______. *Perley's Reminiscences of Sixty Years in the National Metropolis.* 2 vols. Philadelphia: Hubbard Bros., 1886.

Porter, Horace. *Campaigning with Grant.* New York: Century, 1907.

Pratt, Fletcher. *Stanton, Lincoln's Secretary of War.* New York: W. W. Norton & Co., 1953.

Pratt, Harry E. *Concerning Mr. Lincoln.* Springfield, Ill.: Abraham Lincoln Assoc., 1944.

Randall, James G., and Currant, Richard N. *Last Full Measure.* New York: Dodd, Mead & Co., 1955.

Randall, Ruth Painter. *Mary Lincoln.* Boston: Little, Brown & Co., 1953.

Rankin, Henry B. *Intimate Character Sketches of Abraham Lincoln.* Philadelphia: J. B. Lippincott & Co., 1924.

Raymond, Henry J. *The Life and Public Services of Abraham Lincoln.* New York: Derby & Miller, 1865.

Reid, Whitelaw. *Ohio in the Civil War.* Vol. 2. Cincinnati: Moore, Wilstach & Baldwin, 1868.

Rice, Allen Thorndike, ed. *Reminiscences of Abraham Lincoln by Distinguished Men of His Time.* New York: North American Review, 1888.

Richards, D. J., *The Story of Abraham Lincoln's Assassination.* Los Angeles: Cresent, n.d.

Riddle, Albert Gallatin. *Recollections of War Times, Reminiscences of Men and Events in Washington, 1860–1865*. New York: G. P. Putnam's Sons, 1895.

Roscoe, Theodore. *The Web of Conspiracy*. Englewood Cliffs, N. J.: Prentice Hall, 1959.

Ross, Ishbel. *The President's Wife*. New York: G. P. Putnam's Sons, 1973.

Sandburg, Carl. *Abraham Lincoln, the War Years*. Vol. 4. New York: Harcourt, Brace & Co., 1939.

———, and Angle, Paul. *Mary Lincoln, Wife and Widow*. New York: Harcourt, Brace & Co., 1932.

Searcher, Victor. *The Farewell to Lincoln*. Nashville: Abingdon, 1965.

Segal, Charles M. *Conversations with Lincoln*. New York: G. P. Putnam's Sons, 1961.

Seitz, Don C. *Lincoln, the Politician*. New York: Coward–McCann, 1931.

Seward, Frederick W. *Reminiscences of a War-Time Statesman and Diplomat*. New York: G. P. Putnam's Sons, 1916.

———. *Seward at Washington, 1861–1872*. New York: Derby & Miller, 1891.

Shea, John D. G., ed. *The Lincoln Memorial: A Record of the Life, Assassination and Obsequies of the Martyred President*. New York: Bruce & Huntington, 1865.

Shutes, Milton. *Lincoln and the Doctors*. New York: Pioneer Press, 1933.

Simon, John Y., ed. *The Personal Memoirs of Julia Dent Grant (Mrs. U. S. Grant)*. New York: G. P. Putnam's Sons, 1975.

Starr, John W., Jr. *Further Light on Lincoln's Last Day*. Harrisburg, Pa.: Privately printed, 1930.

———. *Lincoln's Last Day*. New York: Frederick A. Stokes, 1922.

———. *New Light on Lincoln's Last Day*. Harrisburg, Pa.: Privately printed, 1926.

Stephenson, Nathaniel Wright. *Lincoln*. Indianapolis: Bobbs–Merrill, 1922.

Stevens, Walter B. *A Reporter's Lincoln*. St. Louis: Missouri State Historical Society, 1916.

Stewart, William M. *Abraham Lincoln, the Man and the War President*. New York: Fords, Howard & Hulbert, 1888.

———. *Reminiscences of William M. Stewart*, ed. by George Rothwell Brown. Washington, D. C.: Neale, 1908.

Stoddard, William O. *Abraham Lincoln, the True Story of a Great Life*. New York: Fords, Howard & Hulbert, 1884.

———. *Inside the White House in War Times*. New York: Charles L. Webster & Co., 1890.

Swanberg, W. A. *First Blood*. New York: Charles Scribner's Sons, 1957.

Tarbell, Ida M. *The Life of Abraham Lincoln*. 2 vols. New York: McClure, Phillips & Co., 1904.

Thayer, William R. *The Life and Letters of John Hay*. Vol. 1. Boston: Houghton Mifflin, 1915.

Thomas, Benjamin. *Abraham Lincoln*. New York: Alfred A. Knopf, 1952.

________, and Hyman, Harold M. *Stanton: The Life and Times of Lincoln's Secretary of War*. New York: Alfred A. Knopf, 1962.

Townsend, George A. *The Life, Crime and Capture of John Wilkes Booth*. New York: Dick & Fitzgerald, 1865.

*Trial of John Surratt in the Criminal Court for the District of Columbia*. 2 vols. Washington, D. C.: French and Richardson; Philadelphia: J. B. Lippincott & Co., 1867.

Truett, Randle Bond. *Lincoln, the Story of the Assassination*. Arlington, Va.: 1949.

Turner, Julian, and Turner, Linda Levitt. *Mary Todd Lincoln, Her Life and Letters*. New York: Alfred A. Knopf, 1972.

U. S. Congress. *Assassination of Lincoln. Report*. Washington, D. C.: 1866.

________. House. *Impeachment Investigation*. House Report no. 7. 40th Cong., 1st sess. Washington, 1867.

U. S. Department of State. *The Assassination of Abraham Lincoln*. Washington, D. C.: Government Printing Office, 1866.

U. S. War Department. *War of the Rebellion: A Compilation of the Official Records of the Union and Confederate Armies*. 128 vols. Washington, D. C.: Government Printing Office, 1880–1901. Unless otherwise noted, all references cited are from Series 1.

Ward, William Hayes. Introduction to *Tributes to Abraham Lincoln from His Associates: Reminiscences of Soldiers, Statesmen and Citizens*. New York: Thomas Y. Crowell & Co., 1895.

Warden, Robert Bruce. *An Account of the Private Life and Public Services of Salmon P. Chase*. Cincinnati: Wilstach, Baldwin & Co., 1874.

Warner, Ezra J. *Generals in Blue*. Baton Rouge: Louisiana State University Press, 1964.

Weichmann, Louis J. *A True History of the Assassination of Abraham Lincoln and of the Conspiracy of 1865*, ed. by Floyd E. Risvold. New York: Alfred A. Knopf, 1975.

Welles, Gideon. *Diary*. 3 vols, ed. by Howard K. Beale, assisted by Alan W. Brownsword. New York: W. W. Norton & Co., 1960.

Whipple, Wayne. *The Story Life of Lincoln*. Philadelphia: J. C. Winston, 1908.

Whiteman, Maxwell. Biographical introduction to *While Lincoln Lay Dying*. A facsimile reproduction of the first testimony taken in connection with the assassination of Abraham Lincoln as recorded by Corporal James Tanner. Philadelphia: Union League of Philadelphia, 1968.

Wilson, Francis. *John Wilkes Booth*. Boston: Houghton Mifflin, 1929.

Wilson, Rufus Rockwell. *Intimate Memories of Lincoln*. Elmira, N. Y.: Primavera, 1945.

________. *Lincoln Among His Friends*. Caldwell, Ida.: Caxton Printers, 1942.

Woods, George. *Essays, Sketches and Stories Selected from the Writings of G. B. Woods*. Boston: James R. Osgood & Co., 1873.

## V. Newspapers, Journals, and Periodicals (other than those named in III)

*Boston Herald*
*Boston Post*
*Boston Weekly Advertiser*
*Brooklyn Eagle*
*Burrell's Washington (Ia.) Press*
*California Daily Register*
*Chicago Record-Herald*
*Cleveland Plain Dealer*
*Danville (Ill.) Commercial News*
*Elgin (Ill.) Courier News*
*Elizabethtown (S.D.) News*
*Frank Leslie's Illustrated Newspaper*
*Harrisburg (Pa.) Evening News*
*Kansas City Star*
*Los Angeles Times*
*Madison (Ind.) Courier*
*Minneapolis Journal*
*New Bedford (Conn.) Standard*
*New York Herald*
*New York Herald Tribune*
*New York Post*
*New York Tribune*
*Oakland (Calif.) Tribune*
*Pensacola (Fla.) Journal*
*Philadelphia Bulletin*
*Philadelphia Inquirer*
*Philadelphia Public Ledger*
*Portsmouth (N. H.) Herald*
*The Presbyterian*
*Reading (Pa.) Eagle*

*Richmond Times–Dispatch*
*Richmond Whig*
*St. Louis Globe–Democrat*
*Sioux City Journal*
*Sioux Falls (S. D.) Argus*
*Springfield (Mass.) Republican*
*Worcester (Mass.) Telegram*

## VI. Press Associations and Syndicates

*Associated Press (AP)*
*International News Service (INS)*
*Newspaper Enterprise Association (NEA)*
*North American Newspaper Alliance*
*United News*
*United Press (UP)*

# Index

*Bold numbers indicate illustrations.*


Abbott, Dr. Ezra W. (physician at bedside) 146, 147, 151, 153

Anderson, Mary Jane (renter behind theatre) 68, 70

Anderson, Major General Robert 32

Armstrong, Mrs. Nelson (of play staff) 126

Arnold, Congressman Isaac N. 59

Arnold, Samuel (kidnap conspirator) 66

Ashmun, George, of Massachusetts 56–57, **58**, 59

Atzerodt, George A. (conspirator) 66, 67, 79, 134

audience reaction to Booth's shot 104, 107, 109, 113, 114

Augur, General Christopher C. (Washington Department commander) 131, 136, 142

Ballauf, Daniel (present at play) 109

Bangs, C. C. (volunteer messenger) 138

Barnes, Dr. Joseph K. (Surgeon General of the Army) 137, 151, 153, 155, 157; examines Lincoln, 147; on autopsy 168

Bates, David Homer (manager, War Telegraph Office) 140

Bedee, Captain Edwin E. (Lincoln bearer) 124; trouble over lost dispatch 166–67

"Beggar's Opera" 41

Berghaus, Albert (artist for *Frank Leslie's Illustrated Newspaper*) 105, 109, 127, 131, 149–50

Bersch, Carl (painter of *Lincoln Borne by Loving Hands*) 128–29

*Black Hawk Mining Journal* 21

Blakeslee, Francis D. (saw Lincoln at *Montauk*) 49

Bolton, Lieutenant John T. (present at play) 106, 107; climbs to box 119; clears way for bearers 124; sends for cavalry 135

Booth, Asia *See* Clarke, Asia Booth

Booth, Edwin (brother of John Wilkes Booth) 63, 65

Booth, John Wilkes **64**; illegitimacy, early characteristics, influence of gypsy 63; determination to be remembered 64–65; skills as horseman and swordsman, amours, attitude toward slavery, presence at Harper's Ferry 65; services to South and plan to kidnap Lincoln 66; incensed at Lincoln's last speech, decision to murder 66; interrupts business conversation at Glover's 66–67; first movements on April 14 67; leaves note for Vice President Johnson, meets Thomas R. Florence, sees Michael O'Laughlin, visits Mrs. Surratt, gets mail at Ford's 68; orders saddle horse 69; tries again to see Johnson, talks to Mrs. Surratt, checks stable behind theatre, talks to lady, observes preparations for President party at Ford's, takes drink at Taltavull's 70; sees James Ford 71; suggestions for Joseph Hazelton 76; gets stationery from Henry Merrick, writes letter 76–77; meets Colonel C. F. Cobb, gets horse, chats with Charles Warwick, James Maddox and James Ferguson 77; gives letter to Matthews 77–78; rides after Grant, learns of latter's departure, meets John Devenay 78; has tea at hotel, makes meaningful remarks to George Bunker and William Withers and meets with fellow conspirators 79; in and out of theatre before murder 93–94; asks time of night 94; final drink order 96; weapons 99; observed approaching state box 98–100; inside passage 100; shoots President, wounds Major Rathbone, drops to stage 102; describes action in diary 105; crosses stage 107; recognized 109, 114; wounds William Withers 112; hits and kicks Peanuts John, escapes down alley 112; shot at Garratt's barn 134; identified as assassin 141, 145

Booth, Junius (brother of John Wilkes Booth) 65

Boozang, James (newspaper messenger boy) 145

Boser, Joseph (unidentified witness) 146

Brinkerhoff, Captain Roeliff (present at play): sees Booth enter corridor 99; describes actor's descent 106; 124

Brooks, Noah (*Sacramento Union* correspondent) 89; invited to replace John Nicolay 53; declines theatre invitation 54; comments on Lincoln's dread of "scene" 84

Brown, Mrs. William A. *See* Porterfield, Miss

Browning, former Senator Orville H. 45; fails on late call to see Lincoln 59–60

Browning, William (Vice President's secretary) 67

Bruce, Sir Frederick (new British minister) 40, 59

Buckingham, John E. (night doorkeeper at theatre) 73, 94, 96, 117, 118

Bunker, George (National Hotel clerk) 73, 79

Bunn, John W. (Springfield merchant) 15

Burke, Ned (Lincoln coachman) 60

Burroughs, Joseph ("Peanuts John") (chore boy at Ford's) 72, 78, 93–94, 111, 117

Butt, Harley (present at play) 113

Byrne, Charles Francis (actor) 117, 123

cabinet, Lincoln's: characterized 31; April 14 meeting 31–38

Campbell, Judge John A. (Confederacy's Assistant Secretary of War) 22, 23

Carland, Louis J. (Ford's former costumer): testimony at John Surratt trial 95–96

Carpenter, Francis B. (artist) 14, 89

Cartter, Chief Justice David Kellogg (of District Supreme Court) 139; takes testimony at Petersen house 142

Chase, Chief Justice Salmon P. 155

Chittenden, L. E. (Register of Treasury) 42

Clark, William T. (in whose room Lincoln died) 131, 151

Clarke, Asia Booth (sister of John Wilkes Booth) 63, 64, 65, 66

Cloughly, Alfred (gave testimony) 142–143

Cobb, C. F. (Booth schoolmate) 77

Coggeshall, Colonel William T. (editor, *Ohio State Journal*) 46

Cole, Congressman Cornelius 3, 19

Colfax, Schuyler (Speaker of the House) 3, 17, 21; conferences with Lincoln 19–23, 56–57; unforgiving toward Rebel leaders 20; speeches in West 21–22; declines theatre invitation 57; leaves Petersen house 153

Conness, Senator John 138, 143

Cooper, Robert (artilleryman) 94; supports Sergeant Dye's testimony 95

Corey, John (Lincoln bearer) 124

Covel, J. A. (present at play) 120

Crane, Dr. Charles H. (Assistant

Surgeon General) 137, 151, 153, 169
Crawford, Lieutenant Alexander McL. (present at play): disturbed by Booth 97–98; requested to restrain crowd 118; tells Laura Keene to bring water 121; remarks on Lincoln's wound 123; asks crowd to fall back 124; makes statement to Judge Cartter 142; associated with lost dispatch 165–66
Creswell, Senator John A. J. 25; conferences with Lincoln 23–25, 42–43
Crook, William H. (Lincoln bodyguard) 48; notes changes in Lincoln's mood 54; urges Lincoln not to go to theatre, hears the President's farewell 55; bitterness toward John Parker 164–65
Curtis, Dr. George D. (Assistant Surgeon, U.S.A.) 169

Daggett, Albert (State Dept. clerk) 142
Daly, Judge Charles P. 58; expects to see Lincoln 57; reason a mystery 59; advice may have averted war with British 59
Daly, Mrs. Charles P. 59
Dana, Charles A. (Assistant Secretary of War) comments on Lincoln 32; seeks Presidential decision 45; takes Stanton's dictation 140
Davis, Jefferson (President of Confederacy) 24, 26, 41, 68
Debonay, John (scene-shifter at Ford's) 93, 116, 146
Deering, John (present at play) 92
Deery, John (Booth friend) gets Booth box at Glover's 67
DeMotte, Daniel (present at play) 83, 106
Dennison, William (Postmaster General) 31, 32, 38, 153
Devenay, John (Booth friend) 78, 105, 146
Dix, General John A. (Commanding General, New York City) 140
Dixon, Mrs. James (Mary Lincoln friend): goes to Petersen house 138; describes scenes at deathbed 139, 148; seeks to console Mary 159
Dole, William P. (Commissioner of Indian Affairs) 10
Downs, John A. (present at play) 96
DuBarry, Mrs. Helen (present at play) 84, 136
Dunn, Alfonso (White House doorkeeper) 60–61
Dye, Sergeant Joseph (gave testimony) 94–95

Eckert, Major Thomas T. (Superintendent of Military Telegraph) 28; declines Lincoln's invitation to be guard 29; directs telegraph service after assassination 140; explains interruption of service 141; at deathbed 153
Emerson, E. A. (actor) 82, 83, 103, 114, 117, 123, 126
Evans, Mrs. J. A. (actress) 82, 86, 103, 113, 126

Faber, Hermann (hospital steward) 151
Farwell, Leonard J. (former Governor of Wisconsin) 146
Ferguson, James P. (restauranteur, present at play) 77, 100, 105, 109, 113, 142, 144, 168
Ferguson, William J. (call boy and actor at Ford's) 70, 76, 82, 84, 105, 110, 113, 123, 126
Field, Maunsell (Assistant U. S. Treasurer) 153, 157, 160
Fletcher, John (stableman) 146
Flood, William (sailor, present at play) 48–49, 106, 109, 119, 126
Florence, Thomas R. (editor, *Daily Constitutional Union*) 68
Forbes, Charles (White House footman) 60, 83, 86, 92, 98
Ford, Frank (son of Harry Clay Ford): explanation of hole in Box 7 and wall niche for bar 73, 75
Ford, Harry Clay (Ford's treasurer): comments on Booth, teases him 68;

approves publicity notice 70; directs preparations of Presidential box 72–73; says Booth always wanted Box 7 86; challenged by Booth 93; informs James Ferguson of theatre party 100; sees Booth on stage 105; recalls action while decorating box 106; gets help from Mayor Wallach 118
Ford, James (theatre business manager) 68, 70, 71
Ford, John T. (owner of theatre) 71, 72; explains origin of bar 76; describes *Our American Cousin* 90; comments on Booth's leaps 107
Ford's Theatre **69**; alley behind **111**; boxes and early history 71; description of reconstructed theatre 72; seating capacity 72, 82; preparations for Presidential party, and furnishings in state box 72–73; hole in door of Box 7 73–75; niche in wall near passageway door 75; ticket prices 81
Fort Sumter celebration 32
Francis, George (Petersen house resident) 129; parlors used while Lincoln lay dying 132, 139
*Frank Leslie's Illustrated Newspaper* 105, 109, 125, 127, 149–50
Fraser, Robert (Grover's messenger) 55–56
Freudenthal, Mrs. Lenora H. (present at play) 135

Gatch, Captain Oliver C. (present at play) 99–100, 114
Gifford, James J. (Ford's Theatre builder) 72; testimony at John Surratt trial 95–96
Gile, Colonel George W. (Veteran Reserve Corps): attempts to help Crawford get missing dispatch 165
Gobright, Lawrence (Associated Press correspondent) 105, 120
Gourlay, Jeannie (actress) 93, 96, **103**, 110, 117, 123
Gourlay, Maggie (actress) 103
Gourlay, Robert (present at play) 93
Grant, General Ulysses S. **36**; note from Lincoln 10; approves Robert for staff 16; at Appomattox 16–17; invited for theatre party 28; congratulated by cabinet 32; instructions to Confederate soldiers 33; thoughts concerning trade 34; disappoints Lincoln 38–39; followed by Booth 78
Grant, Mrs. Ulysses S., **39**; declines theatre invitation 39–40; claims she saw Booth at lunch 70; identifies horseman as Booth 78
Griffiths, Jabes (Lincoln bearer) 124
Grover, Leonard (theatre partner) 56, 67
Gurley, Dr. Phineas D. (Lincoln's pastor) 137, 151, 153, 157, 159

Hackett, James H. (actor) 89
Hale, Bessie (Booth's "lady love") 65
Hale, Senator John Parker (new minister to Spain) 26, 65
Halleck, General Henry W. (Union Chief of Staff) 153
Hampton Roads Conference 23, 45
Hanscom, S. P. (editor, *National Republican*): delivers dispatch 92, 96, 165
Hansell, Emrick (messenger stabbed by Paine) 134
Hardie, Brevet Brigadier General James A. (Chief of Inspector General's Office): action related to lost dispatch 167
Harlan, James (Secretary of Interior nominee) 10
Harris, Clara **82**; theatre guest 60; Mary's "dear friend" 81; position in box 86; in joyful mood 92; calls for help 113, 117; helps William Flood 119; denies Laura Keene was in box 123; escort arranged 124; acts to save fiancé's life 132
Harris, Senator Ira 81
Harris, General T. M. (present at play) 105
Hart, Miss M. (actress) 83
Hawk, Harry (male star of play) 82, 83, 96, **101**, 103, 105, 116–17, 142, 143–44

Hay, John (Lincoln secretary) **13**; on President's mail 9; on assassination missives 12; fears for President 14; has nickname for Lincoln ("the Tycoon") 15; writes orders and pardons for President 43, 44; goes to Petersen house 138; present at deathbed 151, 153; associated with lost dispatch 165, 166, 167
Haynie, General Isham N. **50**; visits with Lincoln 49; at deathbed 153
Hazelton, Joseph (Ford's program boy) 76, 83, 84
Heiss, William H. (commercial telegraph superintendent): interrupts telegraph service 141
Henry, Dr. Anson G. (friend of Lincoln family) 53
Herold, David E. (conspirator) 66, 67, 79, 134, 146
Herron, George S. (prisoner-of-war) 43
Herron, the Reverend S. D. 43
Hess, C. Dwight (theatre partner) 55, 66, 67
Hess, Mrs. C. Dwight (visitor to White House) 26, 67
Hess, Courtland (actor) 95–96
Howard, William A. (Detroit postmaster) 23
Howell, William T. (subject of Lincoln note) 10
Huntoon, Dr. Andrew Jackson (present at play) 109, 114

illustrations: Ashmun, George **58**; Booth, John Wilkes **64**; Booth crossing stage at Ford's **108**; Booth weapons **97**; Colfax, Schuyler **21**; Creswell, Sen. John A. J. **25**; Daly, Judge Charles P. **58**; deathbed **159**; deathbed scenes **150, 154, 156, 158**; Eckert, Maj. Thomas T. **28**; Ford's Theatre **69**; Ford's Theatre, alley behind **111**; Gourlay, Jeannie **103**; Grant, Gen. Ulysses S. **36**; Grant, Mrs. Ulysses S. (Julia) **39**; Harris, Clara **82**; Hawk, Harry **101**; Hay, John **13**; Haynie, Gen. Isham N. **50**; Johnson, Vice President Andrew **42**; Keene, Laura **91**; Lamon, Ward Hill **60**; Leale, Dr. Charles A. **122**; Lincoln, President Abraham **2, 3, 4**; Lincoln, President Abraham, last writing of **58**; Lincoln, President Abraham, and family **17**; Lincoln, Mary **85**; *Lincoln Borne by Loving Hands* **130**; map of Washington, D.C. on April 14–15 **8**; Nicolay, John **13**; Oglesby, Gov. Richard J. **50**; Paine, Lewis, confronting Fredrick Seward **133**; Paine, Lewis, in custody **134**; Petersen, William **128**; Petersen, William, house of **125, 152**; Presidential box at Ford's Theatre **74**; Price, Eli K., and $500 check **11**; Rathbone, Maj. Henry **82**; Seward, Frederick W. **34**; Seward, William H. **35**; Safford, Henry **128**; Stanton, Edwin M. **27**; Taft, Dr. Charles Sabin **121**; Taltavull's Star Saloon **69**; Welles, Gideon **37**; Withers, William **110**
Irving, Henrietta (actress): attacks Booth 65

Jameson, Lieutenant James B. (Light Guard commander) 126, 135
Jaquette, Isaac (present at play) 118
Jefferson, Burtell M. (Chief of Police in Washington): supplies police log for April 14–15, 1865, and charges against John Parker 163, 164
Johnson, Vice President Andrew **42**, 67, 68, 70, 79, 134, 149; his meeting with Lincoln and hard attitude toward South 41; at Lincoln's bedside 146–47
Johnson, Charles H. (present at play) 107
Johnston, Confederate General Joseph E. 27

Keene, Laura (female star of play) 83, **91**; career highlights 90–92; near prompter's box 105, 109; struck by

Booth 110; loath to accuse actor 117; pleads for order 118; takes water to box 120–21; holds President's head 123

Kellogg, William Pitt (Chief Justice, Nebraska Territory) 55

Kent, William (present at play) 118, 119, 121, 123

King, Dr. Albert F. A. (physician present at play): aids in box 118; helps carry Lincoln 124; records pulse and respiration 146, 147; at deathbed 151, 153

Kinney, Constance (with Mary Lincoln at Petersen house) 139, 153, 159

Kinney, Mrs. Mary (with Mary Lincoln at Petersen house) 138–39, 153, 159

Knox, James Suydam (present at play) 84; chases Booth 115; tells of horror and dispair 136; interviewed by police 146

Laird, Thomas A. (War Department telegrapher) 140

Lamon, Ward Hill (U. S. Marshal in District of Columbia) **60**; concern for Lincoln's safety 14, 61

Leale, Dr. Charles A. (surgeon who attended Lincoln) 84, **122**; sees Booth enter corridor 98–99; notes his escape 107; goes to Lincoln's aid 118; discovers wound 119–20; helps move President 124, 126; efforts to make Lincoln comfortable 131; makes thorough examination 136; clears wound frequently, sends for key persons 137; describes Mary's last visit 148; at deathbed 151, 153, 155, 157

Lee, General Robert E. 7, 16, 68

*Leslie's Illustrated Newspaper* see *Frank Leslie's Illustrated Newspaper*

Lincoln, Abraham: "last pictures" **2**, **3**,**4**; in family picture **17**; appearance 7, 9; as story teller 5, 24, 25–26, 51; knowledge of Bible 7; his office 9; mail 9–10; notes written on April 14 10, 12; Mary's worries over him 12; his indifference to threats 12, 14–15, 61; guards for 14; his signature and attitude toward name 15; meals with family 15; endorsements of day 15, 24; signs commission for Robert 16; eagerness for war reports 16; ideas for Robert 17; conferences with Schuyler Colfax 19–23, 56–57; messages to Major General Godfrey Weitzel 19, 22; message to miners 20, 57; relations with Judge John A. Campbell 22–23; conference with Senator John A. J. Creswell 23–25; attitude toward Jefferson Davis 24, 26; signs orders, releases and pardons 24, 43, 44, 51; call from Charles M. Scott 26; kindliness 26, 46; visits to War Department 27–29, 54: meets with cabinet 31–38; relates strange dream 33; desires unity, reanimation of states before Congress meets and treatment of Southerners as fellow citizens 36, 37; thinking of his "soldier boys" 38; disappointed by Grant 39; arranges to meet British minister 40; conference with Creswell and Thomas Swann 42–43; has Hay write orders and pardons 43, 44; talks with former servant 44; conference with General Singleton 44–45; "when you have an elephant by the hind leg" 45; signs Congressman Rollins' petition 46; ride with Mary 47–49; thoughts of future 47–48; memories of past 48; visits *Montauk* 48–49; chats with General Haynie and Governor Oglesby 49, 52; fondness for *Nasby Papers* 51; inclined to give up theatre 53; depressed, muses on assassination 54; depression gone, but still shows no enthusiasm for theatre 55; says goodbye to William Crook, 55; sees William Pitt Kellogg 55; reported visit from Robert Fraser 55; commission for Alvin Saunders 56; talks with George Ashmun 56–57, 59; writes notes for two Southerners and Senator Stewart

57; last writing 57; invites Stewart, Judge Niles Searles and Isaac Arnold to return 59; best of spirits 81; reception at theatre 84; "pathetically sad appearance" 84; position in box 86; fondness for Shakespeare and comedy 89; arises for coat 92; receives dispatch 92; enjoyment of play and company 100; position when shot 102; last words 102; placed in recumbent position 119; given artificial respiration 120; carried from theatre 124; on improvised stretcher 125, 129; height poses problem 131; pocket contents guarded 136; doctors make full examination 136; steps taken to help President 137; readings of pulse and respiration 146, 147; bullet tracked 147; death approaches 155; breathes last 157; "a look of unspeakable peace" 160

Lincoln, Mary Todd **17**, **85**; worry over husband 12; mode of addressing husband 15; breakfast together 15–16; in family portrait 17; ride with husband 47–49; wants to forego theatre 53; invites Major Rathbone and Clara Harris to replace Grants 60, 81; sends for tickets 68; garb for evening 86; position in box 86; enjoyment of play and company 100; incoherent after assassination 113; appeals to Dr. Leale 119; arrives at Petersen house 132; calls for Robert 137; visits Lincoln's bedside 139, 147, 148; calls Ford's that "dreadful house" 160; accuses John Parker 164

Lincoln, Robert **17**; Army service 16; at Appomattox 16–17; declines father's theatre invitation 56; goes to Lincoln's bedside 138; comforts mother 139, 147; at deathbed 151, 153, 155; seeks to console mother 159

Lincoln, Tad 15, **17**, 49, 53

Locke, David Ross (author: pseudonym, Petroleum V. Nasby) 51

Lucas, Mrs. Virginia (present at play) 118, 126

McAllister, Paul (Washington editor, *New York Tribune*) 145

McCulloch, Hugh (Treasury Secretary) 31, 38, 55, 147, 153

Mace, A. L. (present at play) 106

McGowan, Captain Theodore (present at play) 97–98, 106, 118

Maddox, James (Ford's property man) 70, 73, 77, 78, 120, 146

Mason, Captain Henry W. (present at play) 113

Matthews, John (actor): entrusted with Booth's letter to newspaper 77–78; reaction at shot 103; burns letter 131

Maynard, George C. (War Telegraph employee) 83, 106, 107, 120, 140

Meigs, Quartermaster General Montgomery C. 136, 138, 139, 153

Merrick, Henry (National Hotel clerk): notes Booth looks pale 68; conversation with Booth 76–77; 79

Metropolitan Police Department 135, 145–46; 162–63

Mills, James N. (present at play) 107, 126

*Montauk* 5, 48, 49

Morris, former Congressman James R. 106, 114, 119

Moss, Helen Palmer (visitor to White House): meets Lincoln 26; sees Booth 67

Munroe, Seaton (attorney) 114

Nasby, Petroleum V. (author David Ross Locke) 49, 51

*The Nasby Papers* 51

Neill, Edward D. (Lincoln secretary) 12, 41

newspaper coverage of assassination 105

*New York Herald* 141

*New York Times* 135, 141

*New York Tribune* 9, 136, 145

*New York World* 145

Nicolay, John (Lincoln secretary) **13**; on President's mail 9, and assassination missives 12; fears for Presi-

dent 14; has nickname for Lincoln ("the Tycoon") 15; comments on cabinet 31; to become consul in Paris 53
Notson, (?) (Assistant Surgeon, U. S. A.): present at autopsy 169

O'Beirne, Major James O. (Commander of Provost Guard) 146, 164
O'Brien, James (usher) 83
Oglesby, Richard J. (Governor of Illinois) **50**; visit with Lincoln 49, 52; at deathbed 153
O'Laughlin, Michael (kidnap conspirator) 66, 68
Oldroyd, Osborn H. (museum founder) 106–07
Olszewski, Dr. George J. (Ford's Theatre historian) 73, 75, 83
*Our American Cousin*: history and nature of play 90
Owens, Captain Silas (present at play) 106

Paine, Lewis (conspirator) 4, 67, **133**, **134**; enlisted by Booth, refuses to shoot Lincoln 66; assigned to murder Seward 79; beats Frederick Seward insensible 132; attacks Secretary Seward and latter's attendants 134; arrested 135
Parker, John (Lincoln bodyguard) 83, 146; late for theatre trip 54; starts for theatre 60; leaves post 86; his shoddy record, his dismissal and death 162–165
Payne, Lewis *See* Paine, Lewis
"Peanuts John" *See* Burroughs, Joseph
Pendel, Thomas (White House doorkeeper) 52, 56, 57, 60, 61
Petersen, William (owner of house in which Lincoln died) **125**, 126, 127, **128**, 151
Phillips, H. B. (actor and songwriter) 70, 71, 142, 144
Pierpont, Francis H. (leader of Virginia's rump government) 38
Pillow, Confederate General Gideon 26
police log of assassination 145–46
Polkinhorn, Henry (present at play) 115
Pope, Dr. G. W. (friend of the Harris family): attends Major Rathbone 132
Porter, Lieutenant Colonel Horace (aide-de-camp to Gen. Grant) 16
Porterfield, Miss (present at play) 114–15
Potter, Major Horatio (present at play) 124
Powell, Lewis Thornton *See* Paine, Lewis
Presidential box 72–73, **74**
Price, Eli K. (wrote "mysterious" check to Lincoln) 10, **11**, 161–62
Price, Philip (great-grandson of Eli K. Price) 161–62
Proctor, Thomas (Petersen house resident) 127, 151
Pumphrey, James W. (stableman) 69, 77

Rathbone, Major Henry R. **82**; theatre guest 60; service with distinction 81; murders wife in later years 82; describes audience reaction to Lincoln's assassination 84; position in box 86; in festive mood 92; tries to stop Booth 102, 107, 112; wounded 102; rushes for aid 113; removes bar, seeks Lieutenant Crawford's help 118; bleeds profusely 123, 124; faints at Petersen house, taken to Harris home 132
Raybold, Thomas (Ford's purchasing agent) 71, 73, 76, 86
Raymond, Henry J. (Lincoln biographer present at play) 106
Rhoades, James B. (archivist of U.S.) 162
Richards, A. C. (Washington Superintendent of Police) 83, 109, 117–18, 135
Ritterspaugh, Jacob (theatre carpenter) 78, 112, 116
Roberts, W. H. (present at play) 135
Robinson, George (Seward nurse) 134
Rockwell, Major A. F. (sketched diagram of Petersen house) 152, 153

Rollins, Congressman Edward H. 46
room in which Lincoln died: size, furnishings 131, 149; Booth had used bed 131; depictions of deathbed scene 149, **150**, 151, 153, **154**, 155, **156**, 157, **158**
rumors of assassination 12
Rutherford, Colonel George V. (of Quartermaster's Dept.): testifies to Tanner 142, 144

Safford, Henry (Petersen house resident) 127, 128, **128**, 129, 137, 151
Sample, William (Lincoln bearer) 124
Sanders, Thomas Bradford (present at play) 106, 119, 121, 135
Sanford, Charles A. (present at play) 84
Saunders, Alvin (Governor of Nebraska Territory) 56
Scott, Charles M. (Mississippi River pilot): appeals to Lincoln 26
Searles, Judge Niles (visitor to White House): seeks to see Lincoln 57; gains introduction 59
Sessford, John (Joe) (ticket taker) 94, 105
Seward, Major Augustus H. (son of William H.): wounded by Paine 134
Seward, Frederick (son of William H. Seward) **34**, **133**; acting for father 10, 32, 33; summarizes Stanton's plans 35; reminds President of new British minister 40; beaten by Paine 133
Seward, William H. (Secretary of State) 4, 10, 31, **35**; attitude concerning assassination 12; attacked by Paine 133–34
Shellabarger, Congressman Samuel 5
Sherman, Thomas H. (War Department telegrapher) 84, 120, 126
Sherman, General William T. 27, 33, 54
Simms, Joe (colored helper) 73
Singleton, General James Washington (negotiator for peace) 44–45
Smith, W. R. (present at play) 116
Soles, James J. (Lincoln bearer) 124, 126
Spangler, Edmund (carpenter's helper and scene-shifter) 72, 73, 78, 86, 93, 106, 116, 146
Speed, James (Attorney General) 15, 31, 32, 153
Stanton, Edwin M. (Secretary of War) **27**, 31; concerns over assassination rumors 12; signs Robert Lincoln's commission 16; objects to theatre plans 28–29; has proposals for reconstruction 33, 34, 35, 37, 38; comments on Lincoln 40; feels affection for chief 54; wants Jacob Thompson arrested 45; takes charge at Petersen house 139; dispatches to media 140–41, 144–45; hears testimony 142; at deathbed 151, 153, 155, 157; sobs immortal words 159; associated with lost dispatch 165, 166, 167
Stewart, Joseph B. (present at play) 106, 115–16, 146
Stewart, Senator William M.: calls on Lincoln 57; last-minute goodbye 59
Stimmel, Sergeant Smith (crowd control after shooting) 135
Stoddard, William (Lincoln secretary) 10, 12, 41
Stone, Dr. Robert King (Lincoln family physician) 137, 151, 153, 155; on autopsy 168
Sumner, Senator Charles 56, 138, 143, 146, 151, 153, 155
Surratt, John (kidnap conspirator) 66, 76; trial 95, 96, 115
Surratt, Mary E. (alleged conspirator) 66, 68, 70
Swann, Thomas (Governor of Maryland): has conference with Lincoln 42–43

Taft, Dr. Charles Sabin (an attending surgeon) 92, **121**; lifted to box 119; sees no bleeding 123; helps carry Lincoln 124, 126; probes wound 136; recalls Mary's last visit 148; at

deathbed 151, 153; on autopsy 168–69
Taltavull's Star Saloon **69**, 70, 93, 94, 95, 96, 126
Tanner, James (soldier stenographer) **143**; takes assassination testimony 142–44; observes Mary's grief 148; at deathbed 151, 153, 155, 157, 159
telegraph service, interruption of 141
Thompson, Jacob (Confederate official) 45
Tod, David (Governor of Ohio) 126
Todd, Dr. George B.: sees Lincoln at *Montauk* 49; observes Booth approaching box 98
Todd, Dr. Lyman Beecher (cousin of Mary Lincoln) 159
Truman, Helen (actress) 82, 86, 89, 114, 117, 123
Turner, Mary Ann (renter back of theatre) 70

Ulke, Julius (artist, photographer) 151, 159
Union Light Guard 126, 135
Usher, John P. (Secretary of Interior) 31, 33, 40, 61, 139, 149, 153

Van Alen, General James H. (written to by Lincoln on April 14) 10, 12
Verdi, Dr. T. S. (Seward family's physician) 137
Vey, Mrs. Gerda (donor of Carl Bersch painting) 129
Vincent, General Thomas M. (Assistant Adjutant General) 132, 153, 155

Wallace, Congressman William H. 15
Wallach, Mayor Richard 118
Ward, Samuel R. (present at play) 105
Warwick, Charles (actor) 77, 131
Washington, D.C.: war's-end celebration 7; map of White House–Ford's Theatre area 8
*Washington Morning Chronicle* 145
*Washington National Intelligencer* 136
weather on April 14: 7, 47
Webster, Edwin (political appointee) 43
Weichmann, Louis (boarder at Mrs. Surratt's) 68, 70, 117
Weitzel, Major General Godfrey (Military Governor of Richmond) 19, 22, 23
Welles, Gideon (Secretary of the Navy) **37**; comments on Lincoln 31–32; suggestions for reconstruction 34; quotes Lincoln 36–37; idea on military supervision 38; arrives at Petersen house 139; on walk is pressed for hope 148–49; at deathbed 151, 153
Willard Hotel 69, 77, 78
Willis, Charles L. (present at play) 96, 126
Wilson, Lizzie (assassination suspect) 146
Withers, Reuben (theatre musician) 84
Withers, William (Ford's orchestra director) 70, 71, **110**; hears startling Booth prediction 79; observations on Lincoln's arrival 84; sees Booth approaching box 99; encounter with Booth 110–112; loath to accuse Booth 117
Wood, Charles H. M. (Booth's barber) 67
Woodward, Dr. J. J. (autopsy statement) 168, 169
Wright, Mrs. Annie (wife of Ford's stage manager) 84, 86, 100, 107, 119, 123